Jewelry & Beading Designs For Dummies®

W9-AOD-055

Assorted Stringing Materials

You can definitely go crazy with all the stringing choices out there (and we recommend that you do from time to time). But here's our recommendations for what you should keep on hand.

- Nylon size 4 (black and white)
- Nylon size 2 (black and white)
- 0.014-inch or 0.015-inch and 0.019-inch clear beading wire
- Silamide size A in off-white

Must-Have Findings

When you're looking at rack after rack of findings, it can be hard to know what you really need. Here's a list of items that we always have handy, so we can create jewelry at a moment's notice.

- Assorted clasps (toggle clasps, spring ring clasp)
- 2x2mm tube-shaped sterling crimp beads
- Sterling and gold-filled bead tips
- Ear wires (leverback and shepherd hook styles)
- Head pins
- Assorted sizes of jump rings (5mm to 7mm in gold-filled and sterling)

Semi-Precious Wire to Stock

If you need help deciding which wire you need to get started, here's our list, complete with gauges and hardness.

- Gold-filled 22-, 21-, and 20-gauge round dead-soft wire
- Sterling silver 22-, 21-, and 20-gauge round dead-soft wire
- Gold-filled 24-, 20-, and 16-gauge half-hard wire
- Sterling silver 24-, 20-, and 16-gauge half-hard wire

Approximate Number of Beads Needed for Specific Lengths of Beaded Strands

Bead Size	Length of Beaded Strand									
	6"	8"	10"	12"	14"	16"	20"	24"	28"	32"
3mm	51	68	85	102	119	136	170	204	238	271
4mm	39	51	64	77	89	102	127	153	178	204
6mm	26	34	43	51	60	68	85	102	119	136
8mm	20	26	32	39	45	51	64	77	89	102
10mm	16	21	26	31	36	41	51	61	72	82
12mm	13	17	22	26	30	34	43	51	60	68
14mm	11	15	19	22	26	29	37	44	51	59
16mm	10	13	16	20	23	26	32	39	45	51
18mm	9	12	15	17	20	23	29	34	40	46

JAN 2009 WI

For Dummies: Bestselling Book Series for Beginners

How to Attach a Crimp Bead

The quick and easy way to finish jewelry is to use a pair of crimping pliers and the two-phase crimp method.

1. **Position your strung crimp tube or bead in the lower jaw of the crimping pliers. Squeeze the jaws together to reveal a bent crimp that resembles the lefthand image.**

2. **Move the bent crimp up to the top jaw. Squeeze the jaws together to further flatten the crimp, leaving a professional look, like the one in the righthand image.**

Bead-Weaving Stitches

If you're new to bead weaving, it's helpful to have pictures handy to help you work from one step the next. To use these stitches in projects, take a look at Chapters 6 and 11. We give you lots of opportunities to hone your skills.

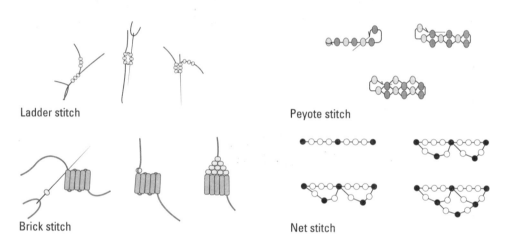

Ladder stitch

Peyote stitch

Brick stitch

Net stitch

Wire-Wrapping Techniques

Wire wrapping is a great way to put your own stamp on your jewelry creations. You can use wire to connect beads, wrap beads, make your own chain or clasps, and so much more. Check out Chapter 8 for some basic projects. Chapter 10 shows you how to fabricate your own components using many of these techniques.

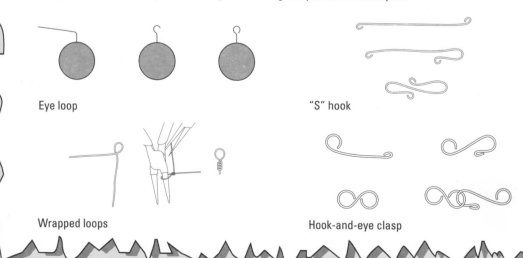

Eye loop

"S" hook

Wrapped loops

Hook-and-eye clasp

Jewelry & Beading Designs
FOR
DUMMIES®

by Heather H. Dismore and Tammy Powley

WILEY

Wiley Publishing, Inc.

Jewelry & Beading Designs For Dummies®

Published by
Wiley Publishing, Inc.
111 River St.
Hoboken, NJ 07030-5774
www.wiley.com

For general information on our other products and services, please contact our Customer Care Department within the U.S. at 800-762-2974, outside the U.S. at 317-572-3993, or fax 317-572-4002.

For technical support, please visit www.wiley.com/techsupport.

Wiley also publishes its books in a variety of electronic formats. Some content that appears in print may not be available in electronic books.

Library of Congress Control Number: 2008931637

ISBN: 978-0-470-29112-2

Manufactured in the United States of America

10 9 8 7 6 5 4 3 2 1

WILEY

About the Authors

Heather H. Dismore is a veteran *For Dummies* author and editor. She's the author of *Jewelry Making & Beading For Dummies* and the coauthor of several titles including *Running a Bar For Dummies* and *Running a Restaurant For Dummies*. She's contributed to many, many other books including *Diabetes Cookbook For Dummies,* 2nd Edition, *Acne For Dummies, Understanding Autism For Dummies,* and *Einstein For Dummies,* all published by Wiley. Her other books include *Start Your Restaurant Career and Start Your Own Personal Concierge Service,* 2nd Edition, both published by Entrepreneur Press.

Heather graduated from DePauw University with majors in political science and English composition. She started making jewelry for friends and family during college as a way to give beautiful gifts on a limited budget. She works in many different mediums, blending them whenever she can.

In her other life, she's an active food writer and trend-spotter in the food and beverage industry and a regular contributor to FoodChannel.com. She can be contacted at heather@ heatherdismore.com. She lives in South Carolina with her husband, two daughters, and dog, who are her first loves, inspirations, and a never-ending source of new material.

Tammy Powley is a writer, designer, and teacher. She attended the University of Central Florida where she earned her master's degree in literature and later her PhD in texts and technology. Tammy works full time as a college English professor, is the author of numerous jewelry-making books, and was the creative consultant for *Jewelry Making & Beading For Dummies.* Tammy also has an extensive background in writing for the Web and has been About.com's Guide to Jewelry Making since 1989. See her Web site at www.tammypowley.com for more information about her publications. Tammy lives in South Florida with her husband and their animal menagerie.

Dedication

We dedicate this book to our families. We love you and know that we couldn't do this without your encouragement and support. Thank you!

Authors' Acknowledgments

Thanks so much to Chrissy Guthrie, our awesome project editor, who gave us great feedback and support all along the way, helping to turn our ideas and designs into reality in the form of the book you have in your hands. Thank you to Vicki Adang, copy editor extraordinaire, whose enthusiasm and attention to detail made sure that you could actually follow our steps to make your own beautiful pieces.

Thanks to Angela Solis, who performed a technical edit of the text and lent helpful suggestions and insights, making the finished product even better.

Several vendors graciously donated supplies we used to create many of the beautiful pieces in this book. A big thank you to Fire Mountain Gems (www.firemoutaingems.com). The folks at Fire Mountain supplied many of the crystals, gemstones (including the gorgeous onyx beads and components), and Hill Tribe Silver, among other things. We truly appreciate your generosity and support. Gary Helwig from Wig Jig (www.wigjig.com) supplied projects for the jig chapter (Chapter 7), as well as some beautiful finished pieces you see there. Thanks so much for everything. And finally, Daphne D. Hess Handcrafted Beads (www.ddhess.com) supplied many of the beautiful lampwork focal beads included in projects throughout this book. Thanks for your amazing glasswork. You're a true artist!

Thanks to everyone who helped bring our pieces to life in the gorgeous artwork in the book, including Kreber, for its work on the color section, and Alicia South, who helped coordinate the art for this book. Special thanks also to Clint Lahnen, supervisor of graphics processing and imaging, for the interior black-and-white photography, and to Rashell Smith, senior graphics technician, for the illustrations.

Thanks to everyone at Wiley who makes the *For Dummies* brand a continued success, including Diane Steele, Joyce Pepple, Kristin Cocks, and Tracy Boggier. A special thank you to Lindsay Lefevere for her work in developing this crafting and pattern series. We think it's a great one!

Publisher's Acknowledgments

We're proud of this book; please send us your comments through our Dummies online registration form located at www.dummies.com/register/.

Some of the people who helped bring this book to market include the following:

Acquisitions, Editorial, and Media Development

Senior Project Editor: Christina Guthrie

Acquisitions Editor: Tracy Boggier

Senior Copy Editor: Victoria M. Adang

Editorial Program Coordinator: Erin Calligan Mooney

Technical Editor: Angela Solis

Editorial Manager: Christine Meloy Beck

Editorial Assistants: Joe Niesen, David Lutton, Jennette ElNaggar

Cover Photos: © Clint Lahnen/Wiley Publishing

Cartoons: Rich Tennant (www.the5thwave.com)

Composition Services

Project Coordinator: Katie Key

Layout and Graphics: Nikki Gately, Melissa K. Jester, Brent Savage, Julie Trippetti, Christine Williams

Special Art: Interior photos by Clint Lahnen; color photograpy: Kreber/Debra Little and Tim Theed. Creative/ Art Direction for color photography–Deborah Pries

Proofreaders: John Greenough, Betty Kish

Indexer: Claudia Bourbeau

Special Help: Alicia South

Publishing and Editorial for Consumer Dummies

Diane Graves Steele, Vice President and Publisher, Consumer Dummies

Kristin A. Cocks, Product Development Director, Consumer Dummies

Michael Spring, Vice President and Publisher, Travel

Kelly Regan, Editorial Director, Travel

Publishing for Technology Dummies

Andy Cummings, Vice President and Publisher, Dummies Technology/General User

Composition Services

Gerry Fahey, Vice President of Production Services

Debbie Stailey, Director of Composition Services

Contents at a Glance

Table of Contents

Introduction

We love making jewelry and beading. We spend hours creating pieces for ourselves, our families and friends, and a few customers here and there. We think you can absolutely find the same joy and satisfaction by pursuing this exciting and versatile craft.

If you have some experience with creating jewelry, *Jewelry & Beading Designs For Dummies* can help you take your skills to the next level. We give you projects of increasing difficulty to help you build on the foundation you have. We help you experiment with skills you may not think to try on your own, all the while coaching you along with step-by-step instructions.

We hope this book inspires you to build up your bead supply so you're ready to create when inspiration strikes. And we want you to have the confidence to create your own custom pieces by altering or building on the designs and easy-to-follow instructions we provide.

About This Book

Jewelry & Beading Designs For Dummies is packed full of projects, more than 70 in all, that span a variety of techniques. Many of the designs include suggestions for varying the projects slightly to create just the right piece to suit you. Whether you want to create a special-occasion piece, say for a wedding, or a new everyday favorite, like the earrings you'll wear twice a week for the rest of your life, you can find it in this book.

No matter what style of jewelry you lean toward, you're sure to find something in the pages of this book that appeals to you. If you're into lots of glitz and sparkle, we've got it. If you're looking for delicate bead-woven pieces, you'll find it here. If you need a simple design with just a few timeless components, you've come to the right place. There's something here for everyone, likely several somethings.

We use several different visual helpers in this book to help you decide what to make, work through the steps, and see many of the finished pieces on models. Here's how they're organized:

- ✔ Each design includes a picture of the finished piece at the beginning of the project. This feature helps you see exactly what all of your hard work will get you.

- ✔ As necessary, we include illustrations of complicated steps in the directions so you don't get lost. You can see exactly what your piece should look like at key points in the process.

- ✔ We created a full-color glossy section of nothing but pictures (okay, and text to describe those pictures, but it's mostly pictures) that are sure to inspire you. We've even grouped coordinating pieces together to help you accessorize with style.

Conventions Used in This Book

We use a few standard conventions to help you navigate this book.

- ✔ *Italics* are used to highlight new words that we define or to emphasize particular terms.

- ✔ `Monofont` is used to point out Web addresses.

- ✔ **Bold** identifies action parts of the numbered steps in the projects and keywords in bulleted lists.

- ✔ When we introduce a new skill that we don't cover somewhere else in the book, we list it within the pattern under the heading "New skill." In that section, we give you the step-by-step instructions to tackle that particular technique. Think of it as a project within a project.

- ✔ We start out the "Materials" section of each project by listing what beads you need for the project. We list them in a consolidated, easy-to-purchase order, rather than the order you use them in. We break beads and findings into two separate lists, but make sure you take a look at both lists before heading to the bead store.

- ✔ We list the tools in each project in the order you use them so you can organize your workspace as appropriate for each project.

- ✔ We include a picture of each design before the instructions so you can soak in the full visual appeal of the piece before you dive into the details.

- ✔ Some of the more advanced projects are pretty involved, so we break down the directions for those designs into smaller chunks. This way, you can focus on one aspect of the project at a time, or if you need to stop to go pick up the kids, you know where a good stopping point is.

Foolish Assumptions

We all gotta start somewhere, right? But if you've never made any jewelry in your life, this may not be the book for you. If you're reading this book, we assume that you have some jewelry-making experience, however basic. Many of the projects in this book are great for beginners, but quite a few of the projects are much easier to tackle if you have some prior knowledge about stringing beads, wire wrapping, and using crimp beads in particular.

If you're brand new to beading and making jewelry, we recommend you take a look at *Jewelry Making & Beading For Dummies* by Heather Dismore with Tammy Powley, creative consultant (Wiley). In it, we cover lots of the basics with great illustrations to help you get up to speed and tackle the more advanced projects included in this book. In fact, we refer to that book often throughout this one as a resource for further information on specific techniques.

How This Book Is Organized

We've included 17 chapters plus an appendix in this book. We've organized those chapters into five separate parts. Part I introduces the basics of jewelry making and beading, and then Parts II, III, and IV detail the designs. The simpler projects are in the earliest part, building to the more detailed projects in the last part. Similarly, within a chapter, the projects tend to be simple at the beginning and increase in difficulty as you get toward the end.

Part 1: Reinforcing Your Jewelry Foundation

Not surprisingly, this part provides a refresher on your gear and basic techniques. It's useful to flip through this part even if you're a fairly experienced jewelry maker. Just survey the material so you have a general idea of what's where so you can come back to it if needed.

Chapter 1 helps you figure out what gear you need and why. It's important to know which pliers do what because we don't go over that again within the actual projects. Chapter 2 jogs your memory about the basic techniques of jewelry making. Here we remind you about the basics of stringing, bead weaving, and wire wrapping.

Part 11: Super Simple Jewelry Projects

Bring on the projects! Here, we pick up the pliers and don't put them down. (Okay, we might put them down, but only so we can pick up another pair as needed.) We organize this part into technique-based chapters. Chapter 3 is dedicated to stringing projects, using different stringing materials, like memory wire, elastic cord, ribbon, and leather. In Chapter 4, we move on to bead crimping, the fastest way to connect findings and terminate strands cleanly and professionally. We use the technique to create everything from basic bracelets and necklaces to a convertible necklace/bracelet.

Chapter 5 shows you how to use traditional knotting to create bookmarks, earrings, and more. Get started with bead weaving in Chapter 6. Look here for help to make a peyote stitch bookmark, ladder stitch earrings, and more.

Use a wire jig to create consistently sized wire components with help from Chapter 7. We give you the steps to create your own changeable necklace and wire components for a double-strand bracelet among other things. Chapter 8 is a mega-chapter dedicated to wire wrapping. We show you how to make many, many projects using this popular technique, including multiple dangle earrings, a wire-wrapped cuff bracelet, and an embellished gemstone pendant.

Part 111: Putting Your Jewelry Skills to the Test

This part of the book represents the bulk of the advanced projects. Several of these projects include new skills and incorporate multiple techniques. We've also included several chapters on creating your own jewelry components.

Chapter 9 starts the part off with pretty straightforward, albeit more complicated projects. These designs take some time, give you great practice in developing techniques covered elsewhere in the book, and offer up beautiful finished pieces. In Chapter 10, you can craft custom jewelry components. This chapter shows you how to make, among other things, your own ear wires and focal pieces.

Chapter 11 covers advanced bead weaving. Here, we build on the techniques we cover earlier in the book to create stunning pieces, including a free-form peyote bracelet and earrings using beads you weave yourself. We dedicate Chapter 12 to making jewelry with polymer clay. Because this medium is so versatile, we really only scratch the surface of what's possible with it, but we do show you how to roll your own beads, use rubber stamps to create pendants, and simulate gemstones.

Part IV: Mixing It Up: Incorporating Multiple Techniques and Materials

This section of the book is dedicated to nontraditional designs. Chapter 13 focuses on non-jewelry items that are created with jewelry-making techniques, like a wire-wrapped ornament and crimped crystal fan pull. We help you take your new skills and eye for design and make the world around you more beautiful with beads.

Chapter 14 is the hot spot for jewelry designs made from nontraditional materials, or materials that you may not think of using in your jewelry designs, like earrings made from items you can find at your local hardware store or pendants made from buttons. We help you begin to look at doodads you find in a whole new way, with an eye toward creating unique and one-of-a-kind accessories. You'll never rummage through the junk drawer the same way again.

Part V: The Part of Tens

This part is made up of three chapters that we hope you find helpful. We give you ideas for storing and caring for all the lovely pieces we know you'll be making soon. We show you a few new places to consider when looking for stuff to bead with. And we help you avoid several common mistakes that jewelry makers make.

Don't forget to check out the appendix if you need help with the details on tying knots or working with a particular kind of finding, like attaching a clasp to a bead tip, for example.

Icons Used in This Book

To make this book even more useful to you, we include a few icons to guide you through the projects. Pay close attention when you see one of these babies pop up.

This icon tips you off to special, helpful information that can save you time by making the project a little easier. We use these to give you a little more information about nuances of a technique or step. Typically these little nuggets contain bits of information that we (and countless other jewelry makers) have found useful through the years.

The Remember icon highlights must-do information in a project. We use it to reinforce key details in the instructions for many of the projects in this book.

Pay particular attention when this icon rears its head. Often we include text here to help you avoid mistakes. Because this is jewelry making and not brain surgery, ignoring the icon won't have life-or-death consequences. But you may have to start a project over, wasting valuable time and materials, if you choose not to heed our carefully crafted advice.

Where to Go from Here

One of the great things about any book in the *For Dummies* series is that you don't need to start at the beginning of the book and read to the end. You can pretty much just jump in anywhere and get going. So flip through the pages and see what projects catch your fancy. Then bead it up.

If, however, you're overwhelmed with the many, many gorgeous projects and really want some direction, here are our suggestions for good starting places:

- ✔ Check out the color photo section in the middle of the book. You've probably already flipped through it. Maybe that's what enticed you to bring the book home with you. Here you'll find pictures of many of the designs we've created for this book, in all their glossy glory. Each photo includes a caption that tells you where to turn to get the step-by-step instructions for creating each piece for yourself.

- ✔ Chapter 2 gives you a refresher in all sorts of technique basics, like making eye loops with wire or basic bead-weaving stitches. It can help you reacquaint yourself with using your tools and materials if it's been a while since you made any jewelry.

- ✔ If you want to focus on a particular technique, check out the Table of Contents to find to the corresponding chapter. Chapter 12 is dedicated to working with polymer clay, for example, while Chapters 6 and 11 focus on bead weaving.

Part I
Reinforcing Your Jewelry Foundation

The 5th Wave   By Rich Tennant

"It's a beginner's jewelry-making kit I put together for you. There are pliers, wire cutters, bandages, gauze, antiseptics..."

In this part . . .

Here we get you started with the basic tools, supplies, and techniques you need to make the beautiful projects in the rest of the book. We give you tips for choosing the right tools for the job. We help you select beads and stringing materials for your own designs as well as for the designs in this book. We introduce you to the wide world of jewelry findings and give you the pros and cons of working with different materials.

Additionally, we get you up to speed in this part with the essential techniques you need to tackle the designs in this book. Most of what you need to know technique-wise is covered here. (If you need any skills that aren't here, we include them with the project or let you know where to get them. Don't worry; we won't leave you hanging.) Look to this part to brush up on how to use crimp beads, bead tips, and other stringing essentials. It also includes great illustrations for conquering several common bead-weaving stitches and wire-wrapping techniques. Feel free to flag or highlight the techniques you use most often so you can refer to them again and again as necessary.

Chapter 1

Gearing Up

In This Chapter

▶ Selecting the right tools and equipment

▶ Creating your collections of beads, stones, and crystals

▶ Figuring out the necessary findings

Get your gear on! Actually making jewelry is the highlight of the creative process, but we think it's almost as much fun to get ready to make jewelry. Think of it as the crafty equivalent of getting new supplies at the beginning of the school year. If you've flipped through a bead supply catalog or browsed an online bead store, no doubt you've seen hundreds of different tools and supplies, which may overwhelm you. In this chapter, we pare down the seemingly endless catalog of gadgets and gotta-haves and give you the real deal on just what you need to get started.

If you want more details about any of the tools, beads, or findings that we talk about in this chapter, please check out our first beading book, *Jewelry Making & Beading For Dummies* (Wiley).

Taking a Look at Essential Tools

Tools vary widely in price range. You can get a basic starter kit with three or four different tools for $15, or you can spend $50 (or more) on a single pair of professional-quality pliers. The most expensive tools are absolutely not necessary when you're just starting out. Look for tools with descriptors like *economy* and *value* to get started.

Picking out pliers

We use three different types of pliers daily in jewelry making: round-nose pliers, chain-nose pliers, and crimping pliers, shown in Figure 1-1a, b, and c respectively. We consider these to be must-have tools.

Figure 1-1:
If you buy only three sets of pliers, these are the ones to invest in.

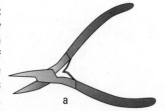
a

b

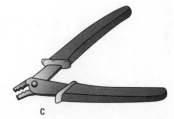
c

- ✔ **Round-nose pliers**, shown in Figure 1-1a, are great for making eye loops and wrapped loops.

- ✔ **Chain-nose pliers,** pictured in Figure 1-1b, are awesome tools to bend wire at a 90-degree angle, a necessary step in creating perfect eye loops. They're also great to open and close jump rings, to tuck in the end of a wrapped loop, or to grab and tighten beading wire prior to crimping. We reach for these pliers constantly.

- ✔ **Crimping pliers,** which appear in Figure 1-1c, help you flatten crimp beads in a clean, neat, professional-looking way. (*Crimp beads* flatten around beading wire to secure findings, beads, and other components onto the wire at a specific point. We cover the basics of the technique in Chapter 2 and have many, many projects dedicated to crimping techniques in Chapter 4.)

Wielding your wire cutters

You need at least one wire cutter, sometimes called *cutting pliers,* in your toolbox to help you cut wire, head pins, beading wire, or even thread in a pinch. Three different wire cutters can come in very handy:

- ✔ **Diagonal cutters** leave the edge of the wire pointed or angled. For the most part, use a diagonal cutter when you need a pointed end or you're going to wrap the wire and the point down.

- ✔ **Flush cutters** create a blunt or flat cut on the end of a wire. These are a great choice to use when the end of the wire may come into contact with your skin. Check them out in Figure 1-2.

  Diagonal cutters and flush cutters are tough to tell apart at first glance; the difference between them is the angle of the cutting blade.

- ✔ **Memory wire cutters (or *shears*)** are stronger than the other two cutters and made specifically to cut the extremely rigid memory wire easily.

Never use diagonal or flush cutters to cut memory wire on a regular basis. *Memory wire* is a rigid steel wire that will quickly dull even the sharpest cutters. If you plan to make memory wire jewelry, invest in some memory wire cutters.

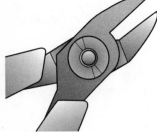

Figure 1-2: Wire cutters make life easier.

You can find wire cutters that cut either from the side or on the end (these end-cut pliers are sometimes called *nippers*). We think side wire cutters are best for general use.

Investigating other hand tools

Depending on what techniques you choose to focus on, you may need a few other items to add the nuances that make finished projects something special.

Wire jigs

You can make wire-wrapped jewelry with pliers and a wire cutter. But if you want to make consistently sized, uniform pieces over and over again, consider a jig. A *wire jig,* like the one in Figure 7-2 in Chapter 7, is the only way to go. In its simplest form, a jig is a board (typically made of plastic) with holes, and you insert pegs into those holes. Then you wrap wire around the pegs. You can change the configuration of pegs to create all sorts of wire-wrapped shapes.

Check out Chapter 7 for details on how to make wire jewelry with a wire jig.

Files

A file allows you to remove any rough or pointy edges that happen when you snip and trim wire. You can shape and smooth sharp metal edges, leaving your pieces ouch-free. Files also come in handy if you decide to pursue more advanced metal-working techniques that are beyond the scope of this book (but really fun!), like working with *precious metal clay* (a malleable clay containing real precious metal that cures to reveal only the precious metal) or metal fabrication techniques.

Some people advocate using a fingernail file in jewelry making. We don't recommend it. They typically aren't hard enough to get the job done. A good set of jewelry files costs around $10 for a set of ten.

Bead reamers

A *bead reamer* is a tool designed to gently increase the size of a bead hole. The rounded tip gradually increases in diameter and is designed to allow you to gently twist the reamer, slowly widening the hole or smoothing out rough edges. Bead reamers seem to work best with natural materials like pearls and gemstones, but they can work on other materials as well. You can get a set for around $5.

If you primarily use crystal, glass, or machined metal beads, you can probably skip this tool. Most of those beads have smooth, consistently sized holes. However, if you move on to cutting your own metal components (like tags, for example), a bead reamer is a great choice to smooth any drill holes you make.

Scissors

Depending on what kind of jewelry you make, scissors can be essential. Bead weaving in particular requires a sharp pair of scissors. Use them to cut thin stringing materials, like silk bead cord and Nymo thread. We've even used them to cut very thin (32-gauge) wire.

Keep a designated pair of scissors with your jewelry-making equipment so you always have them handy. Check out the needlework section of the craft store to find a small pair that will be just right for you.

Hammer

A hammer is great tool to use if you work with precious metals. You can create interesting textures by repeatedly striking metal with the two different ends of the hammer. Or you can actually pound a piece of metal around something, like a *mandrel* (a metal rod) for example, to make rings and cuff bracelets. Look for metal ball-peen hammers with smooth, rounded, or textured heads to make different impressions as you pound.

If, instead, you want to smooth or harden metal pieces without marring them, choose a rawhide hammer, which looks more like a mallet with a wide head. It's made of wood and rawhide and helps you harden and/or flatten metal pieces while keeping them nice and smooth. You can also choose a plastic mallet for this not-so-delicate job.

Anvil and block

If you're pounding on metal with a hammer, you need something to lay the metal on, right? We don't recommend that you just sit down at your dining room table and start banging away. At a minimum, you need a piece of wood to protect your work surface. But when you're ready to take the next step and choose a professional piece of equipment, consider either an anvil or a block.

A *block* is a thick square block of steel (or rubber or wood) with a flat surface for hammering metal. It's handy for hardening your metal designs to help them keep their shape. Or you can use it as a firm surface to pound out cool and interesting textures.

Place a small, folded hand towel under your block to muffle the hammering noise *and* keep the block from damaging your work surface as you bang away. If your block is fairly lightweight, dampen the hand towel before you place it under the block to keep it from sliding around.

In addition to being one of Wile E. Coyote's favorite weapons, an *anvil* is a metal-working tool made from solid steel designed to provide a firm surface for you to hammer away on to shape and mold softer metals. In addition to the flat, block-like top, anvils have *horns* (metal pieces that stick out from the main body of the anvil) with various shapes. Most have a rounded horn to allow you to shape a cuff, for example. Some also have horns with corners of some sort so you can create more-angular designs.

You don't need a big blacksmith-sized anvil. You can find jewelry-sized anvils at many online jewelry stores for less than $30. Depending on the material you choose, a block costs between $10 and $20.

Sorting Out Equipment

In addition to tools, other pieces of equipment are helpful in pursuing your newfound passion for jewelry making. In the following sections, we give you more details about those items, as well as the reasons why we recommend using them.

Keeping things straight with a bead board organizer

An essential design tool, a bead board organizer (typically just called a *bead board*), shown in Figure 1-3, gives you built-in space to lay your bead strands out as you create your design. Typically, it has little compartments to hold and separate several types of beads, plus measurements along the strand compartments to help you keep track of how long your creation is. Some boards have the capacity to lay out as many as five necklace strands and five bracelet strands at the same time — superhelpful if you're designing coordinating accessories.

Consider investing in one of these inexpensive ($5 or less) tools, even if you plan only to follow the designs in this book instead of coming up with your own original creations. You can read the instructions and lay out the beads in the specified pattern, and then you can string them up more quickly and accurately.

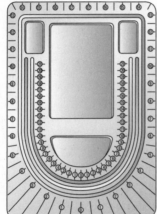

Figure 1-3:
A bead board organizer helps you keep things straight.

Laying down a bead mat

A bead mat is a piece of fabric that serves as place to set your beads. The fabric helps keep the beads from rolling around on the table, and if you drop a bead on your work surface, it's less likely to bounce away from you if you have a mat to cushion it. It's a helpful piece of equipment, especially if you're stringing beads randomly.

You can buy a bead mat from a bead store or make your own from a piece of felt, an old blanket, or even a dish towel. You just need something with a little cushioning power. Cut it or fold it to roughly 9 x 12 inches and bead away.

Using a polishing cloth and some elbow grease

If you work with precious metal, you need a polishing cloth. A *polishing cloth* is a piece of fabric (usually a special weave of cotton) treated with a polishing compound of some sort. Coauthor Heather keeps one on her work table and always gives her wire a quick rub down with one of these before using it in a design. The cloth is way more convenient than using a messy paste or liquid, and unless the metal is severely tarnished, a polishing cloth is usually all you need.

Don't wash your polishing cloth, or you'll remove all the cleaning properties. Just use it until it's covered in black grody tarnish, and then toss it and get a new one.

Very fine steel wood (0000 grade) is great for polishing fine sterling wire as well. It's amazing how it brings out the material's natural shine.

Storing your treasures in a bead box with compartments

You can find many different styles of this quintessential beader's best friend, shown in Figure 1-4, in any craft store. Bead boxes with compartments are great for holding lots of different beads in a small space without mixing them together. You can find simple plastic boxes with 20 compartments, rolling totes that hold multiple bead boxes, or cabinets that hold hundreds of tiny drawers.

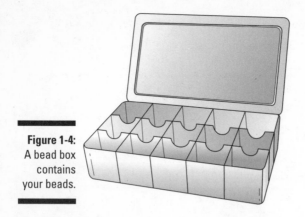

Figure 1-4:
A bead box
contains
your beads.

Getting everything exact with a ruler or tape measure

Even if you choose to buy a bead board marked with accurate measurements, it's handy to keep a ruler or tape measure nearby. Check out the notions section of a fabric or craft store to find a small flexible tape measure that you can keep with your tools. You can find them for around $2.

Getting Your Beads and Stones Together

Ah, beads! These little beauties are probably the reason you're interested in jewelry making to begin with. It's why coauthor Heather got started. She was enamored by the variety of shapes, sizes, colors, finishes, and textures available. Almost every time we pick up a catalog or stroll through a bead store, we see something new, something that inspires us to make a new jewelry piece. In this section, we give you the basics of getting your beads together to get started.

We could talk forever about beads, but we have limited space. Ultimately there's no substitute for reading bead catalogs and visiting your local bead store to continue to develop your knowledge about what's available in the world of beads and figure out what you like.

Selecting bead sizes and shapes

Designing jewelry is definitely an art, rather than a science. Choosing what beads go together in different pieces is really a matter of trial and error, and you'll improve as you get more experience. Certain characteristics (like size, shape, and material) typically come into play when you choose beads for a project.

Why size matters

Because beads are relatively small, individual beads are typically sized in millimeters, designated by the abbreviation *mm*. (Some vendors give the English equivalent in inches for larger pieces.) But strands of beads are typically sold in inches. For example, you may choose to buy a 16-inch strand of 6mm beads, which is roughly 68 beads. Confused yet? To help you out, we include this handy chart, Table 1-1, that lists the bead size, strand lengths, and the approximate number of beads on the strand.

You can also use Table 1-1 to figure out how many beads you need to buy to create a necklace or bracelet of a certain length.

Table 1-1		Approximate Number of Beads Needed for Specific Lengths of Beaded Strands								
Bead Size				**Length of Beaded Strand**						
	6"	**8"**	**10"**	**12"**	**14"**	**16"**	**20"**	**24"**	**28"**	**32"**
3mm	51	68	85	102	119	136	170	204	238	271
4mm	39	51	64	77	89	102	127	153	178	204
6mm	26	34	43	51	60	68	85	102	119	136
8mm	20	26	32	39	45	51	64	77	89	102
10mm	16	21	26	31	36	41	51	61	72	82
12mm	13	17	22	26	30	34	43	51	60	68
14mm	11	15	19	22	26	29	37	44	51	59
16mm	10	13	16	20	23	26	32	39	45	51
18mm	9	12	15	17	20	23	29	34	40	46

Because we want you to be successful in re-creating the designs in this book, we include specific information about the size of each and every bead in each and every project. Just take a look at the materials list at the beginning of each project for the specifics.

Shaping up your options

Beads come in all kinds of shapes. Traditional shapes, like round, bicone, teardrop, and oval, come in all sizes and materials. But other shapes (including hearts, stars, various animals, and leaves) are increasingly popular.

Here's a quick rundown on the shapes we commonly use for the designs in this book:

- **Bicone:** A bicone bead sort of looks like two cones stacked on top of each other with the non-pointy ends touching. The center of the bead is wide, and the tips taper down to a point. You can find *faceted* (having many flat, polished cuts) and smooth bicones. Faceted crystal bicone beads are extremely popular in jewelry design and available just about anywhere that sells jewelry.

- **Cube:** A cube is a square bead with six sides that are exactly the same size. You can find faceted and smooth cubes. Crystal cubes tend to be faceted, but other materials may be smooth or faceted.

- **Nugget:** This bead shape is defined by its lack of shape, strangely enough. The term *nugget* refers to a bead chunk that has no specific dimensions or proportions. Instead, it's a bead (often of a piece of gemstone) with angular edges and sides unequal in length.

- **Round:** Round beads are, well, round — perfectly spherical in fact. Unless otherwise noted, they're smooth. These beads are great all-purpose beads that can be used alone or to provide a visual break between other bead shapes.

✔ **Rondelle:** Rondelles are round-ish beads. They have an overall round shape, but they're typically a bit squished, almost doughnut-like. The hole is drilled through the wider, flatter face of the bead, rather than the round, thinner edge. Often the round edge is embellished in some way, with crystals or a texture. Many spacer beads are rondelles.

✔ **Tube:** Tubes are rounded beads that are longer than they are wide.

Making sense of seed beads

You've probably seen the pouches or tubes of tiny colorful glass beads that line at least one wall of your local bead store. These beads, called *seed beads,* are essential in techniques like bead weaving. Larger seed beads can be strung into standard necklaces, bracelets, earrings, and more. Seed beads have their own set of rules regarding sizing. They have a complicated number system, and after you crack it, you can differentiate these little guys from each other without too much problem.

The larger the size number, the smaller the seed bead. So for example, size 8 seed beads, like the ones we use in the black-and-bright necklace in Chapter 3, are larger than size 11 seed beads, like the ones used in the red hot net necklace in Chapter 11.

In addition to size choices, you can consider color (including some cool inside-out transparent beads) and shape (like hexagonal, square, and triangle) when contemplating your own designs.

Managing materials

The materials you select for a piece significantly impact the look of the design. When you pick out sparkling crystals, rich veiny turquoise nuggets, or sterling silver rondelles, you set the tone for your entire piece.

We can't possibly cover the full range of the amazing materials made into beads these days. We haven't touched on shell, wood, bone, horn, or acrylic. Consider this a recommendation to visit your local bead shop soon.

Gemstones

When you think of the word *gemstone,* you probably think of precious stones like diamonds, rubies, and emeralds. Those gems are indeed gemstones, but for many of us, they're out of our everyday jewelry-making budget. Lucky for us, though, many other gemstones may fill the bill, like pearls, onyx, hematite, or fluorite. You can get high-quality specimens of these semiprecious stones at some surprisingly low prices.

Here are a few things to remember when you're looking to buy some gemstones to spice up your jewelry making.

✔ **Consider what grade you need to purchase.** Coauthor Heather just picked up some peridot and garnet stones (her daughters' birthstones) for a reasonable price because they were small- and medium-grade stones. If by some sad set of circumstance the pieces get lost or broken (they're still pretty young girlies), she won't feel completely distraught because she didn't pay a ton of money for them. On the other hand, if you make high-end pieces with nothing but precious metals and high-quality gemstones, you need to buy and sell accordingly.

✔ **Get to know gemstone lingo.** Terms like *synthetic* (grown in a lab), *simulated* (glass colored to look like gemstones), *natural* (100 percent naturally occurring and untampered with), and *genuine* (created in nature, but may have been altered in some way) have different meanings and should affect the price you pay for the beads.

It's perfectly legal to sell nonnatural stones, but the details of the alteration must be disclosed to the buyer. Get the full scoop before you open your wallet. Don't pay for more than you're getting.

✔ **Buy the right amount for your budget and needs.** This point has two sides. Side one: Typically the more you buy, the less your per-bead price is. Side two: The more you buy, the more you pay in actual dollars. Buy cautiously, but shrewdly, because these beads can be one of your highest expenses.

Glass and crystal

Basic glass beads are economical. Highly faceted rounds and bicones can be a great addition to any project. In fact, you can create gorgeous pieces with nothing but basic glass beads.

Although many glass beads are basic, a few are not. Artists specialize in creating a stunning array of handmade glass beads. Here are a couple of categories to check out:

✔ **Dichroic:** Fashioned into beads, pendants, and charms, these *dichroic* (two-colored) glass pieces have a thin layer of metal infused into them, giving them an iridescent, changing quality as you view them from different angles.

✔ **Lampwork:** Lampwork beads are made with a torch and bead canes in several stages. Often the artist creates the basic shape of the bead, and then adds designs (like flowers, swirls, and bumps) on the surface, almost painting them on with molten glass. Check out an example of a beautiful lampwork bead in the free-form peyote bracelet in Chapter 11.

Crystal is really just glass with lead added to it. (It's perfectly safe because the lead is stabilized in the glass.) Some crystals, often the colorless ones, have a coating applied. The most common coating is *aurora borealis, AB* for short, that gives the crystals an iridescent shine.

Metal

Metal beads add something special to jewelry creations. Back in the day, you had gold, sterling silver, silver plate, or base metal, which was colored to look like gold or silver. (And we had to walk to school uphill, both ways.) But today, even at the neighborhood craft store, you can find many different kinds of metal beads and components. Most stores have a full section of sterling silver beads and components. Some may have gold as well. And almost all have base-metal beads in a variety of finishes designed to resemble antique bronze, patina-fraught copper, or tarnished silver.

Clay

Many fun and funky clay beads are on the market today. Some jewelry artists work exclusively in this versatile medium, making colorful millefiori cane beads. These artists often create jewelry with their custom-made pieces, as well as sell beads for you to use in your own designs. Check out arts festivals and craft fairs to meet polymer clay artists and pick up some of their creations.

We dedicate a whole chapter (Chapter 12) to the joys of polymer clay. We show you how to roll your own beads and create other jewelry components.

Stringing with Wire, Threads, and Cords

If you can string a bead on it, we've probably used it in our jewelry making. If it's used in jewelry making or beading, we've probably used it to do other stuff too. (Coauthor Heather just used beading wire and crimp beads to fix a set of broken wind chimes.)

Wire hardness and size

Did you think all wire was just long and skinny? Not true. If you were to cut a piece of wire and then inspect its cross-section under a microscope, you'd see right away the differences between seemingly similar pieces of wire. That's exactly what we (or rather Fire Mountain Gems and Beads) did to create Figure 1-5. The chart can help you figure out which wire works best for your particular project. To make things easy, we use 22-gauge sterling silver wire for the bulk of the projects in this book.

A general rule of thumb: The higher the gauge number, the smaller the diameter of the wire. So an 18-gauge wire is thicker than a 26-gauge wire.

Figure 1-5:
Wire sizes and shapes.

WIRE SIZE CHART

In reference to wire gauge size numbers, the larger the number, the smaller the diameter of the wire.

Round	Square	
• 26 Gauge	· 26 Gauge	· 22 Gauge
• 24 Gauge	· 24 Gauge	- 20 Gauge
• 22 Gauge	■ 22 Gauge	- 18 Gauge
• 21 Gauge	■ 21 Gauge	- 16 Gauge
• 20 Gauge	■ 20 Gauge	— 14 Gauge
• 18 Gauge	■ 18 Gauge	
• 16 Gauge	24-gauge wire is smaller in	
● 14 Gauge	diameter than 18-gauge wire.	

Source: Fire Mountain Gems and Beads

The term *hardness* refers to how easy (or not) a piece of *precious metal* (gold-filled or sterling silver) wire is to bend into a shape. You can find wire in *dead soft* (very malleable), *half-hard* (sort of malleable), and *full-hard* (not very malleable).

Cords, threads, and other stringing materials

You can find all kinds of cording made from many different kinds of materials these days. Here are just a few of our favorites:

- **Stretchy cord:** We use this quite a bit in the early stringing chapters. You can use it to make pieces that don't need a clasp. Instead, the cord stretches to accommodate hands, heads, or whatever obstacle you need to slip the jewelry over.

- **Leather:** This all-purpose stringing material is great for knotting, or you can choose to terminate it with heavy findings designed to accommodate its girth.

- **Beading wire:** Possibly the best thing to happen to jewelry making in 2,000 years, nylon-coated stainless steel beading wire (typically just called beading wire) is an essential element for most jewelry makers. Its amazing combination of strength and flexibility makes it a great choice for almost any application. Popular brand names of beading wire include Accu-flex, Beadalon, and Soft Flex.

   If you see the term *beading wire* in a materials list, it refers to nylon-coated stainless steel wire. Wire that you can bend and it holds its shape is called simply *wire*. We know it's confusing, but we're going along with the manufacturers on this one.

- **Nymo:** Nymo is a nylon thread used in bead weaving that looks much like the thread used in sewing machines. Smaller amounts are sold on bobbin-sized spools, and it's available in a large variety of colors and thicknesses. Nymo must be *conditioned* (lightly covered in beeswax) before using it to weave.

- ✔ **Silamide:** For those bead weavers who like to skip a step, Silamide is a thread that comes already conditioned and ready to go. Smaller amounts are sold wrapped around display cards, while larger amounts are sold by the spool. It doesn't come in as many colors as Nymo, but it still has a pretty good assortment, such as purple, blue, pink, off-white, black, and brown.

- ✔ **Kevlar:** Nothing beats the strength of Kevlar (as in the material used for bulletproof vests), and some bead weavers love this fact about this strong-yet-thin stringing medium. One drawback is that it's very limited in colors.

- ✔ **Braided thread:** Also often referred to under brand names like FireLine or Power Pro, this is a nylon cord that looks similar to good old fishing line. It's superstrong, and many bead weavers love working with it because it's available in a clear color and thus can be used with any color of beads.

- ✔ **Silk:** The traditional stringing material used for pearls for hundreds of years, silk still really can't be beat for stringing and knotting pearls and other gemstones. It comes in a large assortment of colors. You can buy it wrapped around small display cards, which includes an attached needle, or for those who need to buy in bulk, you can get silk on large spools, sans the needle.

- ✔ **Nylon:** Some bead stringers prefer using nylon beading thread over silk because you don't have as many issues with snagging or stretching because it's not a natural material. Nylon is also a good choice when you want to knot between gemstone beads.

Selecting Your Findings

Without findings, most jewelry would be little more than just a strand of beads. *Findings* — the connectors, clasps, wires, and non-bead components used in jewelry making — give handmade jewelry a professional, quality finish. They allow your pieces to take on a new dimension.

Most findings are made out of metal, but they may be embellished with beads. Metal findings bear some of the stress of wearing the piece (like the pull of gravity). For many years, you could find findings only in precious metal or base metal. Now base metals come in a variety of finishes, like antiqued brass, antiqued bronze, colored wire, weathered copper, and on and on. Experiment with designing with different finishes.

Fascinating fasteners: Clasps

A *clasp* is a jewelry component that allows you to put a piece of jewelry on, take it off, and wear it securely.

Answer two basic questions when choosing a clasp for your project:

- ✔ **How will your piece be worn?** Which is more important: a secure connection (think lobster claw or spring ring) or ease of putting on (toggle clasp or magnetic closure)?

- ✔ **What is the right metal for the job?** At a minimum, you want to coordinate the clasp with the other materials, but you can actually match the clasp to the materials. More and more, manufacturers are creating sets of findings designed to be used together.

Check out Figure 1-6 for our favorite clasp choices.

Figure 1-6:
An assort-
ment of
clasps.

Choosing from a variety of connectors

A *connector* is a component that helps you connect other elements together to make your designs special. So if you want to hang a charm from a bracelet, you need some kind of connector. These jewelry components typically fall into a few general categories we identify in the following sections.

Sometimes components that we traditionally think of as clasps can serve as connectors. Many add-on jewelry components, like charms and pendants, come pre-attached to either a spring ring or lobster clasp (both shown in Figure 1-6), which allows you to quickly and easily connect them to an existing piece of jewelry.

Crimps

Crimps, shown in Figure 1-7, are excellent connectors to have in your jewelry-making stash. In a nutshell, they're designed to let you smash them around a piece of cording to stop a bead (or clasp, charm, and so on) from sliding around on the cord.

Figure 1-7:
Crimp beads
and tubes
help you
make pro-
fessional
jewelry
quickly.

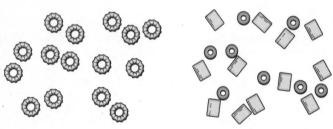

We recommend that you use a set of crimp pliers, shown in Figure 1-1, to flatten these components in the most professional manner. Check out Chapter 5, an entire chapter dedicated to all things crimped.

Jump rings

Jump rings are the consummate connectors. These little, perfectly round loops of metal aren't completely solid; they have a break or opening in them, as shown in Figure 1-8. Using pliers, you can gently twist these open and put them to 1,001 uses. You can connect them to dangles, chain, beads, or anything else with a hole in it.

If you do a lot of work with jump rings, consider investing in a set of pliers, called *jump ring pliers,* designed to help you open and close them easily without warping the nice roundness. For the projects in this book, we don't require these pliers, and instead use two pairs of smooth-tipped pliers (like chain-nose pliers, for example) to open and close them. Take a look at the appendix to see how to open and close a jump ring properly.

Figure 1-8:
Jump rings
allow you to
connect
clasps,
dangles,
and more to
your jewelry
creations.

Bead tips and clamshells

Ever wonder how a simple piece of thread sturdily connects to a metal clasp without an obvious, clunky knot? *Clamshells* and *bead tips,* shown in Figures 1-9a and 1-9b respectively, are the answer. These handy little connectors have a cup to hold knots and a metal hook to wrap around your favorite clasp.

Figure 1-9:
Clamshells
and bead
tips are
great to use
with knot-
ting and
crimping
techniques.

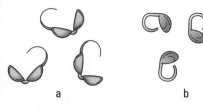

a   b

To get some practice working with bead tips and clamshells, take a look at Chapter 5. We use them in several designs in that chapter.

Spacer bars

These useful findings hold multiple strands of beads together. *Spacer bars* are great for creating cuff bracelets and chokers, or any time you need similarly sized strands of beads to stick closely together. Look for spacer bars with two, three, or more holes to create multistrand masterpieces.

Designing with ear hooks and head pins

You need a few essential items to create the most beloved of all handmade jewelry items — earrings. *Ear hooks* and *ear wires* allow you to hang your creations from your ear lobes. *Head pins* and *eye pins* let you stack beads and hang them with ease.

Ear hooks and ear wires

Ear hooks and ear wires, like most metal components, are available in just about any material and color you can imagine. In general, experiment to see what you like (like anything from the assortment in Figure 1-10), and you can't go wrong.

That "anything goes" rule has one exception. With ear wires and hooks, people tend to have more problems with metal sensitivity, an allergic response to metal. They may be able to wear a loose necklace or bracelet made out of complete junk, but when metal is close to or even inserted into their bodies (like earrings), they have trouble with anything but precious metal. Precious metal is always safe, so when in doubt, go with gold-filled or sterling silver wire.

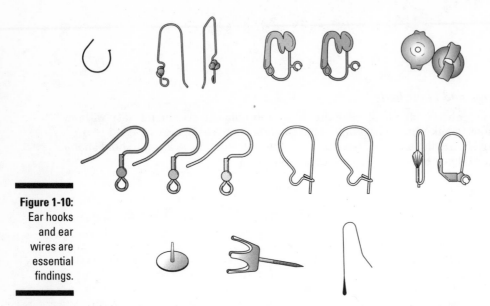

Figure 1-10: Ear hooks and ear wires are essential findings.

Chapter 10 gives you instructions for making your own ear hooks (or turn to Chapter 7 if you want to use a wire jig). Until you feel up to the task, feel free to buy ear hooks ready made at any craft or bead store.

Head pins and eye pins

These findings are terrific for making dangles of all different sizes. The most common use for head pins and eye pins is making the body of an earring, but many designers use them to create dangles for necklaces and bracelets too. They work in basically the same way, but the base of each is slightly different.

- ✔ A **head pin** is a fairly stiff wire with a base on it, designed to allow you to string on beads without them falling off. Often the base, or *head,* is flat, like the one in Figure 1-11a. Some head pins have a jewel or a detailed metal component as the base.

- ✔ An **eye pin** is similar to a head pin, but instead of ending in a head, it terminates with a small loop called an *eye* (check out Figure 1-11b). Eye pins are a great choice if you're planning to connect several dangles together. Use chain-nose pliers to gently open the loops, connect pieces together, and then close them up again.

In Chapter 2, we give you instructions for making eye loops. After you master that, you can use wire to make your own eye pins, customized to any size you need.

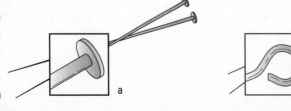

Figure 1-11: Head pins and eye pins.

a

b

Chapter 2

Brushing Up on Bead Stitches and Other Basics

*I*f you don't use it, you lose it, and the first thing to go is the bead brain. Most of us would prefer to spend time beading and making jewelry instead of doing just about anything else that requires our attention — like doing laundry, running errands, or attending to the multiple items on our to-do list. But reality usually dictates otherwise. So it's not surprising that on occasion we need a little review of basic jewelry techniques.

This chapter is a quick reference for basic bead-stringing, bead-weaving, and wire-wrapping methods. You may want to read through it before attempting some of the projects and/or come back to it as you make your way through the rest of the book and need a quick how-to reminder. For example, if you're working on one of the bead-weaving projects and can't remember what the heck a stop bead is, then quickly flip over here for your answer.

If you're a total jewelry-making newbie, you'll find this chapter helpful, but it may not cover everything you need to know. For more details on the basics of jewelry making, see *Jewelry Making & Beading For Dummies* (Wiley).

Getting Down to Bead-Stringing Basics

Most beginners start making jewelry by using bead-stringing methods. Many of these aren't that difficult for the average hobbyists to pick up pretty quickly, but a few take some practice and patience to master. Therefore, we cover them in some detail in the following sections. Specifically, we look at using crimp beads to finish off jewelry pieces, bead tips to finish the ends of strung jewelry designs, and bead knotting to assist in creating secure beaded jewelry items. All three techniques will go a long way in helping you create outstanding beaded jewelry.

Closing a crimp bead

Being able to properly close a crimp bead on the end of a beaded piece of jewelry like a necklace or bracelet can be challenging at first. If you haven't done crimping in a while, remember that this technique does take some practice. It's pretty rare to do it perfectly on the first try.

Although you can flatten a crimp bead with a pair of chain-nose pliers, we recommend using a pair of crimping pliers (see Figure 2-1) to get a more finished look to your beaded designs. The pliers have two notches that you use to close and shape the crimp bead, first pressing the crimp with the second notch on the pliers (labeled as Crimp Phase 1 in Figure 2-1) and then using the first notch (labeled as Crimp Phase 2 in Figure 2-1); therefore, sometimes we refer to this technique as the *two-phase crimp method.* Also, because this method rolls the bead rather than flattens it, the crimps are less likely to scratch the wearer.

Crimp Phase 2

Crimp Phase 1

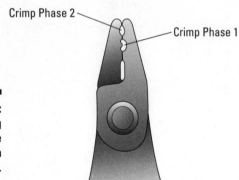

Figure 2-1:
Crimping
pliers are
closed in
two phases.

A quality crimp bead helps you create a quality finish to your strung pieces. Though sterling silver, tube-shaped crimp beads may cost a little more than round, base-metal crimp beads, the added expense is well worth it. You'll find the tube-shaped crimp beads much easier to work with, and as a result, you'll do a much better job fastening the crimp bead, and it will stay securely in place.

It's critical to use the right size of crimp beads with the right size of beading wire and the right size of crimping pliers. Check bead wire manufacturers' Web sites for their recommendations on the proper size of crimp beads, beading wire, and pliers to use together.

To close a crimp bead, follow these instructions:

1. **Insert your beading wire through your crimp bead, and then bring the wire back down through the bead to make a loop of beading wire, as pictured in Figure 2-2.**

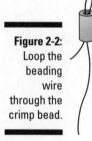

Figure 2-2:
Loop the
beading
wire
through the
crimp bead.

2. **Using the crimping pliers, position the crimp bead in the second notch on the pliers (this is the notch closer to you as you hold the pliers), and close the pliers in one firm motion.**

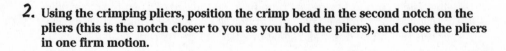

Your crimp bead is now curled, as illustrated in Figure 2-3.

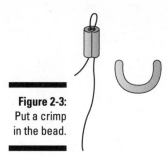

Figure 2-3:
Put a crimp
in the bead.

3. **Position the same crimp bead in the first notch on the pliers, making sure to set the crimp bead on its side. Again, with a firm motion, close the pliers around the crimp bead.**

The crimp bead is now shaped into a rounded tube, like Figure 2-4 shows.

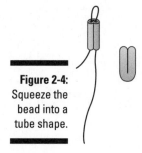

Figure 2-4:
Squeeze the
bead into a
tube shape.

Practice makes perfect — well, just about perfect — when it comes to closing crimp beads. If you haven't done this technique in a while, give yourself a little time to warm up before expecting to make perfectly closed crimp beads again. And if you're ready for some practice, head to Chapter 4, where all the projects require you to work with crimp beads.

Attaching a bead tip

Using a bead tip (see Figure 2-5) is a very popular method for finishing off beaded jewelry. This finding is also sometimes referred to as a *clamshell* because it has cup-shaped pieces on the end that, when open, look like an open clamshell. Some bead tips have two cups (see Figure 2-5a) that hide a knot and look like a bead, while others have just one cup (see Figure 2-5b) and provide a place for the knot to rest in, though you have to look really hard to see it.

Though you can use beading wire with bead tips, jewelry designers usually prefer to use them with silk or nylon cording because this type of cord normally is finished off with a knot. When the clamshell sections are closed around the knot, it looks like a small bead at the end, thus the term *bead tip*. Bead tips are used in some of the bead-weaving projects in Chapters 6 and 11, so these findings can be used for finishing off seed bead jewelry as well as strung jewelry pieces.

Most beginners have pretty good success with bead tips. So, if you have a friend who wants to make jewelry like you do, then suggest he or she start off with these findings instead of using crimp beads.

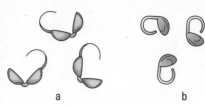

Figure 2-5:
Some bead tips have two cups, while others have one cup.

a   b

To attach a bead tip, follow these instructions:

1. Tie a few overhand knots on the end of your cord (one on top of the other), and with scissors, trim off the excess cord after the knot, leaving the longer cord for bead-stringing purposes.

2. Insert the cord (which should be attached to a beading needle) through the hole in the bead tip, and pull the cord so the knot rests inside the shell of the bead tip, as shown in Figure 2-6.

Figure 2-6:
The knot rests inside the shell part of the bead tip.

3. Dab a little glue on the knot. If you're using the type of bead tip that has two clamshell sides, use chain-nose pliers to carefully close the sides around the knot, as illustrated in Figure 2-7. If you're using the type of bead tip that has just one clamshell side, simply allow the glue to dry while the knot rests in the shell before continuing your stringing.

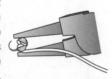

Figure 2-7:
Close the bead tip halves around the knot.

4. After stringing on your beads, attach a bead tip to the other end of the cord. To do this, insert the cord through another bead tip, making sure that the open part of the bead tip is facing away from the beads.

5. Tie another overhand knot, and use a beading awl (see Figure 2-8a) or corsage pin (see Figure 2-8b) to help push the knot into the shell of the bead tip. Trim off the excess cord after the knot.

6. Repeat Step 3 to finish off the bead tip.

Figure 2-8:
These tools
help you
move your
knots.

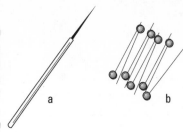

a   b

Only a small amount of pressure is needed to close bead tips. If you press too hard, you can flatten or damage the bead tip, and it won't be secure enough to use. If this happens, it's back to the drawing board.

Knotting between beads

Tying knots between beads is a skill that's considered a little more advanced than just plain bead stringing, but it really isn't all that difficult. Like most jewelry-making methods, it just takes some time. After you get enough knots knotted, you'll increase in both skill level and speed. If you want to take your bead stringing to the next level, mastering knot tying is a must-know skill, and you'll find a few projects that incorporate this technique in Chapter 5. Tying good knots:

- ✔ Creates a better drape or swag for your beads.

- ✔ Secures them better, especially if the strand breaks.

- ✔ Keeps the beads from being damaged because they won't rub up against each other on the beading cord. This is especially important when working with porous beads such as pearls.

Knotting can add a significant amount of extra length to a beaded design, so keep this in mind when you set your beads out on your bead board. Although it's not a major deal when it comes to necklaces, because a longer necklace will still fit you, this is superimportant to consider when making bracelets. String it too long and your bracelet could become an anklet.

To tie a traditional knot between beads, follow these instructions:

1. **After you've started your strand of beads and strung on your first bead, tie a loose overhand knot, as illustrated in Figure 2-9.**

Figure 2-9:
Start with a
loose knot.

2. **Insert either a beading awl or corsage pin into the knot (see Figure 2-10).**

Figure 2-10:
A corsage pin is inexpensive and available at most craft stores.

3. **Keeping the pin inside the knot, push the knot toward the bead, making sure to get it as close as possible to the bead. See Figure 2-11 for an example of this.**

Figure 2-11:
Slide the knot up next to the bead.

4. **After you have the knot up against the bead, hold the knot with the fingers of one hand, and use the other hand to pull the pin out of the knot. Then use your fingers and the pin to tighten the knot up against the bead some more.**

Some jewelry designers really like to use a knotting tool called the Tri-Cord Knotter. It's available at most beading supply companies and is about $50. This tool is designed to help you make the knot and push it up against each bead in one quick motion, so for anyone just starting out with knotting, it's a very handy tool. Accompanying kits, which include multimedia instructional materials, are also available for this unique jewelry tool.

Boning Up on Bead-Weaving Basics

Stitches are the stars of bead weaving. Brick stitch, net stitch, and peyote are very popular and usually some of the first techniques that come to mind for those who know at least a little something about weaving with tiny glass treasures called *seed beads*.

However, before you get started bead weaving, you need to know some other basics, such as how to thread a needle and condition thread, which will help you successfully complete bead-weaving projects. Without them, the stitches just aren't possible. No matter how well you've mastered a stitch, it doesn't matter much if you can't do something like finish off the threads when you're finished. In the following sections, we take a good look at some of the basic bead-weaving techniques you need to make your seed bead designs secure and complete, as well as review some of the basic stitches, which you'll find used in projects in Chapters 6 and 11.

The eye of a needle used for bead weaving is typically much narrower than the eye of an average sewing needle. Therefore, threading it requires a different approach. Instead of holding the needle and trying to insert the thread through the eye, do the opposite: Hold the thread between your thumb and index finger, and bring the eye of the needle to the thread.

Getting in shape: Conditioning your thread

Silamide thread (which we use for the bead-weaving projects in this book) already comes conditioned, but if you want to use something else, like Nymo thread, you'll need to condition the thread before threading your needle with it. You can use beeswax for this or a product called Thread Heaven.

You need to condition threads like Nymo to help keep the thread from tangling as you weave. It also makes it easier to attach your needle and slip on beads because the beeswax or Thread Heaven (whichever you decide to use) covers the thread, creating a smoother thread in general.

To condition thread, follow these instructions:

1. **Cut a piece of Nymo thread to the desired length.**

2. **Take one end of the thread and use your thumb to press it against the beeswax or Thread Heaven.**

3. **With the other hand, pull the thread across the beeswax or Thread Heaven while holding your thumb in place.**

4. **Repeat this a few times, making sure to coat all areas of the thread.**

Getting the go-ahead to use a stop bead

Bead weavers use a *stop bead* to prevent their beads from falling off the thread. You just need one bead for this purpose, and you'll pull it off later, so it's a good idea to use a bead that doesn't match any of the beads you plan to weave together. That way, you can identify the stop bead more easily when you're ready to remove it.

To attach a stop bead, follow these instructions:

1. **After attaching your thread to your needle, insert the needle through your stop bead.**

2. **Bring the needle back around the bottom of the bead, and insert it again.**

3. **Pull the bead down to about 6 to 10 inches from the end of the thread.**

4. **Begin stringing on beads according to the project directions.**

Attaching threads as you keep on weaving on

When you're weaving beads, from time to time you'll need to attach a new thread, because as your beaded piece gets bigger, your thread gets shorter (naturally). Most bead weavers start with a *working thread* that is about 3 feet (plus or minus) long. Superexperienced bead weavers can usually handle starting with a longer working thread, but the rest of us have to be careful, or we'll get more knots in our thread than we know what to do with.

Therefore, one important technique to master is how to attach a new working thread to an in-progress jewelry piece. This method may vary a tad depending on the piece of jewelry you're weaving, but here are the basics when it comes to adding thread.

1. Look for a bead that's pretty close to the *exit bead* where you need the working thread to *exit* (come out of).

Try to pick a bead that you won't have to pass the needle and thread through again, because the more you go through these beads with your needle and thread, the less room there is later in the bead's hole.

2. After locating the bead in Step 1, insert your newly threaded needle up through this bead (making sure to leave at least a 6- to 8-inch thread tail), and keep snaking the needle and thread through other beads in your woven piece as you make your way toward the final bead where you need your working thread to exit from.

Depending on the stitch you're weaving, you may have to snake diagonally through beads or vertically through beads.

3. As you begin snaking your way through the beads, you'll see the threads that are holding previously woven beads together. We call these *bridge threads*. Choose one of these bridge threads, insert the needle and thread around the bridge thread, tie a simple overhand knot, and pull the thread so the tension on the thread is fairly tight and forces the knot into the nearest bead's hole.

4. Go back to snaking your needle and thread toward your exit bead. If you're snaking through a really large area of beads, you may want to repeat Step 3.

5. After you've snaked your way to the exit bead, insert the needle and thread through this bead so your working thread is now located in the exact spot where you ended.

You can continue weaving away at this point, as you were before you had to stop and attach more thread.

Finishing off threads for the big finish

As you weave your beads, you'll wind up with a lot of unfinished threads. Most projects require that you leave thread tails when you start new sections of weaving. Plus, as your working thread gets shorter, you'll have to replace it by attaching a new thread. So at some point, you'll need to finish off all of these leftover threads. You can wait and do them all at the end, or if the extra threads get in your way as you work, you can finish them off periodically.

To finish off the threads, you need to weave them back into your previously woven beads. If you trim them off without weaving first, the beads may become unwoven and fall off the jewelry piece you are making.

We'll start with tails that you've already secured with a knot (see the preceding section), because they're pretty easy to finish off:

1. Attach a beading needle to the tail you need to finish, and start snaking the needle and tail through beads you've previously woven together.

2. After you have a very small piece of thread left — say about an inch long — use a pair of sharp scissors to trim off the thread.

If you need to finish off a tail that hasn't been secured with a knot or if you need to finish off a working thread, here's how to do that:

1. Attach a needle to the thread you plan to finish off.

2. Pick a bead right next to where the thread is exiting the woven piece and snake the needle up through this bead.

3. Keep snaking the needle and thread through some more beads. Choose a *bridge thread* (a thread that's holding previously woven beads together), insert the needle and thread around the bridge thread, tie an overhand knot, and pull the thread so the tension is fairly tight and forces the knot into the nearest bead's hole.

4. Keep snaking your needle and thread through more beads. If you have to insert your needle and thread through a lot of beads, consider repeating Step 3.

5. When you have about an inch of thread left, finish by exiting the needle and thread through one last bead, and use a pair of sharp scissors to trim off the rest of the thread.

You may have noticed we didn't mention using glue to finish off threads. Some weavers do use glue for this, but we don't recommend it. You can get into some real problems with glue when it dries inside the bead holes and soaks into your beading thread. It's not at all unusual, even for a fairly experienced bead weaver, to need to occasionally pull beads out of a piece and weave them again. If you use glue, it's impossible to do this. In fact, some weavers don't even use knots for similar reasons.

Adding fringe as a finishing touch

Fringe is used to accent all kinds of jewelry designs, especially earrings. (Some of the projects in Chapter 6 use this technique.) If your jewelry piece seems to need a little extra zing, consider adding fringe. It's easy to do and a good way to include other types of beads, such as crystals and gemstones, into your bead-weaving jewelry designs.

To make a piece of fringe, follow these instructions:

1. Locate an area on your woven jewelry piece where the bead holes are facing out so you can insert your needle through them.

2. Bring the needle down through one of the beads.

3. Use the needle to add your choice of beads to the working thread.

4. Skipping the last bead, as illustrated in Figure 2-12, insert the needle back up through the beads you added in Step 3.

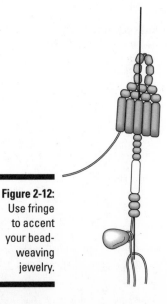

Figure 2-12:
Use fringe to accent your bead-weaving jewelry.

5. Bring the needle back up through the bead you went through in Step 2.

6. Bring the needle down through one of the beads next to this bead and continue adding as much fringe as you want.

TIP

Side-drilled teardrop-shaped crystals are excellent choices for adding to the ends of fringe. You can also use center-drilled teardrop beads. Just include a seed bead after the teardrop bead, and skip this bead when you snake the needle back up through the beads used for your fringe.

The ladder stitch: No climbing required

The *ladder stitch* can stand on its own, but it's also often used for creating a base row for weaving another stitch called brick stitch. *Bugle beads,* long, tube-shaped beads, work really well with the ladder stitch, but you can also use regular round seed beads. You use the ladder stitch to weave a few different pairs of earrings in Chapter 6.

To create the ladder stitch, follow these instructions:

1. Thread a needle with the length of thread you need, add a stop bead (see the "Getting the go-ahead to use a stop bead" section earlier in this chapter), and leave at least a 6-inch tail of thread.

2. Thread on 6 seed beads, and bring the needle up through the first 3 beads, as shown in Figure 2-13.

Figure 2-13:
Start your ladder stitch with just a few beads.

3. Pull the thread taut as you move the beads down to the end of the thread. Continue to tighten the thread tension until the two sets of beads (3 each) are lined up next to each other, as shown in Figure 2-14. Bring the needle back down through the second set of beads.

Figure 2-14:
Tighten the thread tension.

4. With the needle, pick up 3 more beads, and push these to the end of the thread.

5. Bring the needle back through the second set of beads (see Figure 2-15), and then back down through the third set added in Step 4.

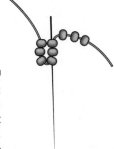

Figure 2-15:
Weave on a
second set
of beads.

6. To reinforce your ladder, thread the needle through the bead sets (these sort of work as the rungs of your ladder) a few times.

You can use either regular round seed beads or bugle beads (which are tubular shaped) for the ladder stitch; however, normally when you use bugle beads with the ladder stitch, you string on one bugle bead at a time instead of multiple beads. Chapter 6 has a project that uses the ladder stitch with bugle beads if you want to see the difference between the two types of beads when using this stitch.

Some bugle beads chip and crack on the ends. Make sure you cull these out of your beads before you start using them. Otherwise, the thread can snag and get cut from these rough areas on the ends of the beads.

Flat even-count peyote stitch: String, skip, string

The peyote stitch has a number of offshoots, but *flat even-count peyote* tends to be the mainstay. The basic concept is pretty simple: String a bead, skip a bead, string a bead, and so on. But if you're new to the stitch or haven't done it in a while and need a refresher, consider using two different colored beads and alternating the colors as you weave with this stitch. It will help you get a better visual idea of how the stitch works. Chapters 6 and 11 include a variety of jewelry designs using peyote.

To weave flat even-count peyote, follow these instructions:

1. Thread a needle with the length of thread you need, add a stop bead (see the "Getting the go-ahead to use a stop bead" section earlier in this chapter), and leave at least a 6-inch tail of thread.

2. With the needle, pick up an even number of beads, as pictured in Figure 2-16.

Figure 2-16:
Start with
an even
number of
beads.

3. String on another bead, skip a bead, and insert the needle through the next bead in the row, as shown in Figure 2-17.

Figure 2-17:
Skip the next bead when inserting the needle.

4. Continue this pattern, picking up a bead and skipping a bead, moving back and forth until you have the number of desired rows. See Figure 2-18 for an example.

Figure 2-18:
Continue the same process for all rows.

The net stitch: Putting some swag in your jewelry

The basic *net stitch* consists of swags of beads connected to a base row of beads. You can create the base row a number of different ways, depending on the design of the beaded piece you're making. For example, you can string a base row of beads and immediately start working back down this base row by adding your swag of beads (as described in these basic review instructions), or you can create a stand-alone base row and include an additional needle and thread to make the swag parts (as described in some of the bead-weaving projects included in Chapters 6 and 11).

As far as the swags go, you can make one simple swag all the way across, as explained in the review instructions, or you can get superfancy and continue to work back and forth creating lots and lots of swag rows. Because the net stitch tends to work up pretty quickly, it's a favorite among bead weavers.

To weave the net stitch, follow these instructions:

1. Thread a needle with the length of thread you need, add a stop bead (see the "Getting the go-ahead to use a stop bead" section earlier in this chapter), and leave at least a 6-inch tail of thread.

2. Thread on the desired number of beads to create your base row, as shown in Figure 2-19.

3. Start to create swags of beads down the base row, moving in the opposite direction so you're weaving the swags down the base row, as shown in Figure 2-20. Do this by adding beads to your working thread, skip a number of beads on the base row, and insert the needle through one bead on the base row.

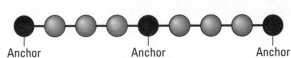

Figure 2-19:
Start with
a base row
of beads.

Anchor $\qquad$ Anchor $\qquad$ Anchor

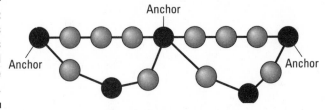

Figure 2-20:
Add swags
of beads
connected
to the base
row.

Anchor

Anchor $\qquad$ Anchor

Creating jewelry brick stitch by brick stitch

Brick stitch is also referred to by some as Comanche stitch because of its link to Native Americans who were some of the first bead weavers in North America. This stitch naturally becomes narrower and narrower until it ends with one bead on the end of the piece (as shown in the brick stitch triangle earrings in Chapter 6). Although you can add and subtract beads to alter the shape of the stitched piece, these instructions just cover the basic stitch.

To weave the brick stitch, follow these instructions:

1. **Thread a needle with the length of thread you need, and create a row of ladder stitch to the desired length (see the "The ladder stitch: No climbing required" section earlier in this chapter).**

2. **String one bead onto the thread, and insert the needle under the thread that joins the first two rungs of the ladder, as shown in Figure 2-21.**

Figure 2-21:
Insert the
needle
between
the rungs of
the ladder-
stitched
piece.

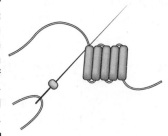

3. **Insert the needle up through the hole in the bead you added in Step 2, and push the bead down so it rests against the ladder section, as shown in Figure 2-22.**

4. **Repeat Steps 2 and 3 as you work back and forth down the ladder until you end up with one bead at the end of the piece, as shown in Figure 2-23.**

Figure 2-22:
Push the bead up against the ladder section.

Figure 2-23:
Continue to work back and forth.

Rounding Out Your Skills with Wire-Wrapping Basics

Wire jewelry techniques are a major help when making all kinds of jewelry. Even if you don't want to make jewelry primarily made of wire, you can use this medium to make findings like ear hooks and clasps (see Chapter 10) that help complete your beaded designs. If you only occasionally use wire when making jewelry, then you'll find this section particularly helpful because it covers some of the fundamental methods you'll use to complete a number of projects in this book. Some of these methods, such as straightening wire, aren't explicitly mentioned in a project because you may not need to do them for every single piece of wire jewelry you make. However, it's still important to have an understanding of them for those times when you need to use them. You'll find lots of wire-related jewelry projects sprinkled throughout this book, including in Chapters 3, 7, 8, and 9.

Don't get bent out of shape: Straightening wire

Sometimes, no matter how much wire work you've completed, you can't help but make a mistake now and then, and you bend a piece of wire the wrong way. Instead of sending it to your scrap pile, you can try to straighten it out first. Nylon jaw pliers (see Figure 2-24) are great for this task. Because the nose of the pliers aren't made out of metal, they won't mark the wire.

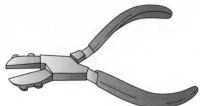

Figure 2-24:
Nylon jaw pliers are great for straightening wire.

To straighten wire, follow these instructions:

1. **Grasp a straight area of the wire with the nylon jaw pliers.**

2. **Pull the wire through them while holding the pliers closed.**

3. **Repeat as necessary until your wire is straight.**

Many vendors who sell wire will take your wire scraps as trade or they'll give a spot price for them. So never throw away even the tiniest amount of silver- or gold-filled wire. Keep similar wire scraps in separate containers. Plastic sandwich bags work really well for this.

Smoothing the rough edges: Filing wire

Metal workers use jewelers' files to file the ends of wire and other forms of metal. These are not at all like your average fingernail file. Jewelers' files are made of high carbon steel and come in different shapes like round, flat, and square. You may not always need to file your wire pieces, but if you find a rough spot, you'll want to do this. Also, it's a good idea to file the ends of your wire a little after cutting it.

To file wire, follow these instructions:

1. **Hold the wire piece in one hand, and hold a flat file in your other hand (your dominant hand).**

2. **Keeping the wire in one spot, pull the file across the end of the wire going in one direction.**

3. **Continue pulling the file across in one direction (not back and forth) until the end of the wire is smooth to the touch and flat.**

Seeing eye to eye: Eye loops

Knowing how to make an *eye loop* is a must-have skill for anyone working with wire. This is especially true if you like to connect beads with wire, because the loops provide a way to easily connect components together. Other than wire, you just need a pair of chain-nose pliers, wire cutters, and a pair of round-nose pliers for this.

We sometimes call this loop the *unwrapped loop* because, essentially, you're making a wrapped loop, but you just aren't wrapping the wire around itself to close the loop. (See the next section for the lowdown on wrapped loops.)

To make an eye loop, follow these instructions:

1. **Use the chain-nose pliers to bend the wire into a 90-degree angle.**

The wire should sort of look like an upside down "L," as shown in Figure 2-25.

Figure 2-25:
Bend the
wire into a
90-degree
angle.

2. **With the wire cutters, trim the bent area of the wire so it's about ½ inch long.**

3. **Using the round-nose pliers, grasp the bent area of the wire with the nose of the pliers and curl the wire toward you so it looks like the example in Figure 2-26.**

Figure 2-26:
Round-nose
pliers help
round the
loop.

4. **Reposition the round-nose pliers inside the loop you started in Step 3, and continue to curl the wire until it's almost closed, as shown in Figure 2-27.**

Figure 2-27:
Continue to
curl the
wire.

 Normally, you don't want to close the eye loop all the way because you may need it to be partially open so you can connect something to it, like another eye loop or a component of some kind. This, of course, depends on the specific jewelry piece you're making.

Winding it up: Wrapped loops

If you want an extra-secure wire connection, the wrapped loop technique is a good choice. It's similar to eye loops (see the preceding section), but it requires that you wrap the wire around itself to close the loop completely. You'll need a few tools for this: chain-nose pliers, round-nose pliers, and wire cutters.

Be aware of what components you plan to connect to each other when using the wrapped loop method. You don't want to close up a wrapped loop only to realize that you needed to slip a component onto the loop before wrapping it closed.

To create a wrapped loop, follow these instructions:

1. **Using the chain-nose pliers, bend the part of the wire where you want to create the loop into a 90-degree angle.**

2. **Grasp the wire at the bent area with the round-nose pliers, and while holding the pliers there, use your other hand to wrap the wire around the nose of the pliers so it looks like the loop in Figure 2-28.**

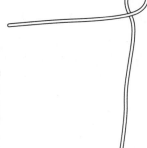

Figure 2-28:
Make the first loop of wire.

3. **With the nose of the round-nose pliers inside the loop (use your index finger to keep the wire in place if necessary), start to wrap the wire around itself, as shown in Figure 2-29.**

   If the wire is soft, you can usually just use your fingers for this, but you can also wrap by using chain-nose pliers, needle-nose pliers, or bent-nose pliers.

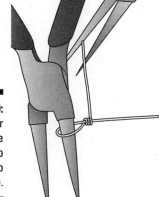

Figure 2-29:
For harder wire, use pliers to help wrap the wire.

4. Continue to wrap the wire until it's as long as you like. Normally, three or four wraps around are fine. Then use the wire cutters to trim off the excess wire so you have a loop that looks similar to the one in Figure 2-30.

Figure 2-30:
Three or
four wraps
of wire is a
good
number to
use.

Part II
Super Simple Jewelry Projects

The 5th Wave   By Rich Tennant

"Oh, I just love jewelry making. I made zipper
pulls for my whole family."

In this part . . .

This part gets you going with the bulk of the beginner and intermediate projects. We've organized these chapters by technique so you can choose a few projects from each chapter to build your beading skill set quickly.

You start out in Chapter 3 with basic stringing projects. After all, most jewelry begins with stringing a bead of some sort onto a cord made of one material or another. Move on to Chapter 4 when you want to string *and* add crimping to your projects. Chapter 5 helps you create cool pieces using knots in traditional and surprising ways.

Chapters 6, 7, and 8 focus on more specific skills — bead weaving, using a wire jig, and wire wrapping, specifically. Designs within these chapters are varied to include basic as well as more-advanced designs. We think no matter what your skill level, you'll find designs that appeal to you and inspire you to get creative.

Chapter 3

Simple Stringing Techniques

● ●

In This Chapter

▶ Making accessories with memory wire

▶ Using simple tools to attach findings to a variety of stringing materials

▶ Creating jewelry with stretchy cord

● ●

Making jewelry is among our all-time favorite ways to spend an afternoon. We love to create beautiful pieces for our friends, families, and customers. Most jewelry pieces start with a single basic technique: stringing a bead on a thread of some kind. Of course, the material the thread is made of can vary wildly, and don't even get us started on the overwhelming options in the bead department. But at its most basic level, stringing is the foundation of jewelry making.

In this chapter, we get you started with beading projects that require just a few tools and materials. You work with memory wire — the wire that's so easy to string that just about anyone can do it. Then we have you try your hand at using other stringing materials, like waxed linen cord, ribbon, and leather. Finally, you can test your hand at using stretchy cord to make jewelry and other items, like a bookmark and napkin rings.

Memory Wire Choker

Using memory wire is one of the fastest ways to get started with making jewelry. *Memory wire* is a hard, rigid wire that holds its shape after stringing beads on it. It's sold in coils that resemble a loose spring. This version of a choker, shown in Figure 3-1, uses neon yellow and green beads that are sure to brighten any mood.

You need heavy-duty wire cutters (and a decent amount of hand strength) to cut through memory wire. If you're going to make several items using memory wire, invest in memory wire shears, which are much easier to use. Using your regular wire cutters on memory wire will dull them quickly, so do so at your own risk.

Figure 3-1:
Create a
necklace in
no time with
color-
coordinated
beads and
memory
wire.

Materials and vital statistics

✔ **Beads:**

- 1 11mm yellow Czech glass nugget

- 16 ¼-inch silver-lined emerald green bugle beads

- 66 gold metallic size 8 seed beads

- 32 size 6 seed beads, inside color turquoise

- 17 3.5mm square transparent yellow seed beads

✔ **Findings:**

- 1½ coils of necklace memory wire

- 1 1½-inch sterling silver head pin

✔ **Tools:** Round-nose pliers, memory wire shears, wire cutters

✔ **Techniques used:** Stringing, using round-nose pliers

This necklace comes together quickly. With a simple twist of the pliers and easy string-ing, you can create your own masterpiece in no time.

Directions

1. **Using your round-nose pliers, make a small loop on one end of the memory wire, like the one in Figure 3-2.**

This loop stops your beads from falling off as you string.

Make sure to form the loop so it curves to the outside (rather than the inside) of the necklace, so it's more comfortable to wear.

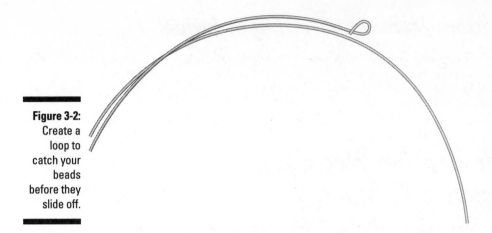

Figure 3-2:
Create a
loop to
catch your
beads
before they
slide off.

2. **String your beads in this pattern of eight beads, shown in Figure 3-3: 1 gold, 1 turquoise, 1 gold, 1 square, 1 gold, 1 turquoise, 1 gold, 1 bugle. Repeat this pattern seven more times, for a total of eight repetitions.**

Figure 3-3:
String your
beads in this
intricate
pattern to
create a
stunning
necklace.

To make sure you don't skip a bead in the pattern, lay them out in order on your bead board, two or three sets at a time. Use the end of the memory wire as a needle to pick up a full set of beads.

3. **Create your focal point by sliding on the glass nugget.**

The nugget falls directly in the middle of the necklace. If yours isn't positioned exactly between the ends, you can always trim the wire at the open end before you close up the necklace.

4. **String the remaining beads in this pattern: 1 bugle, 1 gold, 1 turquoise, 1 gold, 1 square, 1 gold, 1 turquoise, 1 gold. Again, you should have a total of eight repetitions.**

Notice this pattern is the mirror image of the one shown in Figure 3-3. By reversing the pattern, you create a symmetrical design.

5. **Using the memory wire shears, trim the end of the memory wire to ¼ inch. Using the round-nose pliers, make a loop on the end of the memory wire, toward the outside of the necklace, to secure the beads.**

6. **Take the head pin and slide on a gold seed bead, the square seed bead, and then the last gold seed bead. Using your wire cutters, trim the head pin so ¾ inch remains above the beads. Use your round-nose pliers to create an eye loop to complete your dangle.**

Check out Chapter 2 for info on how to make an eye loop.

7. **Slip the eye loop of the dangle onto one of your necklace's end loops for a finishing touch.**

Variation: Memory wire ring or bracelet

You can get memory wire in bracelet, ring, and necklace sizes. Buy extra beads so you can make a matched set of accessories. A little goes a long way; you need roughly 7 inches of beads to make a bracelet and 2 to 3 inches to make a ring. Follow the same pattern in the choker directions to coordinate your accessories perfectly.

Adjustable Leather Necklace with Geometric Pendant

Do you have a favorite necklace that you wish was a little bit longer sometimes and a little shorter at others? This necklace, shown in Figure 3-4, may just be your new favorite. Thanks to an adjustable knot, you can make this necklace longer or shorter to go with whatever neckline you're wearing. Using just a few materials, you can create a new accessory in less than 15 minutes.

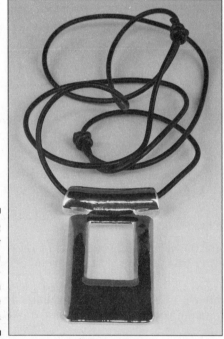

Figure 3-4: Make your own version of this necklace with your favorite pendant.

Materials and vital statistics

- ✔ **Beads:** 1 50x25mm silver geometric pendant with channel *bail* (the loop a pendant hangs by)
- ✔ **Findings:** 30 inches of 2mm black leather cord
- ✔ **Tools:** Scissors
- ✔ **Techniques used:** Stringing, tying an adjustable knot

This necklace may be the quickest project in this (or any) jewelry-making book. But that doesn't mean it lacks style. You can make one of your own in no time.

Directions

1. Slide the pendant onto the cord.

2. Lay both ends of ends of the cord parallel to each other, but pointing in opposite directions. Holding one strand stationary, tie the other strand around it like a figure eight, as shown in Figure 3-5a and b.

a   b

Figure 3-5: Tying an adjustable knot.

 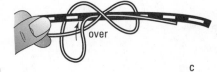   

over

c   d

3. Slip the tail of the figure-eight strand up between the stationary strand and the figure-eight strand, as shown in Figure 3-5c.

4. Pull the knot tight, as shown in Figure 3-5d. Use the scissors to trim any excess cord from the open end of the knot.

   Don't cut the long end of the cord; you need it to make your next knot.

5. Using the other end of the cord, repeat Steps 2 through 4 to make the second knot.

6. Pull the knots apart to make the necklace shorter, or slide them together to make the necklace longer.

Bead and Wire Pendant on Ribbon Cord

Ribbon is one of our favorite materials to use when we make necklaces. It lends a soft femininity to a finished piece, which reminds us of a more romantic time. In this project, featured in Figure 3-6, you use a very basic technique to create a professional-looking closure, literally in seconds.

Materials and vital statistics

✔ **Beads:** 1 bead and wire pendant (We use the pendant that we make in Chapter 8.)

✔ **Findings:**

- 22 inches of 12mm black organza ribbon
- 2 12.5x3mm sterling silver cord end tubes
- 2 sterling silver jump rings
- 1 sterling silver toggle and bar clasp

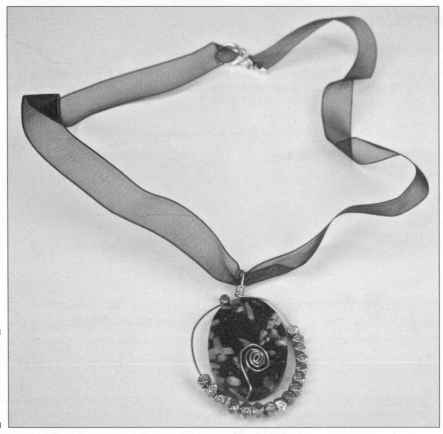

Figure 3-6:
Ribbon is a
great choice
for stringing
necklaces.

✔ **Tools:** Scissors, crimping pliers, chain-nose pliers, flat-nose pliers

✔ **Techniques used:** Stringing, attaching cord ends, opening/closing jump rings

If you prefer, you can substitute ribbon ends for the cord end tubes. They function the same way, but give a flatter look. Coauthor Heather prefers the tubes because she can close the top of the tubes to hide any ribbon edges. See them up close in Figure 3-7.

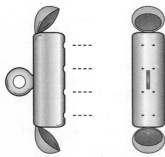

Figure 3-7:
Cord end
tubes help
hide any
errant
ribbon
edges.

Customize your necklace by shortening or lengthening the ribbon as you like. Add the findings and you're ready to wear it.

Directions

1. **Using the scissors, trim the ends of the ribbon flush.**

If the ribbon is angled at all, it won't sit in the cord end properly. The connection will loosen quickly, and the ribbon will fray, undoing all of your hard work.

2. **Slip one end of the ribbon into the cord end tube. Using the front jaw of the crimping pliers (the O-shaped one, not the U-shaped one; see Figure 3-8), gently close the tube around the ribbon.**

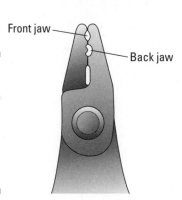

Front jaw — Back jaw

Figure 3-8:
Use the front jaws of the crimping pliers to keep the tube's round shape.

Buy some extra cord end tubes. You get 100 tubes for just a few bucks. Practice gently closing a few spare tubes before you attach one to the ribbon. You can mess up the tube's shape if you apply too much force. For more help with using the crimping pliers, check out Chapter 4.

3. **Use your chain-nose pliers (or your fingers) to close the top and bottom of the tube, hiding the raw edges of the ribbon.**

4. **Slide on the pendant. Repeat Steps 2 and 3 with the other end of the ribbon and the other end tube.**

5. **Using your chain-nose and flat-nose pliers, gently open one jump ring. Slip the jump ring through the loop of the tube, as shown in Figure 3-9. Slide the loop of one half of the clasp onto the jump ring. Close the jump ring with both pairs of pliers.**

6. **Repeat Step 5 with the other cord end tube, jump ring, and clasp.**

Figure 3-9:
Connect the cord end tube to the clasp with a jump ring.

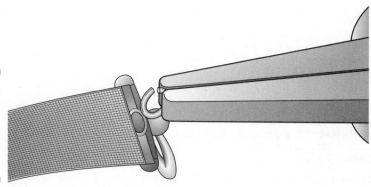

Inspirational Bookmark

You use a supersimple knotting technique to create this quickie bookmark, pictured in Figure 3-10. This project is a great way to use a special bead or two, or even an *orphan bead* (a single bead without a match).

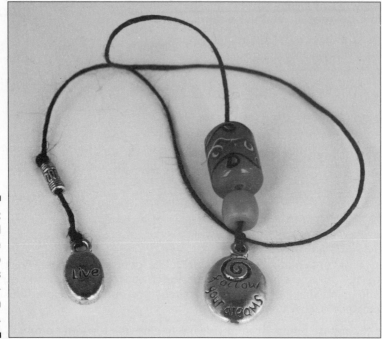

Figure 3-10:
No special tools are required to make this bead-and-charm bookmark.

Keep a stash of these bookmarks made up so you're ready for any occasion. Even an inexpensive paperback feels personal and special when it's accompanied by a stylish, handmade bookmark.

Materials and vital statistics

✔ **Beads:**

- 1 22mm lead-free pewter inspirational charm (Ours says, "Follow your dreams.")
- 1 15mm lead-free pewter inspirational charm (Ours says, "Live.")
- 1 15x2mm turquoise decorative glass bead
- 1 turquoise crow bead
- 1 7x3mm textured sterling silver tube bead

✔ **Findings:** 16 inches of black waxed linen cord

✔ **Tools:** Scissors

✔ **Techniques used:** Stringing, tying an overhand knot

If you can tie your shoes, you can make this bookmark. Gather your beads together and get ready to tie up this easy project.

Directions

1. Using an overhand knot (follow Figure 3-11 as a guide), tie the large charm to one end of the cord. Tie another knot directly on top of the first knot to secure it in place. Trim the excess cord with the scissors.

Figure 3-11:
Add an overhand knot to secure the charm.

Because this cord is waxy, it makes a firm knot that doesn't come untied. No glue is required to hold this one in place. Remember that after the knot is tied, it's tough to untie it, so tighten it carefully.

2. String on the crow bead, followed by the glass bead. Tie an overhand knot above the glass bead. Tie another knot directly on top of the first one.

This double knot makes sure that your beads don't slide up and down the cord. If your glass bead has a small hole, one knot may keep it in place. Use your best judgment.

3. Tie an overhand knot 11 inches above the double knot. String on the tube bead.

The tube bead should rest on the knot.

4. Using an overhand knot, tie the small charm to the open end of the cord. Tie another knot directly on top of the first knot to secure it in place. Trim the excess cord with the scissors.

Variation: Cut glass and silk bookmark

For an elegant variation, substitute faceted briolettes for the charms and silk "bugtail" beading cord for the waxed linen cord. Dress it up with coordinating beads, leaving roughly 11 inches of cord unbeaded to lay flat inside your book. Add a drop of glue to the knots to make sure they stay in place, because silk is quite a bit more slippery than waxed linen.

When coauthor Heather glues knots for these bookmarks, she use Hypo-cement. Take a look at Chapter 5 in *Jewelry Making & Beading For Dummies* to see our complete recommendations for what glue to use when.

28-inch Black-and-Bright Necklace

This festive necklace is inexpensive and right for almost any occasion. Several inches of black seed beads separate a random assortment of brightly colored nuggets in Figure 3-12. The contrast in colors is a fun way to accent any outfit.

Figure 3-12:
Our necklace is 28 inches long, but you can make yours any length you choose.

Materials and vital statistics

✔ **Beads:**

- 245 black size 8 seed beads, approximately 13 grams

- 14 assorted Czech glass nuggets, ranging in size from 8mm to 10mm

✔ **Findings:**

- 1 card of No. 3 maroon silk beading cord, with needle attached

- 2 gold-tone clamshell bead tips

- 1 gold-tone toggle and bar clasp

✔ **Tools:** Scissors, instant glue, chain-nose pliers, round-nose pliers

✔ **Techniques used:** Stringing, tying an overhand knot, using bead tips

This project takes a little time, but the simple pattern is easy to repeat. If you haven't used bead cord with an integrated needle before, this is a great way to get started with it. Grab it and get going!

Directions

1. **Remove all the bead cord from the card.**

This step allows you to save the remaining cord with the needle attached.

If you choose to ignore this advice (and we know some of you will), you can create a needle by coating 2 inches of the cord with clear nail polish. Let it dry for a few minutes, and the lacquer will stiffen the end of your thread. Voilá, instant (almost) needle. This needle isn't nearly as high quality as the one that comes with the cord, so it's definitely not the preferred method.

You can make a matching necklace for your BFF (that's "best friend forever" for those of you who haven't mastered the foreign language of text or instant messaging) with the extra bead cord!

2. Tie an overhand knot on the open end (the end without the needle) of your bead cord. Dab the knot with instant glue. Let the glue dry for a minute or so, and then trim the excess cord with your scissors.

3. Thread the bead tip onto the cord, and then slide it over the knot. Using your chain-nose pliers, close the clamshell to hide the knot.

4. String 25 seed beads followed by 1 nugget.

5. String 15 seed beads, followed by 1 nugget. Continue this pattern until your necklace reaches 26 inches, ending with a nugget. Add 25 seed beads.

6. Slide the remaining bead tip onto your beading cord.

Make sure the clamshell's "mouth" is facing away from your beads and toward the needle end of the cord, so it will clamp down over the knot you tie in Step 7.

7. Tie an overhand knot as close to the clamshell as you can. Add a dab of instant glue to the knot. Allow the glue to dry a minute or so, and then trim the excess cord with your scissors. Using your chain-nose pliers, close the clamshell to hide the knot.

We use a needle to help get the knot superclose to the bead tip. Take a look at Chapter 5 to see this trick in action.

8. Use your round-nose pliers to attach the bead tip to the bar clasp. Repeat with the second bead tip and the toggle clasp.

Variation: Crimped black-and-bright necklace

You can create this same look by using crimp beads (rather than bead tips) to secure the clasp. Take a look at Chapter 4 for all the ins and outs of using crimp beads, tubes, and tools.

Variation: Monochromatic black-and-bright necklace

Consider using nuggets of a single color, rather than an assortment. Add more visual interest by varying the size or shape of the nuggets, but use only one color.

Wooden Bobble Bracelet

Using stretchy beading cord is one of the simplest ways to make jewelry and other beading projects. This easy bracelet, shown in Figure 3-13, uses a basic repeating pattern of two different beads sizes for a simple, classic look.

Don't skimp on using the full length of beading cord listed in the next section. You need a little extra to tie the knots securely and easily. It's always better to have a little extra than not enough. Trust us.

Figure 3-13:
This all-
wood
bracelet has
an earthy,
organic feel.

Materials and vital statistics

✔ **Beads:**

- 7 22mm round wooden beads
- 7 8mm round wooden beads, assorted pattern

✔ **Findings:** 13 inches of 0.7mm diameter clear stretchy beading cord

✔ **Tools:** Binder clip, instant glue, scissors

✔ **Techniques used:** Stringing, tying a square knot

Initially, you may feel like you're making this bracelet too long, but because the large wooden beads are round, they take up more room inside the bracelet. And because this bracelet is stretchy without a clasp, you need to be able to slip your hand through it. The inside diameter of the bracelet is much smaller than actual length of the bracelet before you connect the ends and tie it together.

Directions

1. **Attach your binder clip to one end of the stretchy cord.**

The clip stops the beads from falling off the other end as you string them. Take a look at Figure 3-14 to see the clip in action.

Figure 3-14:
Using a
binder clip
with
stretchy
cord is like
having an
extra hand.

2. **String one large bead, then a small bead. Repeat this pattern until you string all the beads.**

   At this point, you can twist the two ends together several times, and then use the binder clip to temporarily "tie" them together and try on the bracelet. The clip will hold the bracelet fairly securely, allowing you to slip it on and off, and even let you tighten it so you can get a pretty good feel for how the finished project will look. But don't take off for yoga class wearing the bracelet this way, or you'll lose your beads!

3. **Tie the ends of the cord together using a square knot.**

   Take a look at Figure 3-15 for help making a square knot. See Chapter 5 for step-by-step instructions on creating a square knot.

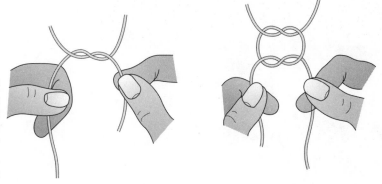

Figure 3-15:
Tie a square knot with both ends of the cord.

The knot itself should be tight, but don't pull the cord supertight. If the cord doesn't stay fairly stretchy, you may break it when you slide your hand through.

4. **Holding both ends of the cord together, tie an overhand knot (refer back to Figure 3-11) and tighten it as close to the square knot as you can.**

5. **Apply instant glue thoroughly to both knots to secure them further. Allow the glue to dry for 5 minutes.**

   This step may seem like too much, but because the large beads are so large, the cord stretches *a lot* when you put this bracelet on. The glue makes sure that the knots hold tight under the strain.

6. **Using your scissors, trim the ends of the cord to ¼ inch.**

   Sometimes when we're feeling lazy, we snip the cord with our wire cutters instead of tracking down the scissors. Over time, this dulls your cutters, so do so at your own risk. If you want, you can keep a cheap pair of wire cutters around just for this kind of job.

7. **Slip the knots into a large wooden bead to hide them.**

We recommend letting your stretchy cord items cure overnight before wearing them. This curing time gives the glue in the piece a bit more strength.

Variation: Wooden bobble and smoky quartz bracelet

You can make this bracelet a little more glamorous by using 11mm smoky quartz barrels in place of the smaller wooden beads. These bigger beads add a little length to the finished piece, so definitely try it on to confirm your fit before you tie it off, glue the knots, and snip the ends. If it's too long, try it with one fewer set of beads.

Confetti Napkin Rings

These napkin rings, in Figure 3-16, take their name from the brightly colored bead mixture that reminds us of confetti. This project is a great way to use the "bead soup" mixes that your local bead store sells by the tube. (If you're like coauthor Heather, a bead soup mixture may form in one of the drawers where you keep your beads, because they invariably get spilled when someone with little hands helps you put them away.) Just choose a color mix you like and have at it. You use stretchy cord to make these simple yet elegant napkin rings that can adorn your table in no time.

Figure 3-16: Brightly colored beads make these napkin rings a beautiful choice.

Materials and vital statistics

✔ **Beads:**

- 16 assorted Czech glass nuggets, ranging in size from 8mm to 10mm with large center holes

- 32 inches of assorted small beads, seeds, and bugles in assorted sizes and coordinating colors

✔ **Findings:** 8 8-inch strands of 0.5mm diameter clear stretchy beading cord

✔ **Tools:** Binder clip, instant glue, scissors

✔ **Techniques used:** Stringing, tying a square knot

With these materials, you have enough supplies to create four napkin rings. Feel free to make as many as you want. Each individual napkin ring uses four nuggets, 8 inches of other beads, and two 8-inch strands of stretchy cord. We used brightly colored nuggets separated by about an inch of beads randomly strung to create these must-have entertaining accessories.

Directions

1. **Attach your binder clip to one end of 2 strands of stretchy cord to keep your beads from sliding off while you're working.**

To see how this works, take a gander at Figure 3-14.

2. **Feed both strands through the center of one nugget. Separate the strands. String approximately 1 inch of beads on each strand.**

It's not absolutely essential that you string exactly 1 inch of beads. It's more important that both bead sections are close to the same length, so they lie nice and flat.

3. **Feed both strands of cord through the next nugget.**

4. **Repeat Steps 2 and 3, using 4 nuggets and 8 inches of beads total.**

5. **Remove the binder clip, being careful to hold all 4 ends of the cord together. Tie a square knot as close to the beads as you can. Apply instant glue to the knot.**

It's virtually impossible to hide this knot inside your nugget because you already have two strands running through it. Do your best to create a neat knot, and your guests will just assume it's a clear seed bead.

6. **Start over with Step 1 to complete the remaining napkin rings.**

Magic Bookmark

This bookmark uses clear stretchy cord, so it looks like the beads magically float on top of the book cover, while the invisible cord wraps around the book, holding your place, as shown in Figure 3-17.

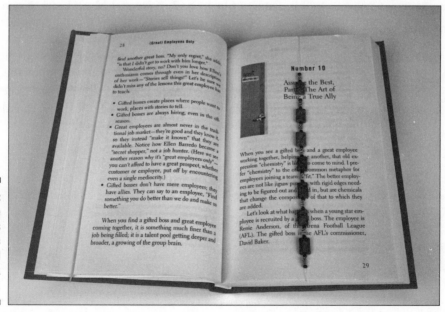

Figure 3-17: Amaze your friends with this magical book accessory.

Don't stretch the cord too tightly when you finish the piece, because you don't want to overstress the cord. You want to be able to firmly hold the pages but not snap the cord and lose your beads.

Materials and vital statistics

- **Beads:**
  - 7 11x7mm puffed rectangle gemstone beads
  - 8 5mm Thai silver barrel beads
  - 16 black size 8 seed beads
- **Findings:** 16 inches of 0.5mm diameter clear stretchy beading cord
- **Tools:** Binder clip, instant glue, scissors, mass-market size paperback book (optional)
- **Techniques used:** Stringing, tying a square knot

You use a technique similar to creating stretchy bracelets when you make this bookmark, but with two significant variations. First, you use a lot more cord because the book is bigger than your wrist. And second, you fill only one side of the cord with beads so your book closes easily.

Directions

1. **Attach your binder clip to one end of the stretchy cord.**

   The clip stops the beads from falling off the other end as you string them. Take a look at Figure 3-14 to see how this works.

2. **String your beads in this order: 1 black bead, 1 silver, 1 black bead, 1 gemstone. Repeat the pattern six more times for a total of seven repetitions. Add 1 black, 1 silver, and 1 black bead to finish the beads.**

   This bead pattern runs the length of a standard mass-market size paperback, roughly 6¾ inches x 4 inches. If you have a larger book, you can continue the pattern to your desired length, adjusting the cord length as necessary.

3. **Fold the beaded cord in half. Using both ends of the cord, tie an overhand knot about 6 inches from the middle of the cord, as shown in Figure 3-18.**

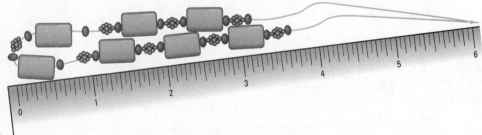

Figure 3-18: Tie an overhand knot to connect the ends of the bookmark.

4. **Apply instant glue thoroughly to the knot. Allow it to dry for a minute or so, and then trim the ends near the knot.**

Game Time Double-Strand Stretch Bracelet

For this whimsical bracelet, featured in Figure 3-19, you use dominos accented with seed beads and spacers configured to remind us of *X*'s and *O*'s in tick-tack-toe. You build on your stringing skills a bit by crisscrossing two strands through a large spacer bead to create the black *X*'s. No worries, though; we know you can handle it.

Figure 3-19:
Wear this bracelet to your next family game night.

Materials and vital statistics

✓ **Beads:**

- 6 30x15mm domino beads, double side drilled, ivory color with black dots
- 6 5x8mm silver rondelle spacer beads
- 96 black size 8 seed beads

✓ **Findings:** 2 12-inch strands of 0.5mm diameter clear stretchy beading cord

✓ **Tools:** 3 binder clips, instant glue, scissors

✓ **Techniques used:** Stringing, tying an overhand knot

Take this project slow to keep your strands straight and the beads in the right order on the right strands.

Directions

1. **Attach one binder clip to one end of a strand of stretchy cord. Repeat with a second clip and a second piece of stretchy cord.**

The clips make sure your beads stay on the cord as you string them. Check out Figure 3-20 to see both binder clips at the ready to perform their duties.

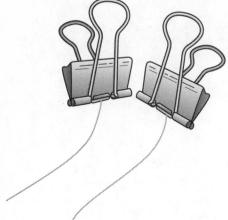

Figure 3-20: Two binder clips keep your strands separate and secure.

You may think it'd be easier to use one clip to hold both pieces of cord. In Step 6, when you tie the bracelet together, you'll appreciate the separate clips. It's much easier to tie the strands if you don't have to try to separate one strand from the clip without dumping the other one.

2. **Thread 4 seed beads onto each strand.**

3. **Feed one strand through the top hole of a domino. Feed the other strand through the bottom hole of the domino. Snug the domino to the seed beads, as pictured in Figure 3-21. Follow with 4 seed beads on each strand. Feed both strands through 1 spacer bead.**

Figure 3-21: Feed the strands through the spacer bead to make the first half of the X.

4. Separate the strands and feed 4 more seed beads onto each, as shown in Figure 3-22.

Figure 3-22:
String more seed beads on separate strands to create the second half of the X.

5. Repeat Steps 3 and 4 using all the beads.

6. Attach the last binder clip to the bottom strand of the bracelet. Remove the binder clip from the starting end of the top strand. Holding both ends of the top strand together, tie a loose overhand knot (refer back to Figure 3-11). Using a needle if necessary, snug the knot as close as you can to the spacer bead. Apply instant glue to the knot. Allow it to dry a minute or so, and then snip off the excess cord with your scissors.

Here's where the extra binder clips come in handy. Unless you're an octopus (and there's nothing wrong if you are — be proud), you can't hold all four ends of the cord at the same time. The clips hold both ends of the bottom strand while you tie, snug, and glue the top strand.

7. Remove the remaining binder clips. Holding both ends of the bottom strand together, tie a loose overhand knot. Using a needle if necessary, snug the knot as close as you can to the spacer bead. Apply instant glue to the knot. Allow it to dry a minute or so, and then snip off the excess cord with your scissors.

If you need help with making knots and using needles to slide them into place, check out Chapter 5.

8. Hide the knots by gently pulling them inside the spacer bead.

If your knots don't fit inside the bead, don't worry. Because you used clear cord, no one will notice them.

Variation: Slightly smaller game time bracelet

The design above makes an 8-inch bracelet, which may feel too loose for some people. If you'd prefer a tighter fit, make a 7-inch version by changing the pattern slightly, using three seed beads each time rather than four. You need to use 72 seed beads total for the smaller bracelet. Who knew that by eliminating one bead in a pattern, you could shrink your bracelet a whole inch?

Chapter 4

Bead Crimping

. . . .

In This Chapter

▶ Using crimps to finish off strands

▶ Separating bead units with crimps

▶ Creating design elements with crimps

. . . .

*B*ead crimping is a relatively recent development in jewelry making and beading. *Crimping* is simply the process of squeezing or flattening specially designed beads and tubes to secure jewelry elements (like clasps or beads) in a particular spot on a stringing material. Most often, it's used to finish a jewelry piece in a clean, professional manner.

What would modern jewelry making be without crimping? Sure, you could knot, solder, and wire wrap, but no other technique gives you the professional-looking results in so little time with so little expense. All you need are crimp beads and tubes and a $14 pair of crimping pliers.

We really do recommend investing in crimping pliers, rather than using chain-nose pliers to flatten crimp beads. The crimp made with the real deal is a much more professional-looking element and makes a tremendous difference in your finished work.

In this chapter, you put your crimping pliers to good use and start off with several projects that use basic crimping skills; you create connections between clasps and your beaded length of wire. Then we give you three more-advanced designs that incorporate crimps as design elements rather than just the hard-working findings they are.

If you need a refresher on using crimping pliers the right way (using a two-phase crimp method), check out Chapter 2.

Metallic Bead Bracelet

The metallic bead bracelet, shown in Figure 4-1, uses crimps in their most basic way — to attach clasps to completed jewelry pieces. You use a simple pattern of matte metallic beads, glass beads, and spacers to create a quick but cute accessory.

You can use the techniques in this project to create an endless variety of accessories. Just switch up your beads, make up your own pattern, and design your own creations.

Figure 4-1:
Create this simple bracelet in less than 20 minutes by using crimps.

Materials and vital statistics

✔ **Beads:**

- 6 8mm navy matte metallic round beads
- 12 5mm gold daisy spacers
- 12 6mm khaki matte metallic round beads
- 5 10mm faceted round beads, amber with brown spots

✔ **Findings:**

- 2 gold crimp tubes
- 1 gold hook-and-eye closure
- 9 inches of 0.014-inch diameter nylon-coated stainless steel beading wire

✔ **Tools:** Crimping pliers, chain-nose pliers, wire cutters

✔ **Techniques used:** Crimping, stringing

This project is so quick, you could make one of these bracelets to match your outfit before you head out to work in the morning. Stringing and crimping combine in a simple, yet elegant design.

Directions

1. **Slide one crimp tube onto the beading wire. Follow it with the connecting loop of one half of the hook-and-eye closure. Fold the beading wire back over itself, and slide the tail back through the crimp tube, as shown in Figure 4-2.**

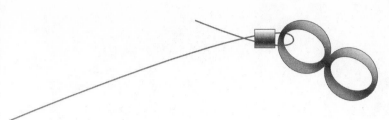

Figure 4-2:
Make a loop with the beading wire to connect your clasp.

2. Using your crimping pliers, close the crimp using the two-phase method to secure one end of the clasp.

3. String the beads in this pattern: 1 khaki, 1 spacer, 1 navy, 1 spacer, 1 khaki, 1 amber. Repeat the pattern four times, for a total of five repetitions.

As you're stringing, use your beads to cover the tail of your beading wire. Snug the beads up next to the crimp bead cover and allow the wire tail to slide inside as many beads as necessary to cover it. This keeps the pesky tail from poking you when you wear the piece.

4. String on the last beads in this order: 1 khaki, 1 spacer, 1 navy, 1 spacer, 1 khaki.

5. Slide on the remaining crimp tube followed by the other half of the clasp. Fold the tail of the beading wire over the clasp, and reinsert it through the crimp bead. Continue to feed the wire through several other beads.

6. Pull the wire taut by using the chain-nose pliers, as shown in Figure 4-3.

Figure 4-3:
Pull the slack out of the beading wire by using chain-nose pliers before flattening the crimp.

7. Use the crimping pliers to create a two-phase crimp. Cut the excess wire with the wire cutters. Tuck any remaining tail into the closest bead to keep it from poking the wearer.

Black Pearl Bracelet

Pearls and crystals are always a terrific combination, and this bracelet, pictured in Figure 4-4, is no exception. Here you use Swarovski crystal pearls (Swarovski covers one of its world-class crystal beads with "highly luminous pearlescence") instead of natural pearls. These crystal pearls are a fun change when you want the beauty of pearls without the expense of naturally perfectly round pearls or the challenges of working with irregularly drilled, cheaper natural pearls.

Figure 4-4:
The classic combination of crystal and pearls gets a makeover with black pearls and tiny pink crystals.

In this project we use crimps to terminate our strand and attach our clasp. Then we take another design step and add *crimp covers* to cover the flattened crimps. The crimp covers we chose look like small silver beads in the finished design.

Materials and vital statistics

✔ **Beads:**

- 15 6mm round Swarovski crystal Tahitian pearl beads

- 28 3mm rose faceted bicone crystals

- 14 4mm sterling silver smooth disc beads

✔ **Findings:**

- 2 silver-plated crimp tubes

- 9 inches of 0.014-inch diameter nylon-coated stainless steel beading wire

- 1 sterling silver heart and arrow toggle and bar clasp

- 2 3mm silver-plated crimp covers

✔ **Tools:** Crimping pliers, chain-nose pliers, wire cutters

✔ **Techniques used:** Stringing, crimping

Flattened crimp beads are fine, but you can jazz them up a bit with crimp covers, like those in this project. The covers make the crimps almost invisible, leaving the design clean and elegant.

Directions

1. **Slide one crimp tube onto the beading wire. Follow it with the connecting loop of one half of the clasp. Fold the beading wire back over itself, sliding the tail back through the crimp tube, as shown in Figure 4-2 earlier in the chapter.**

2. **Using your crimping pliers, close the crimp using the two-phase crimp method to secure one end of the clasp.**

3. **Use the front jaw of the crimping pliers to secure a crimp cover over the flattened crimp bead, as shown in Figure 4-5.**

   The crimp cover looks just like a round silver bead after it's closed.

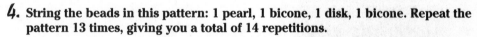

Figure 4-5: Adding a crimp cover hides a flattened crimp.

4. **String the beads in this pattern: 1 pearl, 1 bicone, 1 disk, 1 bicone. Repeat the pattern 13 times, giving you a total of 14 repetitions.**

   As you're stringing, use your beads to cover the tail of your beading wire. Snug the beads up to the crimp cover and allow the wire tail to slide inside as many beads as necessary to cover it.

5. **String on the last pearl bead. Follow it with the last crimp tube and the other half of the clasp. Fold the tail of the beading wire over the clasp and reinsert it through the crimp bead. Continue to feed the wire through several other beads.**

6. **Pull the wire taut by using the chain-nose pliers, as shown in Figure 4-3 earlier in this chapter.**

   Pull the wire fairly tight, but leave a little room for the beads to have some movement. Otherwise, your bracelet may be too stiff to lie flat against your wrist.

7. **Use the crimping pliers to create a two-phase crimp. Cover the flattened crimp with the other crimp cover, using the front jaw of the crimp pliers to secure the cover.**

8. **Use the wire cutters to cut the excess wire. Tuck any remaining tail into the closest bead.**

Variation: Color-mix pearls bracelet

Create a quick variation of this bracelet by substituting a contrasting color of 6mm pearls for the pink crystals. Choose from creams, rose, light blues, coppers, and burgundies. Separate a mix of colors using spacer beads for an almost instant accessory.

Convertible Claspless Necklace or Bracelet

It's true. This piece of jewelry can be a bracelet or a necklace, in a variety of lengths, to fit just about any neckline (or neck size). The secret to this design, shown in bracelet form in Figure 4-6, is the faceted magnetic hematite beads. We designed the bead pattern so that approximately an inch of beads separates the magnetic beads from each other. You wrap the piece around your wrist (or neck), and the magnetic beads grab each other, securing the piece into place.

Figure 4-6:
Wrap this piece any way you want, to go with any outfit.

Materials and vital statistics

✔ **Beads:**

- 23 7x5mm faceted hexagonal tube beads, magnetic hematite

- 22 6mm faceted bicone Swarovski crystals in assorted pinks and greens

- 44 5mm silver-plated smooth disks

- 46 4mm round hematite beads

- 44 3x2mm round tube hematite beads

✔ **Findings:**

- 34 inches of 0.014-inch diameter black nylon-coated stainless steel beading wire

- 2 silver-plated crimp beads

✔ **Tools:** Crimping pliers, chain-nose pliers, wire cutters

✔ **Techniques used:** Crimping, stringing

Bracelet or necklace? What will it be today? Tough choice, but what a great problem to have! After you string all of these beads (in the specified pattern) on the long piece of wire, you can coil the finished piece around whatever appendage fits your mood.

Directions

1. Slide one crimp tube onto the beading wire. Follow it with one round hematite bead. Fold the beading wire back over itself, sliding the tail back through the crimp tube, as shown in Figure 4-7.

Figure 4-7:
Secure this strand with a round bead rather than a formal clasp.

Because this necklace/bracelet doesn't have a clasp, these round beads termi- nate the strand (one at each end). You secure them in the same spot where you'd place a clasp, but they're really just holding all the beads on the wire.

2. Using your crimping pliers, slide the crimp bead down as close to the stop bead as you can, and then close the crimp using the two-phase method to secure it.

3. String your beads in this pattern of eight beads, shown in Figure 4-8: 1 round, 1 round tube, 1 hexagonal tube, 1 round tube, 1 round, 1 disk, 1 bicone, 1 disk. Repeat this pattern 21 times, so you end up with 22 sets.

Figure 4-8:
Follow this pattern along the length of beading wire.

4. Slide the remaining crimp tube onto the beading wire. Follow it with the last round bead. Fold the beading wire back over itself, sliding the tail back through the crimp tube. Thread the wire down through the next three beads, pulling it out under the first hexagonal bead, as shown in Figure 4-3 earlier in this chapter.

5. **Use the chain-nose pliers to pull the wire taut. Cut the excess wire using the wire cutters. Tuck the wire tail into the next bead if necessary.**

Don't pull the wire excessively tight. You want to keep a little bit of extra wire (roughly 2mm or so) to maintain flexibility in your finished piece. It needs this little bit of give to be able to wrap in smaller diameters.

Swarovski Crystal and Sterling Frame Necklace

You use just a few elements to create this special-occasion piece, featured in Figure 4-9. Simple, smooth sterling frames are paired with highly faceted sparkling crystals. Instead of using crimps to simply end the strand elegantly, you can use them to help define design elements, in this case, stationary bead units.

Figure 4-9: Space out these perfectly paired bead units to create a high-end necklace in no time.

These sterling silver frames are fairly expensive. This design is a great way to use them economically because you space a few of them out over a long section of necklace. Flattening crimps on either side of a bead holds it securely in place. Leaving space in between these gorgeous bead units really lets each one shine.

Take care to hang this necklace up when you're not wearing it. Don't just toss it in a jewelry box, or you're likely to kink it. After it's kinked, it can't be unkinked. You'll have to remake it.

Materials and vital statistics

✔ **Beads:**

- 11 8mm khaki Swarovski crystal faced cubes
- 10 4mm khaki Swarovski crystal faced cubes

✔ **Findings:**

- 1 Hill Tribes silver smooth toggle (18mm) and bar (21mm) clasp
- 44 silver-plated crimp beads
- 30 inches of 0.014-inch diameter silver nylon-coated stainless steel beading wire
- 2 3mm silver-plated crimp covers
- 11 12x12x3.5mm square sterling silver frames, 2 holes

✔ **Tools:** Crimping pliers, wire cutters, binder clips (optional)

✔ **Techniques used:** Crimping, stringing

This necklace takes a bit more time than some of the other projects in this chapter because we use several crimps instead of the standard two (one for each end of the strand). The extra time is worth the effort, though, when you're wearing this sparkling beauty.

Directions

1. Slide one crimp bead onto the beading wire. Follow it with the connecting loop of the bar end of the clasp. Fold the beading wire back over itself, sliding the tail back through the crimp bead, as shown in Figure 4-2 earlier in this chapter. Create a crimp with the two-phase crimp method, using the crimping pliers.

2. Trim the excess wire as close to the crimp bead as you can, using your wire cutters. Using the front jaw of the crimping pliers, cover the flattened crimp and tail with one of the crimp covers.

3. String your beads and findings using this pattern: 1 crimp bead, 1 frame with larger cube inside (as shown in Figure 4-10), 2 crimp beads, 1 smaller cube, 1 crimp bead. Repeat this pattern nine times, so you end up with ten repetitions.

Don't crimp any of the crimp beads yet. String them on your wire just like they're any other bead without their superpower, which is the ability to beautifully and quickly stop beads and findings from sliding off with a single (well, actually a two-phase) squeeze.

Figure 4-10:
Frame these sparkling crystal cubes with stunning sterling silver.

4. Finish stringing by adding another crimp bead, a frame with a larger cube inside, and another crimp bead.

5. Slide the remaining crimp bead onto the beading wire. Follow it with the connecting loop of the toggle (circle) end of the clasp. Fold the beading wire back over itself, sliding the tail back through the crimp bead. (Refer to Figure 4-2 earlier in this chapter.) Use your crimping pliers to create another two-phase crimp. Using your wire cutters, trim the excess wire as close to the flattened crimp as possible.

   At this point, you have flattened only two crimp beads (the ones holding your clasp in place). The remaining 42 are sliding around on your necklace.

6. Connect the clasp to create a closed necklace as if you were wearing it. Hold the necklace up, and fold it in half to locate its center point.

   The centermost frame containing a cube is the center point of your necklace. You should have 5 frames, 5 smaller cubes, and 21 open crimp beads on each side of this unit.

7. Situate the center bead unit at the center of your necklace. Using the crimping pliers, flatten the crimp beads on either side of the middle frame, as shown in Figure 4-11, using the two-phase crimp method.

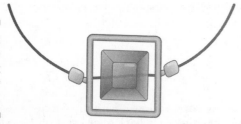

Figure 4-11:
Create the center point of your necklace.

If you're having trouble crimping with the extra beads on the wire, slide them away from the center bead unit, and secure them in place with the binder clips if necessary.

8. Slide the next bead unit (1 crimp bead, 1 smaller cube, and another crimp bead) toward the center bead unit. Decide how far you want this unit from the center bead unit. Crimp it into place.

   We spaced our bead units between ½ and ¾ inch apart.

9. Repeat Step 8, this time sliding a bead unit down on the other side of the center unit.

   Situate this unit symmetrically in relation to the unit you created in Step 8, as shown in Figure 4-12.

10. Repeat Steps 8 and 9 using the remaining beads.

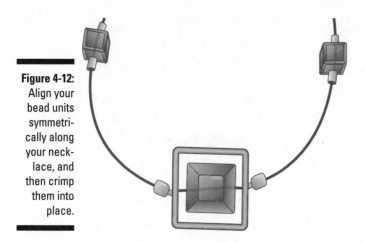

Figure 4-12:
Align your bead units symmetrically along your necklace, and then crimp them into place.

Variation: Adding crimp covers

After you flatten your crimp beads, you can cover them with silver-plated crimp covers, using the front jaw of your crimp pliers. Take a look at the black pearl bracelet instructions earlier in this chapter to see how they work. Because the covers look like round silver beads, they make a nice contrast with the square frames and cubes. Just another design element for you to try.

Variation: Swarovski crystal and sterling frame earrings

Create a quick and easy set of coordinating earrings by using a head pin in place of the beading wire, and 2mm silver round beads in place of the crimp beads. Slide a silver bead onto the head pin. Follow it with a frame with a larger cube inside. Top it off with the last silver bead. Create an eye loop (check out Chapter 2 for details), and slide your creation onto an ear wire. Make one more to complete the set.

Front Dangle Hematite and Sterling Silver Necklace

To create the sophisticated look of this piece, shown in Figure 4-13, you use beads of roughly the same size (5x3mm tube beads), but vary the material and texture. Rajasthani silver components add a hand-worked charm that's not possible with machine-made beads. You work the necklace as two separate lengths of wire connected at two points, through the twisted oval at the center and again at the clasp. The two dangles, terminated with crimps, add to the overall elegance of the design.

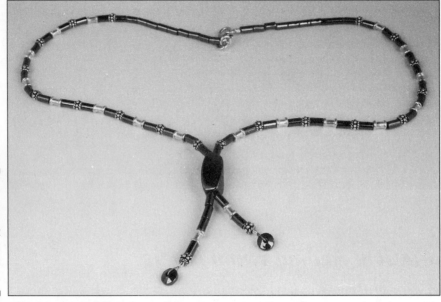

Figure 4-13:
Hematite
and hand-
wrought
silver beads
make a bold
statement.

Materials and vital statistics

✔ **Beads:**

- 2 6mm hematite rondelles

- 20 4mm Rajasthani sterling silver rondelles

- 18 5x3mm Rajasthani sterling silver smooth tubes

- 60 5x3mm hematite tubes

- 1 18x9mm hematite twisted oval

✔ **Findings:**

- 2 14-inch pieces of 0.014-inch diameter silver nylon-coated stainless steel beading wire

- 4 silver-plated crimp beads

- 1 sterling silver S-clasp

- 2 sterling silver jump rings

✔ **Tools:** Crimping pliers, binder clip, chain-nose pliers, wire cutters

✔ **Techniques used:** Crimping, stringing

In this project, you work from the dangles up. The crimp and the disk bead you string in the first step work to terminate the strands and create a stop bead. It's similar to the technique used in the convertible claspless bracelet or necklace earlier in this chapter.

Directions

1. Slide a crimp bead onto one length of the beading wire. Follow it with one hematite rondelle. Fold the beading wire back over itself, sliding the tail back through the crimp bead, as shown in Figure 4-2 earlier in this chapter.

2. String on the beads in this order: 1 silver rondelle, 1 hematite tube, 1 silver tube, and 1 hematite tube, as shown in Figure 4-14. Set this strand aside.

3. Repeat Steps 1 and 2 with the remaining length of beading wire. Add 2 more hematite tubes. Lay both strands next to each other, as shown in Figure 4-15.

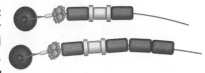

You add two more hematite tubes to the second length of beading wire to create one long and one short dangle. It adds more visual interest in your finished necklace instead of having both dangles the same length.

4. Feed the open ends of both beading wires through the twisted oval, as shown in Figure 4-16.

5. Place a binder clip on one side of the beading wire above the twisted oval. On the other length of wire, string beads in this pattern: 1 hematite tube, 1 silver tube, 1 hematite tube, 1 silver rondelle. Repeat the pattern eight times for a total of nine sets. Follow the pattern with 1 hematite tube, 1 silver rondelle, and then 10 more hematite tubes.

The binder clip helps you keep your wire and beads secure through the twisted oval while you're working on the other side.

6. **Slide on one crimp bead and one jump ring with "S" clasp attached. Fold the beading wire back over itself, sliding the tail back through the crimp bead. Slide the beading wire down through two tube beads. Using your chain-nose pliers, pull the tail taut, as shown in Figure 4-17.**

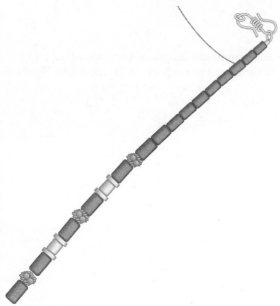

Figure 4-17:
Pull the tail out through two beads with your chain-nose pliers.

7. **Using your crimping pliers, flatten your crimp using the two-phase crimp method. Using your wire cutters, trim the excess wire under the second hematite tube and tuck any remaining tail into the third bead.**

8. **Remove the binder clip from the second length of wire. Repeat the stringing pattern detailed in Step 5.**

9. **Repeat Steps 6 and 7 to complete your necklace.**

Constellation Crimp Necklace

The dazzling array of crystal, beads, and crimps in this necklace, featured in Figure 4-18, doesn't form an actual constellation, but it reminds us of sparkling stars. Crimps take center stage in this light and airy creation, making it look much tougher to create than it is. In this project, the crimps are design features, not simply jewelry findings. They serve both to anchor design elements (like the bicone beads and arrows along the main length of wire) and to create delicate ends to the apparently errant wire strands.

Although this design isn't difficult to create, it does take some time, so set aside a few hours of uninterrupted time to crimp away if possible!

Figure 4-18:
Create this beautiful crimped necklace with your pliers and a bit of patience.

Materials and vital statistics

✔ **Beads:**

- 40 3mm gold-plated round beads

- 10 6mm faceted bicone Swarovski crystals in assorted browns

- 9 14x17mm smooth arrow beads, topaz-colored glass

✔ **Findings:**

- 1 22-inch length of 0.014-inch diameter black nylon-coated stainless steel beading wire

- 20 2-inch lengths of 0.014-inch diameter black nylon-coated stainless steel beading wire

- 62 gold-plated crimp beads

- 2 gold-plated clamshell bead tips

- 1 gold-plated lobster claw clasp

- 1 gold-plated chain tab

- 1 gold-plated jump ring

✔ **Tools:** Crimping pliers, wire cutters, chain-nose pliers

✔ **Techniques used:** Stringing, crimping, using bead tips

The finished piece contains 62 strategically placed crimps, but it may take you a few more, especially if you're new to crimping. Because you're moving the crimps around, often with your pliers, they can accidently get crimped on the edge of a piece of wire, for example. You may need as many as another 10 to 15 crimps to account for accidents.

This intricate-looking necklace is made of one long length of wire, decorated with several short pieces of wire (along with crimps and beads, of course). You create this piece from the middle of the wire out to the ends by repeating a simple pattern that involves layering the short pieces of wire along the main wire.

Directions

1. Slide one crimp bead onto the long length of beading wire. Situate it at approximately the middle of the wire. Slide a short length of beading wire through the same crimp bead so the crimp bead rests at approximately the middle of the short piece of wire, as shown in Figure 4-19. Use the crimping pliers to flatten the crimp bead, using the two-phase crimp method.

Figure 4-19:
Crimp your bead in the middle of both the short and long wires.

2. String one gold bead on one side of the short length of wire. Add a crimp bead. Flatten the crimp bead at the very end of the wire. Repeat on the other side of the short wire, as shown in Figure 4-20.

Figure 4-20:
Add gold beads to both ends of the short wires and crimp the ends to secure them.

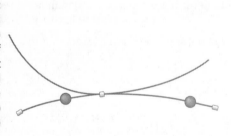

3. String an arrow onto one end of the long wire. String on a crimp bead. Slide a short length of wire through the crimp bead, situating the bead at the middle of the short piece of wire and about ¾ inch from the last crimp bead on the long length of wire, as shown in Figure 4-21. Using the crimping pliers, flatten the crimp using the two-phase crimp method.

Use your crimping pliers to situate the crimp bead exactly where you want it before you flatten the crimp. If you try to move the bead into place with your hands, and then pick up the pliers and try to crimp, you'll invariably move the bead out of position. Save yourself the extra step and use your pliers.

Figure 4-21:
Your next
crimp bead
performs
double duty,
securing the
arrow and
the next
short wire.

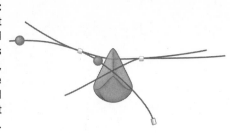

4. **Add a gold bead and crimp bead to each end of the short wire, like you did in Step 2. Flatten the crimps at the ends of the short length of wire to secure the gold beads, as shown in Figure 4-22.**

Figure 4-22:
Add gold
beads and
crimp them
into place to
begin to
layer short
wire pieces.

If any of your flattened crimps seem a bit loose, especially the crimps on the ends of the short wires, give them an extra squeeze with the chain-nose pliers. This step flattens them almost completely, eliminating any wiggling or sliding around.

5. **Repeat Steps 3 and 4, using a crystal instead of the arrow.**

6. **Repeat Step 5, alternating between crystals and arrows over the length of the necklace, until you run out of short wire lengths.**

Don't worry if your spacing between crimps isn't perfect. You layer so many pieces of wire, beads, and crimps that small variations aren't going to matter.

7. **Slide a bead tip onto one end of the long length of wire.**

Make sure the open mouth of the clamshell is pointing away from the beads and toward the open end of the wire so you can close the clamshell over the flattened crimp.

8. **Slide on a crimp bead. Using your crimping pliers, flatten the crimp approximately ¾ inch from the last flattened crimp, roughly the same spacing used throughout the necklace. Using the wire cutters, trim the excess wire flush with the flattened crimp, as shown in Figure 4-23.**

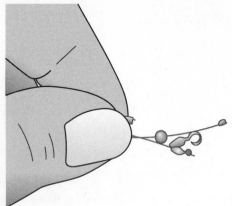

Figure 4-23:
Use a crimp to terminate your strand. Trim away the excess wire.

9. Use the chain-nose pliers to close the clamshell over the flattened crimp.

10. Repeat Steps 7 through 9 on the other end of the long length of wire.

11. Use the chain-nose pliers to connect the jump ring to the lobster claw. Close the jump ring. Slip the closed jump ring onto the loop of one bead tip. Use the chain-nose pliers to close the loop, connecting the jump ring to the bead tip, as shown in Figure 4-24.

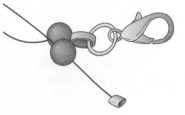

Figure 4-24:
Connect the lobster claw to the bead tip with a jump ring.

12. Use the chain-nose pliers to connect the loop of the other bead tip to the small hole of the chain tab to complete the necklace.

If you don't have a chain tab handy, feel free to substitute a gold-plated jump ring. Our clasp came with a matching chain tab, so we used it, but a jump ring would work just as well. Just make sure your metals match for this particular design.

Variation: Crystal constellation necklace

Create a stunning display by using 4mm faceted bicone crystals in a single color in place of all the other beads. Crystals could line the main wire, as well as dangle from the short pieces of wire. The single color and size of the crystal would create a bold and sparkly finished piece.

Constellation Crimp Earrings

We created these earrings, shown in Figure 4-25, to coordinate with the constellation crimp necklace. We didn't copy the design completely because the crimp ends of the short pieces of wire poked a little too much behind the ears. But by using matching components and similar techniques, both pieces coordinate nicely.

Figure 4-25: These easy-to-create earrings coordinate with the constellation crimp necklace.

Materials and vital statistics

- **Beads:**
  - 4 6mm faceted bicone Swarovski crystals in assorted browns
  - 2 14x17mm smooth arrow beads, topaz-colored glass
- **Findings:**
  - 2 5-inch lengths of 0.014-inch diameter black nylon-coated stainless steel beading wire
  - 6 gold-plated crimp beads
  - 2 gold-plated ear wires
- **Tools:** Crimping pliers, wire cutters, round-nose pliers (optional)
- **Techniques used:** Stringing, crimping

If you made the coordinating constellation necklace, you can definitely appreciate the relative speed and ease of this fun earring project. You use many of the same beads to create a coordinated look, but you skip the short wire pieces and opt instead for a single long loop with strategically placed crimps.

Directions

1. Slide one arrow onto one piece of beading wire. On either side, slide on a crimp bead, followed by a crystal, as shown in Figure 4-26.

Figure 4-26:
Slide your beads onto one piece of wire.

2. Feed both ends of the wire through another crimp bead, as shown in Figure 4-27.

Figure 4-27:
String both ends of the wire up through the crimp bead.

3. Form a loop at the top and feed the tails of both ends of the wire back down through the crimp bead, as shown in Figure 4-28.

At this point you have four strands running through one crimp bead.

4. Crimp the bead into place, using your crimping pliers. Trim off any excess wires with your wire cutters.

Figure 4-28:
Create a
loop and
stick the
tails back
down
through the
crimp bead.

5. Using your crimping pliers, position one of the loose crimp beads under one crystal above the arrow. When the crimp bead is positioned where you want it, crimp it into place. Repeat the process for the second crystal, as shown in Figure 4-29.

We positioned our first crystal about 15mm from the teardrop and the other about 18mm away. We like to stagger these a bit rather than place them exactly symmetrical.

Figure 4-29:
Crimp the
crystals into
place.

6. **Slip the loop onto an ear wire, using your round-nose pliers if necessary, to complete the earring.**

7. **Repeat Steps 1 through 6 to make a matching earring.**

Before crimping the top crimp of your second earring, make sure you compare the length of the loops to your first earring. Use your round-nose pliers if necessary to help adjust the top loop and overall length of the earring before crimping the bead into place.

Variation: Crystal constellation earrings

You can make a pair of earrings to go with the crystal constellation necklace discussed in the variation from the previous project. Simply use 4mm faceted bicone crystals in a single color in place of all the other beads. Choose crystals that match those you chose for the necklace.

Chapter 5

Bead Knotting

· ·

In This Chapter

▶ Using knots and bead tips to terminate strands

▶ Creating bead units with knots

▶ Knotting with nontraditional materials

· ·

Knotting is one of the oldest techniques in jewelry making. Before there was wire, stainless steel strands, and crimp beads, there were knots. In fact, knots are among the earliest embellishments in our human quest to beautify and distinguish ourselves from our fellow humans.

In this chapter, you spend some time working with the noble knot and putting the different varieties to use in stylish ways. You work with overhand knots, figure-eight knots, and lark's head knots, just to name a few, to craft earrings, bracelets, necklaces, and bookmarks. And we show you ways to include knots in different styles of jewelry designs.

If you need help making knots, take a look at the appendix. We cover different kinds of glues and how to use them in *Jewelry Making & Beading For Dummies* (Wiley). (We used Hypocement for the projects in this chapter, but you can use whatever suits your fancy.)

Semiprecious Stone Knotted Earrings

Bead cord may not seem like the first choice for making earrings, like the pair made with snowflake obsidian and fluorite in Figure 5-1, but it's such an easy stringing material to work with, we think you should give it a try. Knotting this thin black cord gives the illusion of tiny black beads separating and supporting the round beads, adding an elegant design element to these simple earrings.

Materials and vital statistics

✔ **Beads:**

• 4 7mm snowflake obsidian round beads

• 6 5mm clear fluorite round beads

✔ **Findings:**

• 2 gold-plated clamshell bead tips

• 2 gold-plated ear wires

• 7 inches of No. 6 black nylon bead cord

✔ **Tools:** Glue, scissors, ruler, needle, chain-nose pliers, round-nose pliers

✔ **Techniques used:** Stringing, tying overhand knots, using bead tips

Figure 5-1:
Snowflake obsidian and fluorite make these easy earrings extra special.

One 2-meter card of beading cord makes this project and the triple-wrap necklace later in this chapter. Talk about materials synergy!

We chose nylon bead cord for this project because we wanted something that's easy to string and doesn't fray or stretch much. Nylon lasts longer than traditional silk beading cord (which typically lasts a few years), so it's a good option for these earrings that we think you'll want to wear several times a week.

Directions

1. **Unwrap the full card of bead cord. Tie a double overhand knot in the open end (the one without the needle) of the cord. Apply a dab of glue to the knot. Trim off the extra tail with the scissors.**

Even though you need only 7 inches of cord, we recommend that you unwrap the full length of cord from the card and work from the tail. That way, if you have any left over (and you will if you start with a new 2-meter card), you still have the needle attached. Reduce, reuse, recycle!

2. **String on one fluorite bead. Tie an overhand knot 5mm above the fluorite bead. Slide on an obsidian bead. Tie an overhand knot 5mm above the obsidian bead. Repeat using 5 beads total, ending on a fluorite bead.**

Even though you use glue on the first knot in Step 1, you don't need to apply glue to the knots within the piece. The glue keeps the cord's edges from fraying or untying, so you need glue only on knots at the beginning and ending of strands.

3. **Slide a clamshell bead tip onto the bead cord with the mouth of the clamshell open toward the needle. Tie a double overhand knot in the bead cord, but before tightening the knot, insert a needle and slide the knot into the clamshell, as shown in Figure 5-2.**

   Use a needle to adjust and place the knot exactly where you want it. Simply slip the needle into the knot before tightening it completely. Then using the needle, slide the knot into place.

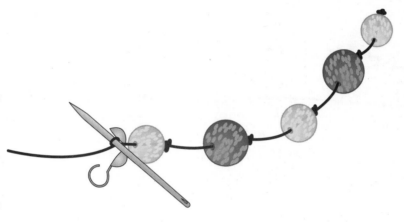

Figure 5-2:
Use a needle to slide your knot into place.

4. **Apply a dab of glue to the knot. Use the scissors to trim away the extra cord. Use the chain-nose pliers to close the clamshell over the knot, as shown in Figure 5-3.**

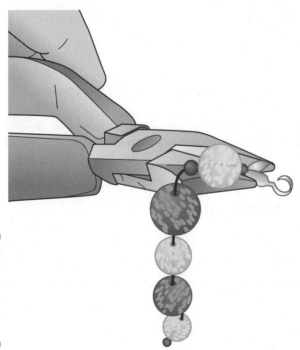

Figure 5-3:
Close the clamshell with the chain-nose pliers.

5. Slip the loop of the clamshell onto the loop of one ear wire. Using your round-nose pliers, close the clamshell loop, securing the ear wire.

6. Repeat Steps 1 through 5 to create a second earring to complete the set.

When you're making the second earring, do your best to create symmetrical spacing between the beads on the earrings so they match. Lay your first earring out, and lay the second one next to it. Use your needle again to place your knots in the appropriate place, as shown in Figure 5-4.

Figure 5-4:
Use your
first earring
as the
model to
create the
second.

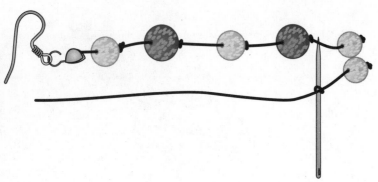

Variation: Semiprecious stone knotted bracelet

You can make a coordinating bracelet with your extra bead cord. To keep the bead spacing consistent with the earrings, you need 9 inches of bead cord, 7 obsidian beads, and 8 fluorite beads. String them in an alternating pattern, beginning and ending with a fluorite bead. Tie knots on both sides of each bead (instead of only under the bead as you did with the earrings) to hold it in place. Choose a lobster claw or a toggle and bar clasp to finish the bracelet, and you're done!

Silk Bookmark with Beads and Charms

Just because a bookmark's a necessity doesn't mean it can't be pretty, like the one in Figure 5-5. In this stylish embellishment for your favorite tome, you use chandelier earring components to create custom charms.

Materials and vital statistics

✔ **Beads:**

- 10 4mm red crackle glass beads
- 10 5mm silver-textured oval tube beads

✔ **Findings:**

- 2 base metal chandelier findings with 1 top loop and 5 bottom loops
- 10 1-inch base metal head pins
- 12 inches of 1mm black silk bead cord

✔ **Tools:** Round-nose pliers, wire cutters, scissors, glue

✔ **Techniques used:** Creating eye loops, stringing, tying a figure-eight knot

Figure 5-5:
Let a beautiful bookmark hold your place while you're off creating more jewelry.

This bookmark uses wire wrapping and knotting for a stylish combination. You can add extra beads to lengthen the wire dangles or create new color combinations if you want.

Directions

1. **Create your bead dangles. String one spacer bead, followed by one glass bead, onto one head pin. Using your round-nose pliers, create an eye loop. Trim any excess wire with the wire cutters. Repeat this step nine times using all the beads and head pins.**

Jump back to Chapter 2 for help making eye loops.

2. **Using the round-nose pliers, connect a head pin's eye loop to a bottom loop of the chandelier finding. Repeat, using all the dangles and bottom loops on the chandelier findings, as shown in Figure 5-6.**

You can use ready-made charms in place of creating your own embellished findings. Just skip Steps 1 and 2, and then jump to Step 3 with your own charm.

Figure 5-6:
Embellish
the chande-
lier findings
with beaded
dangles.

3. **Thread your bead cord through the top loop of the chandelier finding. Tie a figure-eight knot, as shown in Figure 5-7. Using the scissors, trim the extra cord near the knot. Apply glue to the trimmed knot.**

Figure 5-7:
Tie a figure-
eight knot in
four simple
steps.

4. **Repeat Step 3 with the other end of the cord and the other embellished chandelier finding to complete the bookmark.**

Two-Strand Elastic Crystal Bracelet

You use your old friend stretchy cord to create this elegant bracelet, shown in Figure 5-8. In this case, spacer bars connect the strands into a single cohesive unit. The shimmering crystals create elegant black-and-white stripes that are incredibly versatile, making the bracelet appropriate for almost any occasion.

Figure 5-8:
Elastic gets
a makeover
with elegant
crystals.

Materials and vital statistics

✔ **Beads:**

- 30 6mm clear AB faceted coin crystals

- 30 6mm black faceted coin crystals

✔ **Findings:**

- 2 12-inch pieces of 0.5mm diameter stretchy cord

- 6 10mm gold-plated 2-hole spacer bars

✔ **Tools:** 2 binder clips, needle, scissors, glue

✔ **Techniques used:** Stringing, tying an overhand knot

Use binder clips to help you keep the beads on the cord while you move and manipulate the strands. They come in especially handy when you tie the knots at the end.

Directions

1. **Place a binder clip on one end of each piece of stretchy cord. Slide 5 crystals onto each cord in this order: 1 black, 1 clear, 1 black, 1 clear, 1 black, as shown in Figure 5-9.**

Figure 5-9:
Work with
both strands
at the same
time.

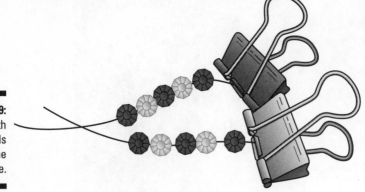

2. **String 1 spacer onto both strands, as shown in Figure 5-10.**

   The spacer bar connects the two strands, keeping them together as one bracelet. This completes the first bead section.

Figure 5-10:
A spacer
bar con-
nects the
strands and
keeps the
crystals
lined up
properly.

3. **Reverse the pattern, and string beads onto each strand in this order: 1 clear, 1 black, 1 clear, 1 black, 1 clear. Slide on 1 spacer to complete the second bead section.**

4. **Repeat Steps 1 through 3 using the remaining beads until you have a total of 6 bead sections.**

5. **Remove the binder clip from one strand. Place it at the open end of the other strand.**

   At this point, one strand is open on both ends; the other is secured with binder clips at both ends. The binder clips hold the second strand together while you tie off the first one.

6. **Take both ends of the open strand, and holding the two ends together, tie an overhand knot. Before tightening the knot completely, insert a needle into the knot and slide it as close as you can to the next bead. Take all the slack out of the stretchy cord, pulling it taut. Apply a dab of glue to the knot.**

   When you remove the slack from the cord, make sure all the beads are touching the beads next to them, but don't overstress the cord. Remember, you still need it to stretch a bit more to slip it over your hand.

7. Remove the binder clips and repeat Step 6 with the other strand.

8. Allow the glue to dry, and then snip the excess cord with your scissors. Tuck the knots into neighboring beads for a clean, professional look.

Variation: Crystal checkerboard bracelet

You can make a quick variation of this bracelet using the exact same supplies listed in the original pattern. Instead of stringing the top and bottom strands to match, stagger the pattern. So, a clear crystal in the top strand rests on a black crystal in the bottom strand, and so on. Instant checkerboard!

Variation: Gemstone bead bracelet

Substitute pearls and onyx for the crystals to make a gemstone version of this must-have accessory. Other good gemstone combinations include jade and carnelian, peridot and rose quartz, or coordinating colors of jasper.

Shell and Husk Heishi Bracelet

Here's a quick project for the favorite guy in your life. Pictured in Figure 5-11, this bracelet is made from black lip shells and, believe it or not, coconut husks! These natural, earthy materials are a natural fit for an everyday bracelet. Because the beads are the same shape, the subtle differences in size and color provide the contrasting texture, which is the piece's most distinctive design element.

Figure 5-11: The natural materials in the bracelet work well together.

Materials and vital statistics

✔ **Beads:**

- 3–4 inches of 4–5mm brown coconut heishi beads

- 3–4 inches of 4–5mm black lip shell heishi beads

  Because heishi beads often vary in width, we typically measure them in inches instead of by individual beads.

✔ **Findings:**

- 1 card of gray No. 4 silk bead cord with needle attached

- 2 base metal bead tips

- 1 base metal lobster claw

- 1 base metal jump ring

✔ **Tools:** Needle, glue, scissors, round-nose pliers

✔ **Techniques used:** Stringing, tying a double overhand knot, working with bead tips

We designed this 9-inch bracelet (the clasp measures about ½ inch) to fit an average-size man and allowed for a loose drape. If you're making this for a woman, size it to about 7½ inches. If you're fitting a larger man, consider a 9½-inch or larger bracelet. Or create a kid's version at roughly 6 inches.

Directions

1. **Unwrap the full length of bead cord. Tie a double overhand knot in the open end (the end without the needle attached) of the cord. Apply a dab of glue to the knot. Slide on a bead tip so the knot rests inside the cup of the bead tip.**

2. **Begin stringing beads in this pattern: 1 black lip shell, 1 coconut. Repeat the pattern until the bracelet measures 8½ inches or the desired length.**

3. **String on the remaining bead tip with the cup open toward the needle. Tie a double overhand knot. Before tightening the knot, slip a needle into the knot. Use the needle to slide the knot down into the cup of the bead tip. Remove the needle, and apply a dab of glue to the knot. Trim away the excess bead cord with the scissors.**

   Refer back to Figure 5-2 if you need to see how to use the needle to move the knot.

   Rewrap the silk bead cord onto the card it came with so you know exactly the size, brand, and color of the cord when you use it next time. Wrap it tail first so you can tuck the needle in on the outside.

4. **Slip the connecting loop of the lobster claw onto the loop of one bead tip. Using the round-nose pliers, close the loop, securing the clasp. Repeat the process using the jump ring and the other bead tip.**

Triple-Wrap Necklace

One of our favorite things about the triple-wrap necklace in Figure 5-12 is its randomness. There's no pattern to follow, no measurements to make (after you get your materials together, of course). Just good ol' stringing with a few knots thrown in for good measure. So start up the DVD player and get busy. Depending on how quickly you string, you could be done in a single episode of your favorite prime-time drama or reality series.

This project isn't called "triple wrap" for nothing. You can wear the 42-inch necklace as is, or wrap it around your neck up to three times for a layered choker. It's also a fun bracelet wrapped around your arm. Our favorite way to wear it is double-wrapped, with one wrap acting as a choker and the other part hanging nice and long.

Figure 5-12:
Wear the triple-wrap necklace at several different lengths.

Materials and vital statistics

✔ **Beads:** 42 inches of brown bead mix, assorted sizes of your choice

In our design, we use a bead assortment that weighs roughly 45 grams. Our beads range in size from No. 6 seed beads to 8mm beige faux pearls.

✔ **Findings:**

- 2 gold-plated clamshell bead tips
- 48 inches of No. 6 black nylon bead cord
- 1 gold-plated toggle and bar clasp

✔ **Tools:** Glue, needle, scissors, chain-nose pliers, round-nose pliers

✔ **Techniques used:** Stringing, tying an overhand knot

Create this long necklace by using nothing but random beads and a few findings. How's that for quick and easy?

Directions

1. **Unwrap the full length of bead cord. Tie a double overhand knot in the open end (the end without the needle attached) of the cord. Apply a dab of glue to the knot. Slide on a clamshell so the knot rests inside the clamshell, and the loop points away from the cord, as shown in Figure 5-13a. Apply a dab of glue to the knot. Trim away the excess bead cord using the scissors.**

2. **Using the chain-nose pliers, close the clamshell over the knot, as shown in Figure 5-13b.**

Figure 5-13:
Tie a knot and situate it inside the cup of the bead tip.

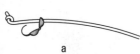
a

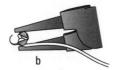
b

3. **String your beads any way you see fit until you use all the beads. When the strand is complete, slide on the remaining clamshell, this time with the clamshell open to the needle side of the bead cord.**

4. **Tie a knot and slide it down so that it fits inside the bead tip. Trim the knot with scissors, and apply a dab of glue to the knot. Close the clamshell over the knot with the chain-nose pliers.**

5. **Using your round-nose pliers, gently open the loop of one bead tip. Attach one end of the toggle clasp to open loop, and then close it using the pliers. Do the same with the other bead tip and the other half of the clasp.**

Variation: 4mm bead strand

Although we love the randomness of the original design, you can create a more ordered look by using beads that are the same size. For this project, 4mm round beads are a great choice because they're small enough to be comfortable in any of the various wrapping configurations you may wear. The instructions are the same, but instead of choosing the random bead mix, choose 42 inches of 4mm round beads and string them up!

Gemstone Nugget and Beading Wire Knotted Necklace

If you've made any kind of jewelry before, you're probably familiar with beading wire. It's a flexible wire made up of several strands (anywhere from 7 to 49 individual strands) of stainless steel covered in nylon. Most often used in stringing and crimping necklaces and bracelets and the like, this versatile material can also be used in knotting projects, like the necklace featured in Figure 5-14.

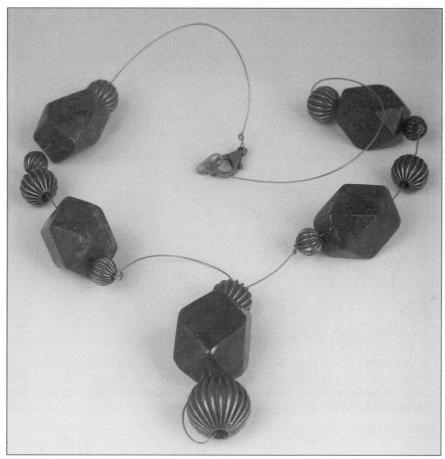

Figure 5-14: This chunky design owes much of its appeal to thin but mighty beading wire.

Materials and vital statistics

✔ **Beads:**

- 5 15–23mm large brecciated jasper faceted nuggets
- 1 15mm corrugated base metal round bead
- 5 10mm corrugated base metal round beads
- 4 6mm corrugated base metal round beads

✔ **Findings:**

- 2 base metal (to match the corrugated beads) crimp beads

- 1 base metal (to match the corrugated beads) chain tab

- 26 inches of 0.014-inch or 0.20-inch diameter nylon-coated stainless steel beading wire

  We chose silver beading wire, but you can choose any color that coordinates with your nuggets and beads. The wire is exposed for significant chunks throughout this project, so your choice really matters this time!

✔ **Tools:** Ruler, crimping pliers, wire cutters

✔ **Techniques used:** Stringing, tying an overhand knot, crimping

In this project, you string beads and knot the beading wire at staggered increments along the wire to create bead units, exposing sections of wire along the way. The exposed wire shows off the chunky nuggets and beads nicely.

Directions

1. String the 15mm corrugated bead onto your beading wire. Position the bead in the middle of the wire, as shown in Figure 5-15.

Figure 5-15:
Slide your bead to the middle of your wire.

2. String both ends of the wire through one nugget. Snug the nugget down as close to the corrugated bead as you can. Follow the nugget with a 10mm corrugated bead, stringing both ends of the wire through the bead, as detailed in Figure 5-16.

This unit is the center of your necklace.

Figure 5-16:
Feed both ends of wire back through one end of the nugget to create your dangle.

3. Tie a double overhand knot approximately 2 inches above the center bead unit in one side of the wire. Tie a double overhand knot approximately 1 inch above the center bead unit in the other side of the wire, like the ones in Figure 5-17.

Figure 5-17: Use knots to create separate bead units along your wire.

4. Slide 1 6mm corrugated bead, 1 nugget, and 1 10mm corrugated bead onto each side of the wire.

5. Repeat Steps 3 and 4, using the remaining beads. Vary the spacing for your knots as you see fit.

6. On one side of the wire, slide on one crimp bead, followed by the lobster clasp. Feed the tail of the wire back through the crimp bead, as shown in Figure 4-2 in Chapter 4. Adjust the placement of the crimp bead so one side of the necklace measures 10 inches from the clasp to the *top* of the center bead unit, as shown in Figure 5-18.

See Chapter 4 if you need a refresher on working with crimp beads.

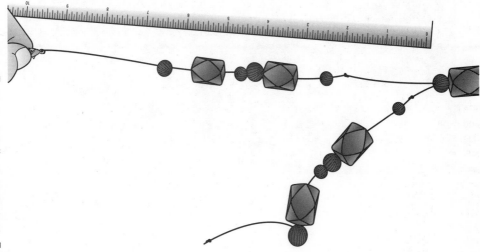

Figure 5-18: Measure from the top, not the bottom, of the dangle to get an accurate measurement.

We designed this necklace to measure 20 inches, so half the length is 10 inches. If you want a longer or shorter necklace, now's the time to make an adjustment. For an 18-inch necklace, this half should measure 9 inches; for a 22-inch necklace, this half measures 11 inches, and so on.

Make sure to measure from the top of the dangle bead unit to get an accurate fit. The dangle itself is about 1¾ inches long, but it doesn't count in the overall length of the necklace.

7. **Using the crimping pliers, flatten the crimp, securing the clasp into place. Using the wire cutters, trim the excess wire so it's flush with the crimp bead.**

8. **Repeat Steps 6 and 7 with the chain tab (instead of the lobster clasp) on the other side of the wire to finish the necklace.**

You may be surprised that we terminated this necklace with crimp beads, because this chapter is, after all, about knotting. Although the beading wire forms strong knots within a piece, we don't trust it to hold this heavy piece together. If you'd prefer to use knots, feel free to give it a shot, but keep a resealable plastic bag handy in case you need to collect scattered nuggets later.

Ceramic Pendant and Button Knotted Necklace

This necklace, shown in Figure 5-19 is full of knots. Don't worry, you don't have to untangle them. Instead, they're part of the design. In fact, the knots keep the small tag charms spaced out along the length of the necklace.

Figure 5-19: Use knots to hold the tags in place on this necklace.

Materials and vital statistics

✔ **Beads:**

- 1 46mm round ceramic pendant
- 2 10mm corrugated metal beads, with extra large holes
- 6 11mm metal round charms, jump ring attached
- 6 11mm metal diamond charms, jump ring attached
- 6 15mm filigree metal charms, jump ring attached

✔ **Findings:**

- 28 inches of 1mm rubber cord
- 25mm stamped toggle and bar clasp
- 2 large (designed for 2mm stringing material) silver-plated crimp beads

✔ **Tools:** Ruler, 2 pairs of chain-nose pliers, crimping pliers, scissors

✔ **Techniques used:** Stringing, tying a lark's head knot and overhand knot, crimping

Knots are a great design tool to help you hold the charms where you want them. For added design elements, you use a lark's head knot to keep the pendant lying flat against your body.

Directions

1. Using a lark's head knot, tie the pendant to the center of the cord. Holding both strands together, tie an overhand knot, sliding it down to touch the top of the lark's head knot, as shown in Figure 5-20.

Figure 5-20:
Use a lark's head knot and an overhand knot to decoratively attach the pendant.

2. Tie an overhand knot about ¾ inch above the pendant on one strand. Using the chain-nose pliers, open the jump ring on one charm. Slip the open jump ring through the knot.

3. Tie another overhand knot about ¾ inch above the first knot. Slide on a bead. Tie another overhand knot above it.

4. Repeat Step 2 eight more times up the rest of the strand.

5. Slide on one crimp bead. Slip the tail through the hole of one side of the clasp, and then back down through the crimp bead. Using the crimping pliers, flatten the crimp bead using the two-phase crimp method. Trim away any extra cord with the scissors.

6. Repeat Steps 2 through 5 to complete the other side of the necklace.

Chapter 6

Bead-Weaving Stitches

● ●

In This Chapter
▶ Practicing different beading stitches
▶ Weaving beads into jewelry and accessories
▶ Becoming part of the history surrounding bead weaving

● ●

*W*hen you create projects using bead-weaving techniques, you use a needle and thread to stitch tiny little glass beads together. Much like other types of needlework, such as embroidery, you employ different stitches to create jewelry, home décor items, and other decorative art objects.

Some of the most popular bead weaving stitches include peyote, brick (also known as Comanche), ladder, and net. These stitches have a rich history because they were developed by various cultures, like the Native Americans who used bead-weaving methods to adorn their clothing and other objects.

After you conquer the basics of these bead stitch techniques, you'll be amazed at what you can create with just some little beads and a simple needle and thread, and of course, your own imagination. As you work each technique, you become part of the history behind this unique art. However, like any type of jewelry making, practicing the techniques is essential to crafting quality artwork that you'll enjoy wearing and using in your home.

In this chapter, you get some solid bead-weaving practice under your belt. First, you use the peyote stitch as well as a fringe technique to weave together some Japanese Delica beads and Swarovski crystals to create a bookmark that makes the perfect gift for that bookworm on your list. Then it's time to get into some jewelry making, starting with a pair of ladder stitch earrings, which combine glass bugle beads, seed beads, and crystals. And, because you can never have too many earrings and they happen to be a great way to practice your bead-weaving skills, you use the brick stitch to weave a pair of triangle-shaped earrings that have little dangle crystals on them. Finally, a simple net stitch anklet is a good way to practice more stitch work and end up with a little something sparkly to wear.

Good lighting is always important when making jewelry but even more so when working with small beads like seed beads. Remember to also take breaks now and then to help combat possible eye strain as you work.

If you have trouble threading your needle, try turning the needle so you're going through the other side. The eye of the needle actually has a front and back.

Peyote Bookmark

Peyote is one of the more versatile bead-weaving stitches, so it's often used to create items besides jewelry. Many bead weavers enjoy stitching decorative art objects, home décor items, or other accessories using this stitch. This beaded bookmark project (shown in Figure 6-1) is a good introduction to this stitch technique. The addition of crystals in a mixture of colors, as well as the flower and butterfly shapes, makes this bookmark a bright and cheery spring-themed accessory for any book lover. To change the theme, simply change the beads. For example, if you plan to give this bookmark to the man in your life, earth tone beads would be a better choice.

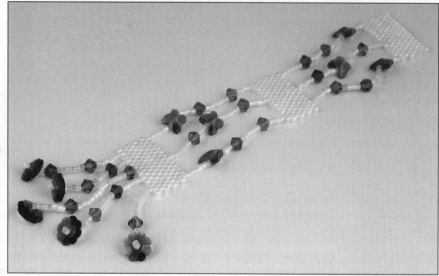

Figure 6-1:
Crystal
butterflies
and flowers
decorate
this beaded
bookmark.

Try to stick with Delica beads when weaving the peyote stitch. Delicas are more square shaped than rounded like other seed beads, so they stack well against each other as you stitch them together, very much like tiny little bricks.

Materials and vital statistics

- ✔ **Beads:**

    - 5 grams of silky satin rainbow white Delicas

    - 6 6mm Swarovski fuchsia butterfly crystals

    - 21 4mm miscellaneous colored Swarovski bicone crystals

    - 5 8mm Swarovski amethyst flower crystals

- ✔ **Notions:** Off-white Silamide thread, size-12 beading needle

- ✔ **Tools:** Scissors, jeweler's cement

- ✔ **Techniques used:** Weaving the peyote stitch, making fringe

This bookmark combines three peyote sections that are connected with strands of beads and then topped off with fringes of flower crystals. The connection strands are also enhanced with butterfly-shaped crystal beads. The crystal beads are amazing when you see them in person.

Creating the peyote sections

1. **Use the scissors to cut about a yard of thread and thread it through the eye of your needle.**

2. **Add what bead weavers call a *stop bead* by bringing the needle up through one Delica bead, and then taking the needle back down through the bottom of the same bead. Leave about a 6-inch tail of thread.**

   A stop bead is used to prevent any beads from falling off the thread when you first start stitching. After you're finished with the project, you can simply pull the bead off the thread to remove it.

3. **Thread 8 Delica beads onto the thread, and push these down until they rest against the stop bead.**

4. **Thread on another Delica bead, skip one bead previously strung on the thread, and insert the needle through the hole of the next bead on the thread, as illustrated in Figure 6-2.**

   So you end up adding a bead and skipping a bead.

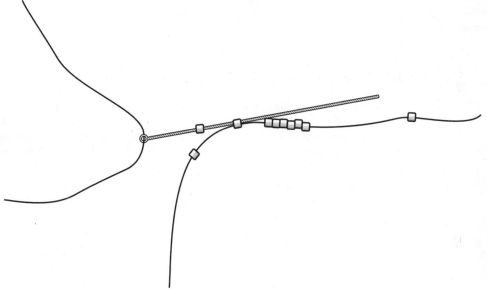

Figure 6-2:
Start your first row of peyote stitch by adding and skipping beads as you weave.

5. **Continue to add a bead and skip a bead until you've worked your way down to the end of the beads on the thread.**

6. **Repeat Steps 4 and 5 eleven more times so you're stitching beads (adding a bead, skipping a bead, adding a bead, skipping a bead, and so on) back and forth across the row of beads.**

   You should end up with a section of Delica beads stitched together as shown in Figure 6-3. Because you started with 8 beads in Step 3, you'll see 4 beads (half as many beads) sticking out like little teeth.

7. **Make two more peyote sections, following Steps 1 through 6, so you have a total of three. Set one aside for later.**

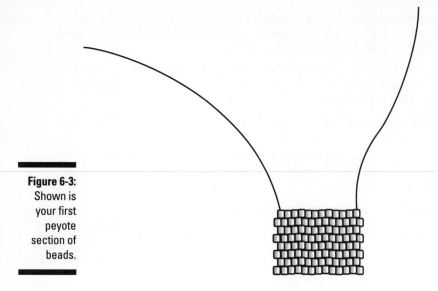

Figure 6-3:
Shown is
your first
peyote
section of
beads.

Piecing the peyote sections together

1. **To start connecting the three peyote sections together, you first need to secure a thread to one of the peyote pieces. Insert your needle and thread any place you like into one peyote section and weave it through the beads to one end. Make at least one knot as you weave to secure the thread to the peyote section, pulling on the thread so the knot is hidden in the beads.**

Make sure to weave so that eventually the needle comes out of one end of the bead section. (See Chapter 2 for more explanation on how to attach and finish off threads while bead weaving.)

Some bead weavers are knotters, and some prefer to weave the threads together as they work with no knots. It's really a personal preference, but we recommend using knots now and then when you have to reinsert a needle and thread into your beadwork. If you pull on the thread, you can pull the knot inside of a bead, and the knots won't be noticeable, so we think it's worth the extra security.

You can also glue knots to secure the thread if you'd like, something we don't usually do. Do not, however, add any glue to knots until you're totally done with any bead-weaving project. After you glue those knots, you can't unweave anything if you make a boo-boo later in the weaving process.

2. **Now that your thread is coming out of one end of a peyote section (as shown in Figure 6-4), string on 4 Delica beads, 1 butterfly crystal bead, 6 Delica beads, 1 bicone bead, 4 Delica beads, 1 bicone bead, and 6 Delica beads.**

Pay attention to the orientation of your butterfly crystal beads. You want to make sure they're all flying in the same direction. This bookmark has a definite top and bottom, as you'll see in the next section.

3. **As illustrated in Figure 6-5, connect this first section and its strand of beads to a second peyote bead section by inserting the needle through the corresponding bead.**

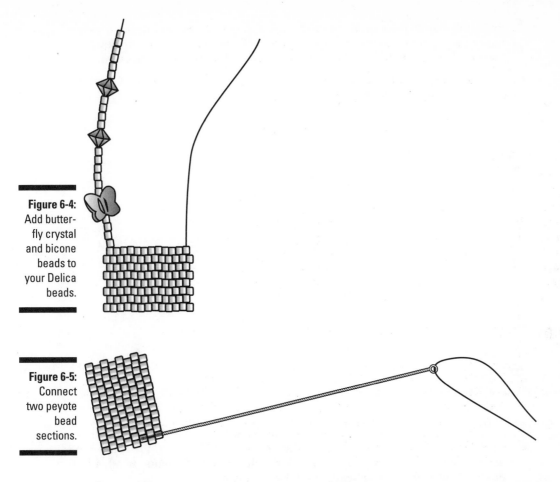

Figure 6-4:
Add butter-
fly crystal
and bicone
beads to
your Delica
beads.

Figure 6-5:
Connect
two peyote
bead
sections.

4. Bring the needle back down through the strand of beads you strung in Step 2
(see Figure 6-6), as well as down through the first bead on the first peyote
section.

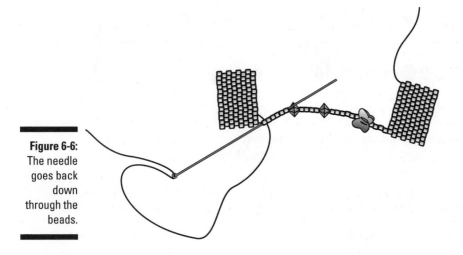

Figure 6-6:
The needle
goes back
down
through the
beads.

5. Bring the needle back up through the bead next to it, and continue to weave until you get to the opposite end of the peyote section and your working thread is coming out of the bead on the very end of the peyote section.

6. Repeat Steps 2 through 5 so you're connecting the two peyote bead sections with two strands of Delica and crystal beads, as shown in Figure 6-7.

Figure 6-7:
Beaded
strands con-
nect both
ends of two
peyote
sections.

7. Following Steps 1 through 6, connect your third peyote section to the other side of the second peyote section. This time, add the beads in the following pattern: 4 Delica beads, 1 bicone bead, 6 Delica beads, 1 bicone bead, 4 Delica beads, 1 butterfly crystal bead, and 6 Delica beads.

See Figure 6-8 for an example of how the piece should now look.

Figure 6-8:
All three
peyote
sections
are now
connected.

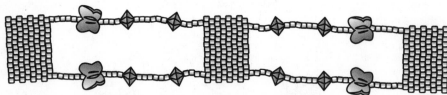

8. Weave the needle and thread through the first peyote bead section, again securing with knots, so the needle comes out of a bead in the top middle of the peyote section.

Unless you're very comfortable working with a thread that is very, very long, most bead-weaving projects require you to periodically finish off an old working thread and weave in a new thread. Three feet is a good general length to start with, but it's up to you and your comfort level to determine how long you like your threads. They need to be long enough to work with comfortably, but not so long that they get tangled up.

9. String on 4 Delica beads, 1 bicone bead, 6 Delica beads, 1 butterfly crystal bead, 4 Delica beads, 1 bicone bead, and 6 Delica beads. Insert the needle up through the center of the second peyote bead section, continuing to weave until you come out the middle of the other side.

10. String on 4 Delica beads, 1 bicone bead, 6 Delica beads, 1 butterfly crystal bead, 4 Delica beads, 1 bicone bead, and 6 Delica beads. Insert the needle up through the center of the third peyote bead section, continuing to weave and knot the thread, and use scissors to trim it off.

Figure 6-9 shows how the six strands of beads connect the three peyote bead sections.

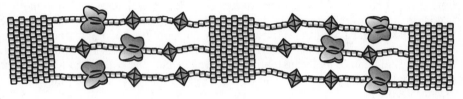

Figure 6-9:
Six strands
of beads
connect
three peyote
sections.

Finishing with fringe

1. Create some fun fringe at the top of the bookmarker. Weave a new working thread into the last peyote bead section so the thread is coming out the top of the peyote section. String the fringe with your choice of beads, making sure to end with a flower crystal bead and a Delica crystal bead.

Each piece of fringe can be any length, number, and combination of Delica beads and bicone crystal beads. In fact, you want to stagger the lengths, making some short and some long, so they aren't all the same length and will have more movement to them. Just make sure each piece of fringe ends with one flower bead and one Delica bead.

2. Bring the needle back down through the flower (skipping the last Delica bead on the strand) and through all the other beads on the strand, as shown in Figure 6-10.

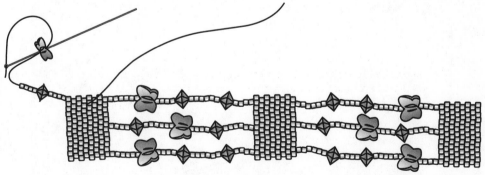

Figure 6-10:
Flower
crystal
beads
dangle from
each piece
of fringe.

3. **Weave the needle down and up through the Delica beads on the top of the peyote bead section to space out the fringe. Continue to follow the same stringing pattern and weaving procedure in Steps 1 and 2 until you have as much fringe as you want.**

   We added five strands of fringe to our bookmark.

4. **Finally, go back and pull off your stop beads (if you haven't already) that you strung at the very beginning of the project, weave in any extra pieces of thread, and use scissors to trim them off.**

Variation: Boy blue bookmark

Blue is the color most often associated as a color for guys. Therefore, for something a little less girlie, apply the same peyote technique just described, but change the bead choice. Instead of silky satin rainbow white Delicas, opt for opaque luster royal blue Delicas. Then substitute clear aurora borealis square crystals for the butterfly and flower crystal beads. Finally, instead of using miscellaneous colored Swarovski bicone crystals, keep them the same size at 4mm, but use different shades of blue bicone crystal beads.

Ladder Stitch and Crystal Earrings

Ladder stitch is better known by your average bead weaver as the precursor stitch to brick stitch. You have to do ladder stitch first before you can start to weave anything using brick stitch. However, ladder stitch can also fly solo if you get a little inventive with it, as we did to create these ladder stitch and crystal earrings, shown in Figure 6-11. Two ladder stitch sections made with *bugle beads* — long, tube-shaped glass beads — are connected with segments of round seed beads and crystals. These earrings actually work up pretty quickly after you get going, so you'll have plenty of time to make more than one pair, one for you and one for a friend.

Figure 6-11: Combine bugle beads and crystals for these ladder stitch earrings.

Double check the ends of bugles beads before you start weaving with them to make sure they're not cracked or nicked around the holes in the beads. Broken areas around the holes can snag and eventually cut through your beading thread.

Materials and vital statistics

- ✔ **Beads:**
  - 6 ¼-inch purple bugle beads
  - 16 size 11 purple rainbow iridescent Japanese seed beads
  - 5 4mm round Swarovski clear aurora borealis crystals
- ✔ **Findings:** 1 pair of sterling silver ear hooks
- ✔ **Notions:** Purple Silamide thread, 2 size-12 beading needles
- ✔ **Tools:** Scissors, chain-nose pliers
- ✔ **Techniques used:** Weaving the ladder stitch

You can use Nymo beading thread if you prefer it to Silamide, but if you use Nymo, you'll need to wax the thread. Silamide comes waxed already, which is one reason we like to use it so much. It means one less step while weaving.

The two most common types of seed beads are Czech seed beads and Japanese seed beads. Although Czech seed beads come in wonderful colors, they're not always uniform in shape. So for beginners, they can be a little more difficult to use than their counterparts from Japan, which are known for their higher quality and more consistent size and shape. That's why you use Japanese seed beads in this project.

Directions

1. Use scissors to cut about a yard of thread and thread it through the eye of your needle.

2. String two bugle beads, and then insert the needle through the bottom of the first bugle bead, as shown in Figure 6-12. Make sure to leave about a 6-inch tail of thread.

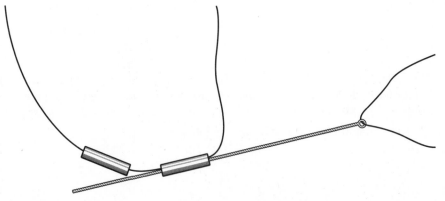

Figure 6-12: Add your first two bugle beads for your ladder stitch.

3. Pull the working thread so both bugle beads line up right next to each other, as shown in Figure 6-13.

Figure 6-13:
The bugle beads line up next to each other.

4. Add another bugle bead, and as shown in Figure 16-14, insert the needle through the second bugle bead.

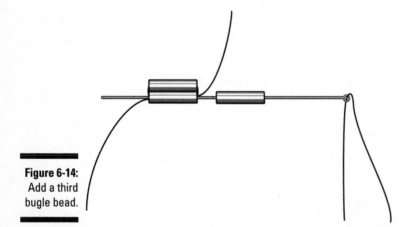

Figure 6-14:
Add a third bugle bead.

5. Insert the needle back up through the third bugle bead (see Figure 6-15). To make sure the beads are nice and secure, thread the needle through each one before continuing.

At this point, you've made your first bugle bead section.

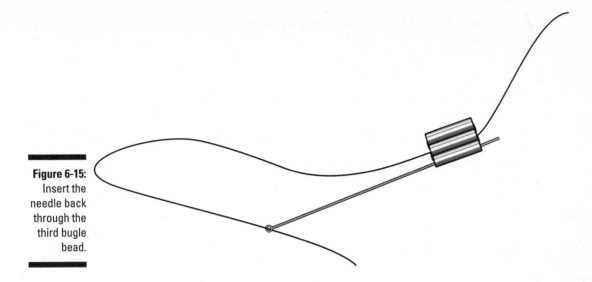

Figure 6-15:
Insert the
needle back
through the
third bugle
bead.

6. **String on 8 Japanese seed beads, and insert the needle through one end of your ladder section, as shown in Figure 6-16.**

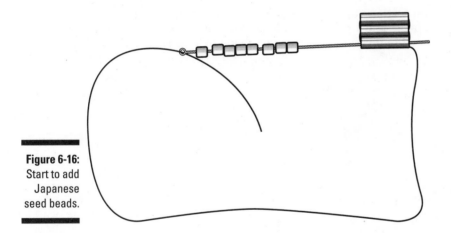

Figure 6-16:
Start to add
Japanese
seed beads.

7. **Insert the needle through the other end of the bugle bead you inserted it through in Step 6.**

This makes a loop of beads as illustrated in Figure 6-17.

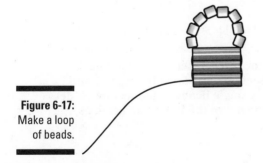

Figure 6-17:
Make a loop
of beads.

8. To reinforce the loop of beads, thread the needle back through the seed beads and bugle bead a few times. Then set this section aside, still keeping the needle on the thread.

    You'll use the needle again in a minute.

9. Use the scissors to cut a 2-foot piece of thread and thread it through the eye of another needle.

10. Repeat Steps 2 through 5 to make another bugle bead ladder section. Weave and trim off the threads (both the working thread, which has the needle attached, and the non-working thread, which is the tail) so your ladder section looks like the one in Figure 6-18.

Figure 6-18:
Make a
second
bugle ladder
section.

11. Pick up the bead section you set aside in Step 8, and string 1 purple seed bead, 1 crystal bead, and 1 purple seed bead. Then insert the needle through the top bugle bead in the ladder section you made in Step 10. See Figure 6-19.

Figure 6-19:
Connect
ladder
sections.

12. String on 1 purple seed bead, 1 crystal bead, and 1 seed bead. Then insert the needle through the opposite end of the bugle bead that the working thread is coming out of.

    This completes the connection to the second ladder section, as shown in Figure 6-20.

13. To again reinforce the beads, at least once or twice, insert the needle back down through the seed beads and ladder section you added in Steps 11 and 12. Then snake the needle through the three bugle beads in the second ladder section so the working thread is now coming out of the last bugle bead, as shown in Figure 6-21.

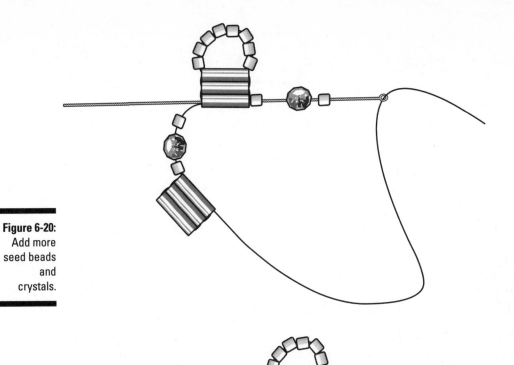

Figure 6-20:
Add more
seed beads
and
crystals.

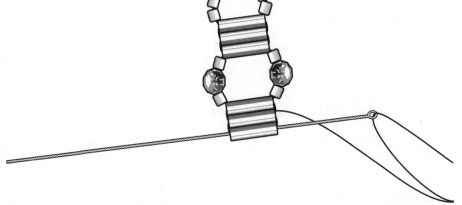

Figure 6-21:
The working
thread is
coming out
of the last
bugle bead.

14. String on alternating purple seed beads and crystal beads until you have 4 purple seed beads and 3 crystal beads on your thread. Insert the needle back through the last bugle bead, as shown in Figure 6-22.

15. As before, reinforce the beads by threading the needle back through the beads you added in Step 14, and then finish off and trim off any excess thread. (Chapter 2 explains how to finish off threads if you need a refresher.)

16. Repeat Steps 1 through 15 to make a duplicate earring.

17. Use the chain-nose pliers to open the loop on an ear hook. Slip the loop of the ear hook onto one of the seed bead loops (the ones you made in Steps 6 through 8), and then, using the chain-nose pliers, close the ear hook loop back up. Repeat this step for the other earring.

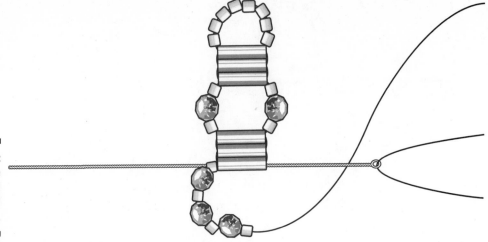

Figure 6-22:
Alternate
purple seed
beads and
crystals.

Variation: More ladder earrings

To add a little something extra to this same ladder stitch earring design, instead of having more 4mm crystals at the bottom of the earrings, use seed beads and a briolette crystal to dangle from the bottom of each earring. *Briolettes* are side-drilled teardrop-shaped beads that come in a huge assortment of colored and clear crystals, as well as gemstones such as amethyst (which would look killer next to the purple beads), smoky quartz, and citrine, to name just a few.

Brick Stitch Triangle Earrings

To weave brick stitch, you first need to use the ladder stitch, so this earring project (shown in Figure 6-23) is sort of a two-for-one deal when it comes to practicing bead weaving stitches. Brick stitch naturally evolves into a triangular-shaped section of beads, unless you add or subtract beads during the process. For this design, we kept the natural triangle shape and accented the bottom with tiny *fringe beads* — small, side-drilled, teardrop-shaped glass beads that often are added to the bottom of fringe. In keeping with the geometric feel of these earrings, the ear hooks are French hoops, so you get the combination of a triangle and circle pattern in each earring.

Figure 6-23:
Hoop ear
hooks
become
a design
element in
these brick
stitch
earrings.

Though colors like off-white and light gray are good general thread colors to keep on hand, try to use thread that matches the beads as much as possible. This way, you'll hardly be able to see the threads that connect all the beads as you weave.

Materials and vital statistics

- ✔ **Beads:**
  - • 5 grams of size 11 turquoise rainbow iridescent Japanese seed beads
  - • 18 clear rainbow glass fringe beads
- ✔ **Findings:** 2 sterling silver French hoop ear wires
- ✔ **Notions:** Turquoise Silamide thread, size-12 beading needle
- ✔ **Tools:** Scissors, chain-nose pliers
- ✔ **Techniques used:** Weaving the ladder stitch and brick stitch

Make sure you have a small pair of extra-sharp scissors when bead weaving so you can get good clean cuts on your thread. Small sewing scissors are handy for this sort of work.

These little triangle earrings are a good way to practice both the ladder and brick stitches.

Beginning with the ladder stitch

1. **Use the scissors to cut about a yard of thread and thread it through the eye of your needle.**

2. **Begin by making a ladder stitch section. String on two seed beads and bring the needle up through the bottom of the first bead, as illustrated in Figure 6-24.**

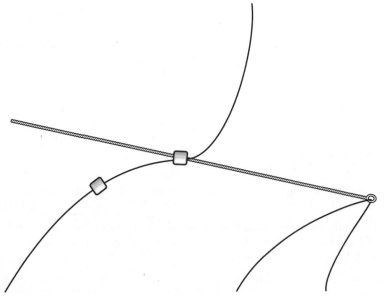

Figure 6-24:
Start the ladder stitch section.

3. Pull the thread so that both beads line up next to each other. Reinforce the stitch by bringing the needle back through the bead next to it, as shown in Figure 6-25.

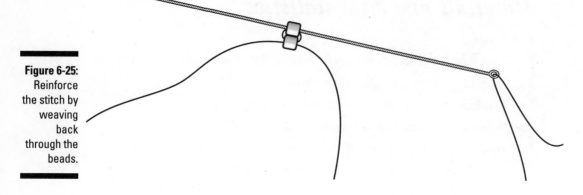

Figure 6-25:
Reinforce the stitch by weaving back through the beads.

4. Continue the ladder stitch until you have connected 9 seed beads, as shown in Figure 6-26.

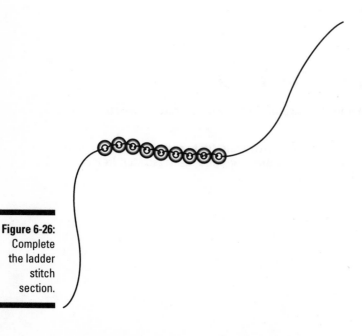

Figure 6-26:
Complete the ladder stitch section.

Adding the fringe beads

1. Insert the needle through the hole in one fringe bead, and bring the needle back up through the first bead in the ladder stitch section (see Figure 6-27).

2. Insert the needle down through the second seed bead in the ladder stitch section (see Figure 6-28), and pull the thread so the fringe bead is close up against the bottom of the triangle.

There should be little to no wiggle room between the fringe bead and the bottom of the triangle.

3. Repeat Steps 1 and 2 until you have added all the fringe beads to the bottom of the ladder stitch section, as shown in Figure 6-29.

At this point, the working thread should be coming out of the top of one end of the ladder stitch section.

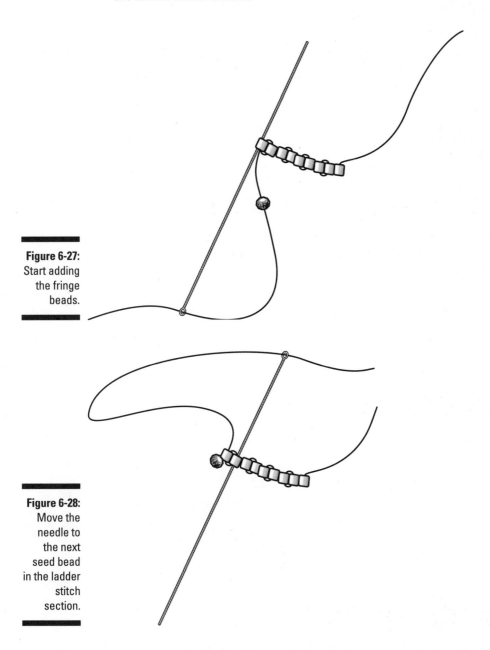

Figure 6-27:
Start adding the fringe beads.

Figure 6-28:
Move the needle to the next seed bead in the ladder stitch section.

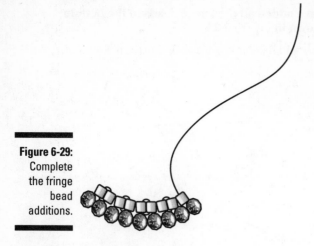

Figure 6-29:
Complete
the fringe
bead
additions.

Building on with the brick stitch

1. String on a seed bead, and insert the needle under the thread that joins the first two beads in the ladder section (see Figure 6-30).

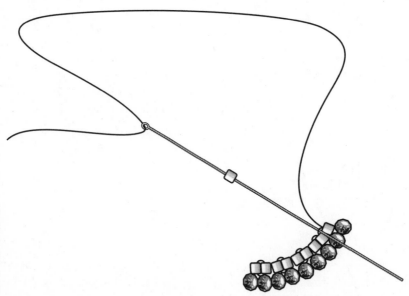

Figure 6-30:
Start the
brick stitch
now.

2. Bring the needle up through the hole of the bead you added in Step 1, as shown in Figure 6-31.

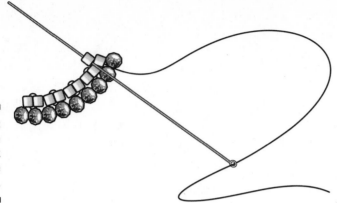

Figure 6-31:
Insert the needle back through the bead.

3. **Pull the thread to snug up the bead so it rests on top of the ladder section (see Figure 6-32).**

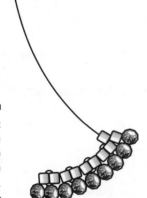

Figure 6-32:
Pull the thread to keep the tension.

4. **Repeat Steps 1 through 3, moving back and forth to weave the beads. You'll notice the beads start to form a triangle. Do this until you have two beads at the top of your triangle, as shown in Figure 6-33.**

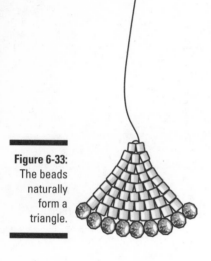

Figure 6-33:
The beads
naturally
form a
triangle.

Finishing with a loop of beads and findings

1. String on 4 seed beads, and insert the needle down through the next bead. Pull the thread so you have a loop of beads at the top of the triangle.

2. To reinforce the loop of beads, snake the needle back through the 4 beads a few times, knot, and tie off the working thread.

3. With the chain-nose pliers, open the loop on the hoop ear hooks, attach the bead loop, and close the ear hook loop back.

4. Repeat all of the steps, starting with the "Beginning with the ladder stitch" section, to make a second earring.

Variation: Mega triangle earrings

When working with the brick stitch, the longer your ladder section is to begin with, the larger your triangles will be when you're finished. To make some extra-large, extra-fabulous triangle earrings — mega triangle earrings — follow the same procedure as described for the brick stitch triangle earrings, but make the ladder stitch twice as long. Instead of 9 seed beads in the ladder, double it to 18. This will result in earrings that are twice as large.

Net Stitch Lacy Anklet

Spice things up a little with a beaded adornment for your ankle. The single net stitch creates a wonderful lacy effect with your seed beads and is one of the easiest stitches to master for beginners. And because we're talking lace, why not get the look of antique white lace by using cream-colored seed beads?

In this anklet project, pictured in Figure 6-34, white seed beads are accented with clear crystal beads and larger pale pink glass beads. Create a swag of seed beads as you connect each station of accent beads around the anklet.

Figure 6-34:
Create a lacy effect with the net stitch.

Materials and vital statistics

- **Beads:**
  - 10 grams of size 11 cream-colored Japanese seed beads
  - 24 4mm light pink glass beads
  - 12 4mm round Swarovski clear aurora borealis crystals
- **Findings:**
  - 5mm sterling spring ring clasp
  - 5mm sterling jump ring
  - 2 sterling silver bead tips
- **Notions:** Off-white Silamide thread, 2 size-12 beading needles
- **Tools:** Scissors, jeweler's cement, pin cushion, chain-nose pliers, corsage pin
- **Techniques used:** Weaving the net stitch

Be extra safe when working with techniques such as netting that require the use of two beading needles. A cushioned work surface or pin cushion can help you keep track of the needle you aren't using as you switch back and forth between them through the weaving process.

This finished anklet is about 10 inches long, and most anklets range from 9 to 10 inches in length, so if you want to make the piece longer or shorter, you'll need to consider this when you make the base row of beads.

Beginning with two needles and one bead

1. **Use the scissors to cut about a yard of thread and thread it through the eye of one needle. Repeat this for the second needle.**

2. **For one needle, pull the thread so it's a double thickness. You'll use this for your base row of beads.**

3. **Holding the ends of the threads that are in both needles (which should be three because one needle's thread is doubled), tie two overhand knots, one on top of the other. String 1 seed bead onto both needles and all three threads. Push the seed bead down so it rests against the knots.**

4. **Insert both needles back through the bottom of the seed bead, and push the bead up against the knots.**

5. **Insert the needles through the hole in one of the bead tips, and pull the threads so the knots and seed bead rest inside one of the shells of the bead tip, as illustrated in Figure 6-35.**

Figure 6-35:
The knots and bead rest inside the bead tip.

6. **Use the scissors to trim off the excess threads, and add a small drop of jeweler's cement (a type of glue) inside the bead tip.**

7. **Use the chain-nose pliers to close the bead tip around the seed bead and knot.**

Stringing the base row of beads

1. **Now you're ready to start adding beads to the doubled thread. Pull the needle with the single thread aside so it's not in your way as you work.**

   Make sure to secure the needle safely, such as in a pin cushion.

2. **On the doubled thread, string on beads in the following pattern: 1 pink bead, 1 crystal bead, 1 pink bead, and 8 cream-colored seed beads, as shown in Figure 6-36. Repeat this pattern 10 times, for a total of 11 repetitions, on the doubled thread. Finish the base row with 1 pink bead, 1 crystal bead, and 1 pink bead.**

3. **To attach another bead tip to the other end of the doubled thread, insert the needle through a bead tip (making sure the opening of the bead tip is facing away from the beads) and one seed bead, and then bring the needle back up through the bottom of the seed bead (see Figure 6-37). Push the seed bead down into the opening of the bead tip, and tie two overhand knots with the doubled threads. Then use the same process as described in Steps 6 and 7 in the preceding section to secure the bead tip.**

   You may find it helpful to insert a corsage pin (which is pretty thick) into the knots, and then pull on the doubled thread as you use the pin to push the knots into the bead tip.

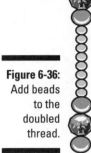

Figure 6-36:
Add beads
to the
doubled
thread.

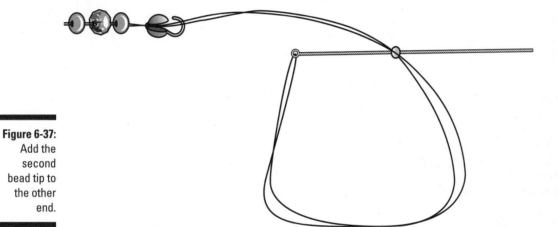

Figure 6-37:
Add the
second
bead tip to
the other
end.

Adding the bead swags

1. Take the needle with the single thread and insert it through the first station of beads, which includes a pink bead, a crystal bead, and another pink bead, as shown in Figure 6-38.

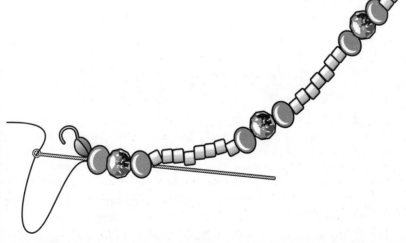

Figure 6-38:
Insert the
single
thread
through
some of the
beads.

2. String 12 cream-colored seed beads onto the thread, and then insert the needle through the next pink bead, crystal bead, and pink bead station, as shown in Figure 6-39.

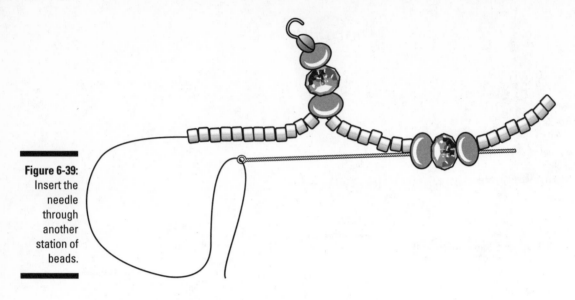

Figure 6-39:
Insert the needle through another station of beads.

3. **Repeat Step 2, moving all the way down the base row of beads, so you have a swag of beads between each bead station.**

Finishing up and adding findings

1. **To secure the working thread, make an overhand knot just past the last crystal bead on the base row, as shown in Figure 6-40.**

   You may find it helpful to use another needle (or corsage pin) inside the knot to help push the knot against the base row thread.

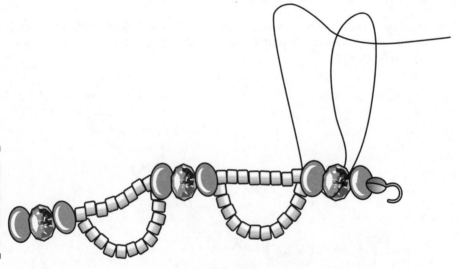

Figure 6-40:
Secure the working thread using an overhand knot.

2. **Thread the needle back through some of the beads on the base row, and tie another overhand knot on the base row as you did in Step 1.**

3. **Snake the needle down through the base row of beads for a few more inches, and use the scissors to trim off the thread.**

4. **Using the chain-nose pliers, close the hook part of one bead tip around a jump ring. Repeat this on the other bead tip to add the spring ring clasp.**

Chapter 7

A New Twist: Wire Jig Wrapping

A wire jig is a really cool piece of equipment used for wire jewelry making. Basically, a *jig* consists of a flat base (often made out of thick clear acrylic, wood, or metal) and lots of pegs that fit into the base. On the average commercial jig these days, you can remove the pegs, which allows you to move them around in an infinite assortment of configurations. After you have your pegs in the right spot, you wrap wire around the pegs to fabricate any number of jewelry elements, such as pendants, earrings, and findings.

Though this book covers a lot of hand-forming wire techniques, some of you may crave a more uniform look to your finished wire jewelry, or maybe you plan to make a lot of the same jewelry pieces over and over again. In these instances, a wire jig is probably the way to go. You can accomplish wire techniques such as unwrapped loops and wrapped loops with this simple piece of equipment.

To help show the assortment of design possibilities, we enlisted the help and creativity of wire jig expert Gary Helwig from www.wigjig.com. Gary has generously provided some wonderful jewelry projects for this chapter that illustrate the wire methods available to jewelry makers who love wire and beads. Gary's jewelry designs show how simple techniques can result in stunning jewelry.

You'll notice a few brand names sprinkled here and there throughout this chapter. That's because we used products from WigJig.com to make these jewelry projects. Although there are other jig manufacturers out in jewelry land, WigJig has been a leader in the jig field for a long time and has some of the best quality products for jig lovers. So that's why we chose WigJig.

Wire Fish and Pearl Earrings

If you've mastered the unwrapped loop technique, then you're ready to make these wire fish and pearl earrings (see Figure 7-1). And if you're still working on the unwrapped loops, don't worry, because these earrings are supereasy but superelegant at the same time. We thought the dangling curved and crossed wires looked like a fish, thus the name. Along with making the earring components, you make the ear wires as well.

By using square or other shapes of wire instead of round wire all the time, you can create subtle design elements in your wire and bead jewelry.

Figure 7-1: Wire, chain, and pearls combine to make an elegant pair of earrings with lots of movement.

Materials and vital statistics

✔ **Beads:** 2 6mm pearl beads

✔ **Findings:**

- 2 gold-filled head pins
- 2 ¼-inch pieces of link chain
- 6 inches of 21-gauge gold-filled dead-soft round wire
- 9 inches of 21-gauge gold-filled dead-soft square wire

✔ **Tools:** Wire cutters, round-nose pliers, nylon jaw pliers, ¾-inch Super Peg, regular jig peg, jig, ruler, jeweler's file, rawhide hammer, anvil or bench block

✔ **Techniques used:** Creating unwrapped loops, using a jig

After you have all of your tools and supplies together, it's time to "get jiggy" (sorry, couldn't resist). We suggest making the ear hooks first, and then making the earring sections.

Crafting the ear hooks

1. **Using the wire cutters, cut 2 3-inch pieces of 21-gauge round wire.**

2. **Use the round-nose pliers to make a small loop on one end of each piece of wire.**

3. **With the nylon pliers, straighten the wire pieces below the loop by pulling each one through the jaws of the pliers as you hold it closed.**

4. **Now it's time to use your jig. Insert a ¾-inch Super Peg into one of the holes on the jig base and a regular size peg next to the larger peg.**

5. **Slip the small loop you made in Step 2 onto the regular size peg, and wrap the rest of the wire around the Super Peg as shown in Figure 7-2.**

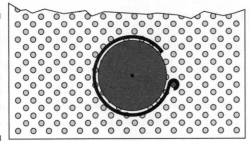

Figure 7-2:
Position two pegs in the jig base, and wrap wire around the larger peg.

6. **Pull the wire off the jig peg. Using a ruler and starting at the small loop, measure 1 inch down on the wire and grasp this point with the tip of your round-nose pliers.**

7. **Continue to hold the wire in this spot with your round-nose pliers, and with your fingers, bend the wire so it's more oval shaped than round.**

   The wire should cross over at the ends as shown in Figure 7-3.

Figure 7-3:
The ends of the wire cross a little at this stage.

8. **Use the wire cutters to cut off the excess wire about ³⁄₁₆ inch before the point where the wire overlaps.**

9. **File the end of the wire you just cut with a jeweler's file.**

10. **Repeat Steps 4 through 9 to complete the second ear hook.**

    You should have a matching set, like the ones shown in Figure 7-4.

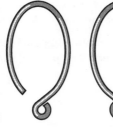

Figure 7-4:
You need two ear hooks, one for each earring.

11. **Finally, to help work harden the ear hooks, set them one at a time on an anvil or bench block, and hammer each one with a rawhide hammer.**

    Set aside the ear hooks while you work on the rest of the earring.

Work harden describes the method for hardening metals. This can be done a few different ways, including heating metal in a kiln or with a torch. Even as you work with the wire, it hardens a little bit, because the more it bends the harder it becomes. One of the easiest methods to work harden wire is to use a rawhide hammer and simply pound on the wire component.

Forming the fish shape

1. Use wire cutters to cut 4 2¼-inch pieces of square wire.

2. With the round-nose pliers, make a small loop on one end of each piece of wire.

3. With the nylon pliers, straighten the wire pieces below the loop by pulling each one through the jaws of the pliers as you hold it closed.

4. Now it's time to use your jig again. With the same peg configuration you used in Step 4 of the "Crafting the ear hooks" section, slip the small loop you made in Step 2 onto the regular size peg, and wrap the rest of the wire around the Super Peg as shown in Figure 7-2. Remove the wire from the jig.

5. Repeat Step 4 for the other pieces of wire.

6. Hold two rounded pieces of wire so one piece is on top of the other piece of wire (superimposing them).

7. To make both pieces the same size, use the wire cutters to trim off any excess wire, and set these aside for later.

   You'll notice the wires look like an elongated letter C.

8. Repeat Steps 6 and 7 for the other two wires.

Keep the matched elongated C wire sections together so you can attach them to the same ear hook in the "Putting all the pieces together" section.

Creating the pearl inset

1. Slide a pearl bead onto a head pin and make a loop at the top using the unwrapped loop technique. Repeat this for the second pearl bead.

2. Take the pieces of chain and slip the unwrapped loop of each pearl head pin segment on to a link on one end of each chain.

Putting all the pieces together

1. Using the round-nose pliers, open up the loop on one of the ear hooks.

2. Slip on one of the elongated C wire sections, one of the chain-and-pearl sections, and the other elongated C wire section, making sure it's pointing in the opposite direction from the first one.

3. Close the loop on the ear hook.

4. Repeat Steps 1 through 3 to finish the other earring.

Variation: Dichro bead fish earrings

Pearls may be classic, but the brightly colored glass beads used in this variation earring project (see Figure 7-5) can really jazz up a design. These bright green beads are made from dichroic glass, which is used in fused glass making as well as lampwork bead making. The techniques used for constructing these dichro bead fish earrings are exactly the same; it's just the beads that are different and there's no chain, so you skip that part of the process. Simply switch the pearl beads for 4mm black crystal beads and 8mm dichroic glass beads, and attach the top of the head pin to the bottom of the ear hooks so the beads are sandwiched in between the fish-style wire components.

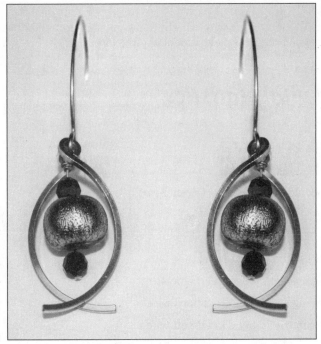

Figure 7-5:
Get a
different
look simply
by using
different
beads.

Changeable Pearl Necklace Strap

A great way to get more versatility from a jewelry piece is to design it so it can be worn in different ways. This changeable pearl necklace strap (see Figure 7-6) incorporates multiple wire-wrapping techniques, such as the "S" scroll and unwrapped loops, to make a necklace that allows you to switch out the pendants. For this particular necklace, you make a pretty pink briolette bead pendant to attach to the strap, but you can create a wardrobe of pendants to mirror your moods.

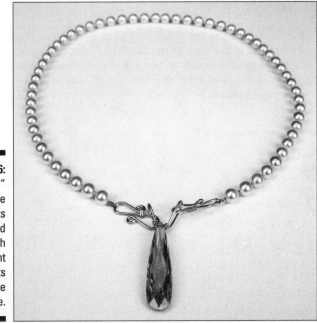

Figure 7-6:
Use the "S"
hook wire
components
on the end
to attach
different
pendants
to the
necklace.

Rawhide hammers are useful for working with wire because you can pound on the wire without scarring it. A metal hammer will make marks in your wire.

Materials and vital statistics

✔ **Beads:**

- 60 6mm pearl beads
- 59 1mm gold-filled beads
- 1 35x10mm pink faceted crystal briolette bead

✔ **Findings:**

- 2 2x2mm gold-filled crimp beads
- 20 inches of 0.019-inch diameter beading wire
- 6 inches of 24-gauge gold-filled dead-soft wire
- 6 inches of 18-gauge gold-filled half-hard wire
- 6 inches of 22-gauge gold-filled dead-soft wire

✔ **Tools:** Wire jig, 2 regular metal jig pegs, 2 ³⁄₁₆-inch Super Pegs, wire cutters, round-nose pliers, chain-nose pliers, crimping pliers

✔ **Techniques used:** Creating unwrapped loops, "S" hooks, and wrapped loops; using crimp beads

Half-hard wire is usually better to use for jewelry components such as clasps because it's not as soft as dead-soft wire and can therefore handle more weight.

This project combines bead stringing and wire work. The wire components are attached to the end of the beaded strap, thus providing a way to change the pendant. You start with the necklace strap and then make a supereasy pendant to attach to it.

Shaping the "S" hook

1. **Place the jig pegs into the jig. Set the Super Pegs into your wire jig so they're positioned diagonally from each other and have about two holes in between each peg. Set the regular jig pegs diagonally in the other direction so your pegs form an X with the regular pegs spaced one hole apart. See Figure 7-7 for an illustration of how your pegs should be placed.**

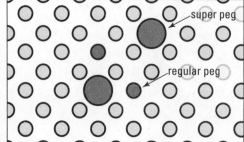

Figure 7-7: The pegs are placed in an X pattern.

2. Use the wire cutters to cut 2 3-inch pieces of 18-gauge wire.

3. With round-nose pliers, make a small unwrapped loop on one end of one of the wire pieces.

4. Place the unwrapped loop onto one of the regular size pegs. Wrap the wire around one of the Super Pegs, then the next Super Peg, and then back down to the second regular peg, as shown in Figure 7-8.

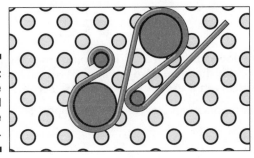

Figure 7-8:
Wrap the wire all around the pegs.

5. Pull the wire segment off the pegs. It should look like Figure 7-9.

Figure 7-9:
This is what the wire looks like when it's first pulled off the jig.

6. Using the round-nose pliers, grasp the middle part of the wire on the unfinished side, and use your fingers to wrap the wire around the nose of the pliers so you have a piece that looks like Figure 7-10.

Figure 7-10:
Round-nose pliers help you finish the ends.

7. With the wire cutters, trim off the excess wire from the unwrapped loop you just made so you have an "S" scroll shape, as shown in Figure 7-11.

Figure 7-11:
Now you
have an "S"
scroll wire
shape.

8. **Insert the 24-gauge wire into one loop in the wire "S" hook, and wrap the wire around the loop twice and the center diagonal wire segment. With wire cutters, trim off the excess wire, which you'll use for the second "S" scroll.**

   This closes one side of the wire component and leaves the other open. See Figure 7-12.

Figure 7-12:
Close up the
wire com-
ponent on
one side.

9. **Repeat Steps 3 through 8 to make a second "S" hook.**

Stringing the strap

1. **Insert the beading wire through and around the closed part of one of the wire "S" hooks, and secure the beading wire with a crimp bead.**

   See Chapter 2 if you need help working with crimp beads.

2. **String the beads, starting with a pearl bead and alternating with a gold-filled bead, until you've used all the beads and ended with a pearl bead.**

3. **Complete the strap by repeating Step 1 to secure the other "S" hook on the end of the strap.**

Fashioning the pendant and finishing the design

1. **Wrap the 22-gauge wire around one of the Super Pegs, and then pull it off.**

2. **Continue to wrap the wire around itself to create a wrapped loop.**

3. **Insert the wire through the hole in the pink briolette bead, and repeat Steps 1 and 2 to finish the other side of the pendant. See Figure 7-13.**

Figure 7-13:
Use a bead
and wire to
make a
simple
pendant.

4. To attach the pendant to the strap, simply slip the open sides of the "S" hooks into the wrapped loops of the pendant, as shown in Figure 7-14.

Figure 7-14:
Connect the
pendant to
the "S"
hooks.

Hematite Link-Up Bracelet

Chain is a wonderful medium to use with beads, and with some simple wire-wrapping techniques, such as the wrapped loop and "S" hook methods, you can make your own chain links out of wire. Then you can use more wire to connect the links with your choice of beads. For this particular project (pictured in Figure 7-15), you combine hematite beads with gold-filled wire for a two-tone effect: the silver color of the beads with the gold color of the wire. Hematite is a favorite stone of many jewelry lovers, and because it's such a neutral color, it goes with everything.

Figure 7-15:
Make your
own chain
links from
wire
using this
interesting
technique.

When you make jewelry gifts, if you don't know someone's color preference, choose neutral colors such as silver, gold, white, and black.

Materials and vital statistics

✔ **Beads:** 7 6mm hematite beads

✔ **Findings:**

- Gold-filled lobster claw clasp
- 12 inches of 20-gauge gold-filled dead-soft wire
- 18 inches of 22-gauge gold-filled dead-soft wire

✔ **Tools:** Wire jig, 3 metal pegs, wire cutters, round-nose pliers, 2 pairs of bent-nose pliers (or you can substitute chain-nose pliers)

✔ **Techniques used:** Creating wrapped loops and figure eights

When you're trying out a particular wire jig pattern for the first time, it's a good idea to use inexpensive wire to practice with first. Copper wire is an inexpensive alternative to silver and gold-filled wire, and it allows you to make mistakes as you practice the technique.

After you've collected all of your tools and materials, you're ready to start wrapping. Hematite is an iron ore gemstone that is dark silver in color, so it contrasts really well with gold-filled wire, giving your jewelry pieces a rich look.

Winding your way to figure-eight links

1. **Insert the pegs into the jig in the pattern shown in Figure 7-16. Two pegs are positioned right next to each other, and a third peg is positioned two pegs away at a diagonal.**

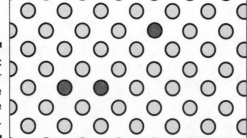

Figure 7-16:
Add your
pegs to the
jig before
starting.

2. **With the wire cutters, cut a 2-inch piece of 20-gauge wire.**

3. **Use the round-nose pliers to make a partial loop on one end of the wire.**

4. **Place the partial loop on the left peg, pull the wire toward the peg in the upper diagonal position, wrap the wire 180 degrees around this peg, bring the wire back down to the third peg, and again wrap it 180 degrees. Your wire should look like a figure eight, as shown in Figure 7-17.**

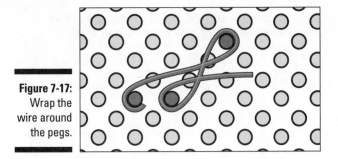

Figure 7-17:
Wrap the
wire around
the pegs.

5. Pull the wire off the pegs and grasp one loop of the figure eight with a pair of bent-nose pliers, as illustrated in Figure 7-18.

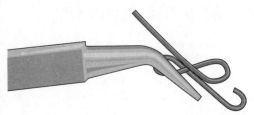

Figure 7-18:
Bent-nose
pliers work
well for
holding onto
wire as you
work.

6. As you continue to hold the wire piece, use another pair of pliers (either bent-nose or chain-nose) to grasp the wire section that has the partial loop, and wrap this around the middle of the figure-eight section, as shown in Figure 7-19.

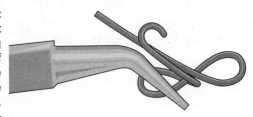

Figure 7-19:
Start
wrapping
one end of
the wire
around the
figure eight.

7. Repeat Step 6, but this time, wrap the other end of the wire, as shown in Figure 7-20.

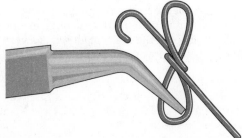

Figure 7-20:
Wrap the
other wire
section.

8. Use the wire cutters to trim off the excess wire, and flatten the wire wrap ends using the chain-nose or bent-nose pliers so you have a completed link section, as shown in Figure 7-21.

Figure 7-21:
You've made
your first
link.

9. Repeat Steps 2 through 8 five more times so you have a total of six links.

Adding beads and building the bracelet

1. Using the wrapped-loop technique, start a wrapped loop with 22-gauge wire, but before wrapping it closed, slip one link onto the loop.

   It's always easier to work with a longer piece of wire, rather than cut your wire into small pieces to make each component. This also limits waste. For example, when making a component like a figure-eight section, start with 12 inches of wire, and continue to use the wire for additional components, trimming off the wire after completing one component and before starting another. Eventually, you'll end up with a really tiny piece of wire that you can't work with anymore, but then you just put that in your wire scrap bag (never throw them out because you can sell them back to some vendors as scrap metal). Your fingers will thank you for working with these longer pieces of wire, too!

2. String one hematite bead onto the wire, and again, use the wrapped-loop technique to connect another link. Cut the wire after the pieces are joined.

3. Repeat Steps 1 and 2 until you have seven hematite wire wrapped loops connected to six wire links, but don't close the last wrapped loop just yet.

4. Slip a lobster claw clasp onto the last wrapped loop.

   You use the open loop of the first figure-eight link to close the clasp and join the bracelet ends.

5. Wrap the loop closed, and use the wire cutters to trim off any excess wire.

Variation: Siam crystal link bracelet

If you want to add a little more pop and sizzle to this wire link and wrapping bracelet technique, switch out the beads from neutral hematite to eye-popping Siam red crystals, as shown in Figure 7-22. Use the same amount of gold-filled wire, but use 8mm round faceted Swarovski Siam red crystals in between the links. Siam red is a very deep ruby color, and it's very popular among beaders who like lots of color in their jewelry designs.

Figure 7-22:
Substitute
sparkling
red crystal
beads
for the
hematite.

Double-Strand Onyx and Cloisonné Bracelet

Multiple-strand jewelry pieces, such as bracelets and necklaces, are more popular than ever, but constructing them can be a little challenging if you want the strands to line up next to each other. Though multiple-strand pieces require a little rethinking when it comes to designing them, a wire jig offers one option for tackling this stringing dilemma. By using the unwrapped-loop technique in different configurations, you can create wire components that secure the strands together, like those in this double-strand onyx and cloisonné bracelet project (see Figure 7-23).

Figure 7-23:
Wire
components
help keep
the bead
strands next
to one
another.

To jazz up your gemstone bead designs, look for accent beads such as cloisonné, metal, crystal, wood, and glass. Mix them in smaller amounts with primarily gemstone beads to vary the design and color of your finished jewelry piece.

Materials and vital statistics

🗸 **Beads:**

- 48 6mm onyx beads

- 8 6mm white-and-red cloisonné beads

🗸 **Findings:**

- 4 2x2mm crimp beads

- 1 6mm gold-filled spring ring clasp

- 2 10-inch pieces of 0.019-inch diameter beading wire

- 18 inches of 18-gauge gold-filled half-hard wire

🗸 **Tools:** Wire jig, 3 regular size pegs, wire cutters, round-nose pliers, chain-nose pliers, crimping pliers

🗸 **Techniques used:** Creating unwrapped loops, using crimp beads

Crimping pliers provide a way to first curl and then flatten your crimp beads onto the beading wire. This gives your piece a more professional finish and prevents the crimp beads from scratching you when you wear the bracelet.

As you craft this piece, make the wire components first, and then string up your bead strands. The two wire components each have different purposes in this bracelet. One is used to keep the two strands of beads lined up next to each other. The second wire component connects the two strands to the clasp.

Beginning with one wire component

1. **Insert three pegs into the jig in a triangle pattern, with one hole separating two of the pegs, as shown in Figure 7-24.**

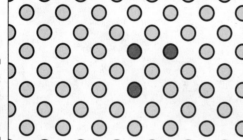

Figure 7-24: Insert pegs into the jig to start.

2. **Using the wire cutters, cut a piece of 18-gauge wire that's 2¼ inches long.**

3. **With the round-nose pliers, make an unwrapped loop on one end of the wire.**

4. **Slip the loop onto the bottom peg. Wrap the wire 180 degrees around the top left peg, and then wrap it 180 degrees around the top right peg, as illustrated in Figure 7-25.**

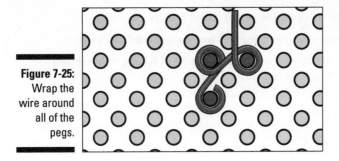

Figure 7-25:
Wrap the wire around all of the pegs.

5. **Pull off the wire piece from the jig.**

   You should have a piece that looks like the one in Figure 7-26.

Figure 7-26:
This is what your wire piece should look like.

6. **Use the wire cutters to trim off the excess wire so you get a component that looks like the one in Figure 7-27. Set this aside for later use.**

Figure 7-27:
Trim off excess wire.

Giving wire components the eye

1. **These wire jig components have an unwrapped loop, or *eye loop*, at either end. Start by pulling out the top left peg on your jig so two pegs are diagonal to one another, with one hole in between them, as shown in Figure 7-28.**

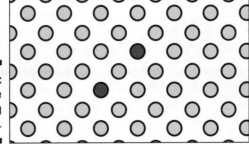

Figure 7-28:
Rearrange your jig pegs.

2. With the wire cutters, cut a piece of 18-gauge wire that's 1⅜ inches long.

3. With the round-nose pliers, make an unwrapped loop on one end of the wire.

4. Slip the loop onto the bottom peg, and then wrap the wire 180 degrees around the top right peg, as illustrated in Figure 7-29.

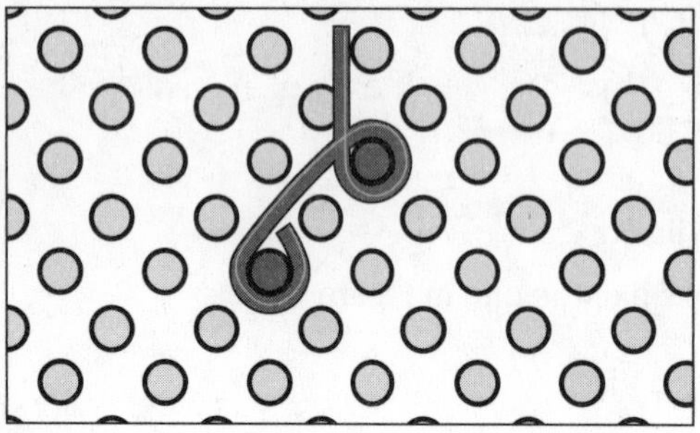

Figure 7-29:
Wrap the wire 180 degrees around a peg.

5. Pull off the wire piece from the jig, and use the wire cutters to trim off the excess wire, so you get a component that looks like the one in Figure 7-30.

Figure 7-30:
Make your second wire component.

6. Insert the tip of your round-nose pliers in one of the loops, and bend the loop back toward the center of the wire a little without opening up the loop. Repeat this for the other side.

This step makes the wire between both eye loops straight so it looks like the component in Figure 7-31.

Figure 7-31:
Bend the loops to move the crossbar to the center of the component.

7. Repeat Steps 2 through 6 four more times so you have a total of five double eye loop wire components. Set these aside for later.

Shifting to stringing, and finally finishing

1. **Using the crimping pliers, attach a crimp bead to one end of each piece of beading wire and create a loop in the wires.**

    Flip back to Chapter 2 if you need a refresher on using crimp beads.

2. **Take one of the eye loop wire components and use the chain-nose pliers to open up both loops. Connect the beading wire loop of one strand to one loop of the wire component, and then do the same with the other strand to the other loop so everything is connected, as shown in Figure 7-32.**

Figure 7-32:
Connect the beading wire strands to an eye loop wire component.

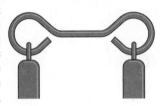

3. **On each strand of beading wire, string 3 onyx beads, 1 cloisonné bead, and 3 more onyx beads.**

4. **Insert the beading wire strands through the eye loops on one eye loop wire component.**

5. **Continue stringing beads and findings in the same order as you did in Steps 3 and 4.**

    You should use all of your beads, as well as four eye loop wire components. These components keep the bead strands together, and the pattern should look like the one shown in Figure 7-33.

Figure 7-33:
Thread on your gemstone and cloisonné beads.

6. **Finish off the ends of both pieces of beading wire with the remaining crimp beads by using the crimping pliers again.**

7. **After you have your crimp beads in place, repeat Step 2 with the final eye loop wire component.**

8. **Take the first wire component you made in the "Beginning with one wire component" section, and using the chain-nose pliers, twist the eye loops about 90 degrees so they face to the side of the component.**

9. Attach the loops on the eye loop wire component to the loops you adjusted in the wire component in Step 8. Then attach the spring ring clasp to the ending wire component so the end of your bracelet looks like Figure 7-34.

Figure 7-34:
Finish the
end with
wire
components
and a clasp.

Variation: Pearl and purple crystal double-strand bracelet

To give your double-strand bracelet a more classic look, switch the black onyx beads with 6mm white pearl beads and the cloisonné beads with 8mm faceted Swarovski tanzanite-colored crystal beads. Add a clasp of your choice, or like Gary Helwig did for the bracelet pictured in Figure 7-35, you can make the hook clasp yourself using wire and a jig. Either way, you have a classic bracelet that you'll find yourself wearing again and again.

Figure 7-35:
This
bracelet
combines
crystals and
pearls.

Chapter 8

It's a Wrap: Wire Wrapping

● ●

In This Chapter

▶ Creating quick and simple earrings with eye loops and wrapped loops

▶ Wrapping your way to beautiful bead components

▶ Fabricating your own pendants with wire

● ●

*P*ick up your pliers and start wrapping! Imagine taking a single (mostly) straight piece of wire and creating delicate loops, clean connections, and wonderful wire effects. In this chapter, you can do that and more. We start with simple but beautiful projects to get your creativity flowing. Even though these projects come together simply and quickly, they're a great foundation to help you build your jewelry-making skills.

The first two projects use just a few beads, a simple pattern, and the most basic of all wire-wrapping techniques, the eye loop and the wrapped loop. Other projects in this chapter build on those basics, and include additional wire-wrapping techniques that help you make dangles of varying lengths to expand your earring wardrobe. Then we show you how to create visual interest by adding a focal point (like a pendant) to your projects with a few easy variations. We also throw in a few longer projects to test your endurance, including making your own necklace completely out of wire, chain, and beads.

No matter which projects you pursue in this chapter, you can quickly add excitement to your accessory wardrobe. With a few simple supplies and tools, you'll be creating beautiful jewelry in no time. (And if you need a refresher on how to make wrapped loops or eye loops, flip back to Chapter 2.)

Eye Loop and Bead Earrings

The *eye loop* technique is one of the easiest wire methods to master, which is great because it has all kinds of applications when you're making jewelry. Dangles, connections, earrings — you name it, and the eye loop is a perfect fit. However, no one else needs to know how easy it is to make something like these yummy Venetian glass and gold-filled bead earrings (see Figure 8-1). They're superquick, and you can make a huge variety of designs simply by using different types of beads. The only real tricky part to the eye loop method is getting the loops sized consistently, which pretty much just takes practice, so you've got a great excuse to make lots of earrings.

Earrings are a perfect project when you have the urge to create but don't have a lot of time. They also require only a small number of supplies.

Figure 8-1:
You can make countless variations on these earrings just by changing the bead sizes and colors.

Materials and vital statistics

✔ **Beads:**

• 4 4mm gold-filled corrugated beads

• 2 15mm square Venetian glass beads

✔ **Findings:**

• 2 gold-filled head pins

• 2 gold-filled ear hooks

✔ **Tools:** Chain-nose pliers, wire cutters, round-nose pliers

✔ **Techniques used:** Creating an eye loop

This is a great project to get you working with basic jewelry components. With just a few beautiful beads and basic tools, you can whip up these earrings in no time.

Directions

1. String your beads by slipping one gold-filled bead onto a head pin, followed by a Venetian glass bead and another gold-filled bead.

2. Make an eye loop at the top of the head pin by using the chain-nose pliers to bend the head pin into a 90-degree angle. Then use the wire cutters to trim off all but about ½ inch of the head pin. Finally, using your round-nose pliers, form an eye loop above the last bead on the head pin.

3. Open the loop a little with the chain-nose pliers, and slip an ear hook onto the loop.

4. Close the loop to secure the ear hook.

   Make sure you close it tightly so you don't lose your beads!

5. Repeat Steps 1 through 4 to make a second earring so you have a matching pair.

Variation: Bali bead caps & bead earrings

Jazz up a simple round bead with a *bead cap*. It's sort of like a little hat that hugs the bead. Slip on one bead cap with the cup facing up, one 8mm round crystal bead, and another bead cap with the cup facing down. Thus, your bead is nestled between the two caps, just like the one in Figure 8-2.

Figure 8-2:
Bead caps give a simple bead a touch of elegance.

Variation: Crystal & carnelian earrings

Add a little glitter to this simple earring project by alternating Czech clear fire-polished 4mm crystal beads with deep rich red 6mm Carnelian beads. By keeping the same findings, but using different beads, you can create a totally different look with the same technique.

Fancy Head Pin Earrings

You don't always have to use the standard variety of head pin — a stick with a flat head on one end. The availability and variety of fancy shmancy head pins these days is outstanding. Using them can add some major design elements to your jewelry. These Swarovski faux pink pearl beads (see Figure 8-3) are teamed up with head pins that have a flower element on the end. To keep with the nature theme, we use sterling leverback ear hooks with a leaf design.

Figure 8-3:
Fancy head pins let you create spectacular designs with a single bead.

Don't shy away from faux pearls, especially if they're made by Swarovski. Although natural pearls are great, manufactured ones have perfectly drilled holes, uniform shapes, and come in great colors as well.

Materials and vital statistics

- **Beads:** 2 6mm Swarovski faux pink pearls
- **Findings:**
    - 2 sterling flower head pins
    - 2 sterling leaf leverback ear wires
- **Tools:** Round-nose pliers, chain-nose pliers, wire cutters
- **Techniques used:** Creating a wrapped loop

For extra bead security, consider using the wrapped loop technique when making earrings. Then, for an added touch, combine the wrapped loop technique with ultrafancy head pins, as this project demonstrates.

Directions

1. **Slide one pearl bead onto one head pin. Using your round-nose pliers, begin the wrapped loop technique by wrapping the wire around the nose of the pliers, but don't wrap the wire around itself. Thus the wrap isn't closed yet.**

2. **Slip the loop on the leverback ear wire onto the head pin.**

3. **Close the wrapped loop, squeezing gently with your chain-nose pliers.**

4. **Trim off any excess head pin using the wire cutters.**

5. **Repeat Steps 1 through 4 for the second earring.**

Variation: Fancy head pin necklace

Fancy head pins aren't just for earrings. Make a matching necklace using eye loops, flower head pins, and Swarovski pearls, and dangle them from a scalloped sterling silver chain. Finish it off with a delicate filigree clasp.

Filigree Hoop Earrings

No matter what type of filigree components you can find, with a little wire and some wrapping, you can turn unique metal elements into fashionable jewelry. You make these filigree hoop earrings (see Figure 8-4) by simply wrapping some wire around the diameter of the hoop sections, and then add smoky quartz crystals and sterling silver ear hooks to the top. The icy color of the silver-plated filigree and silver wire and ear hooks looks great next to the dark crystal accenting the top of the earrings.

To keep your silver looking shiny and new, keep it in an airtight container, like a self-sealing plastic bag. You can also purchase antitarnish strips from most jewelry supply vendors. Cut the strips into small pieces, and then slip one into the plastic bag or container with your jewelry for additional tarnish protection.

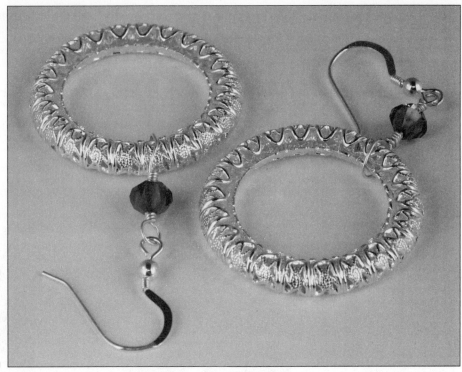

Figure 8-4:
Make your own holiday hoops in minutes.

Materials and vital statistics

- **Beads:** 2 6mm bicone-shaped smoky quartz crystals
- **Findings:**
  - 2 sterling ear hooks
  - 2 silver-plated filigree hoops
  - 2 6-inch pieces of 22-gauge sterling wire
- **Tools:** Round-nose pliers, wire cutters, chain-nose pliers
- **Techniques used:** Creating a wrapped loop

A round filigree metal component is perfect to transform into a hoop earring. You just need a little wire-wrapping know-how.

Directions

1. Tightly wrap a piece of 22-gauge wire around the filigree component, and secure it with the wrapped loop method.
2. Trim off the excess wire of the wrapped loop with your wire cutters as needed, leaving the rest of the unwrapped part of the wire in place.
3. On the unwrapped section of wire, slip on one crystal bead.
4. Begin another wrapped loop on the other side of the crystal.
5. Before closing the loop, add an ear hook.

6. Complete the wrapped loop and trim off any excess wire with the wire cutters.

7. Repeat Steps 1 through 6 for a second earring.

Variation: Gold-filigree wreath earrings

These gold-filigree wreath earrings (see Figure 8-5) are beyond simple. All you have to do is attach an ear hook to any of the open circles around these filigree brass stampings that look very much like woven wreaths of metal.

Figure 8-5: Brass-stamped wreath-style elements turn into instant earrings.

If the loops on the end of your ear hooks aren't large enough to fit around the open circles in the wreath component, just open the loop ends slightly with pliers, and then use the round-nose pliers to make the loop larger. Making a larger loop will shorten the hooks ever so slightly, but will allow the hooks to fit onto the brass-stamped piece.

Double-Dangle Gemstone & Pearl Earrings

When you know and use different wire-wrapping techniques, you can connect various jewelry elements and give movement to a finished jewelry design. Such is the case with these lapis lazuli and pearl double-dangle earrings (see Figure 8-6), which use the wrapped loop technique in addition to the eye loop. The lapis is A-grade, which in gemstone terminology pretty much means practically perfect, and so the dark, rich blue color of the gemstone beads are a perfect contrast to the white pearl beads sandwiched in between them.

When trying to determine if a lapis bead is real or faux, look for silvery-gray veins running throughout. Real lapis lazuli has iron pyrite, also known as fool's gold, in it.

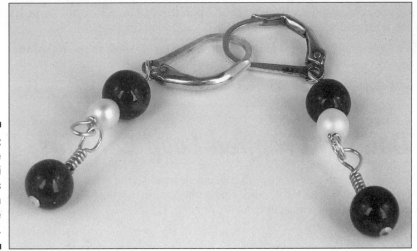

Figure 8-6:
Dark blue
lapis lazuli
contrasts
well with
white
pearls.

Materials and vital statistics

✔ **Beads:**

- 4 6mm lapis lazuli beads
- 2 4mm pearls

✔ **Findings:**

- 2 leverback ear wires
- 2 2-inch sterling head pins
- 2 2-inch pieces of 22-gauge sterling wire

✔ **Tools:** Round-nose pliers, wire cutters, chain-nose pliers

✔ **Techniques used:** Creating a wrapped loop, creating an eye loop

Although wrapped loop sections can be more secure, the extra wrapping adds length to a finished piece of jewelry. Keep this point in mind when you decide which technique to use. Extra length can mean bead sections on the wire don't have as much movement and swag as you may like. If you aren't sure which to use, consider using less expensive practice wire (like copper or craft wire) to make a prototype or just a few beaded sections of the design you envision. Then compare the two and see which seems to have the look you want.

Directions

1. **Slide one lapis lazuli bead onto one head pin, and make a wrapped loop at the top with your round-nose pliers.**

   Set this piece aside for later.

2. **Using your round-nose pliers, make an eye loop on one end of one of the wire pieces, slip on one pearl bead and one lapis lazuli bead, and make another eye loop on the other end of the wire.**

3. Using your round-nose pliers, slightly open the eye loop next to the pearl, slip on the wrapped section made in Step 1, and close the loop.

4. Add an ear hook to the loop next to the lapis lazuli bead at the top of the dangle.

5. Repeat Steps 1 through 4 for the second earring.

Teardrop Double-Wrapped Loop Earrings

Using the wrapped loop technique with a different bead shape gives a new twist on a favorite accessory. With the right beads and a few simple twists of your pliers, you can create beautiful dangle earrings, like those shown in Figure 8-7.

Figure 8-7: Wrapped loops take on a new dimension as they echo the triangular shape of the top of a teardrop bead.

Materials and vital statistics

✔ **Beads:**

- 2 10x22mm faceted glass side-drilled teardrops

- 2 8mm onyx faceted round beads

✔ **Findings:**

- 2 sterling ear hooks

- 2 3½-inch pieces of 22-gauge half-hard silver wire

✔ **Tools:** Round-nose pliers, wire cutters, chain-nose pliers

✔ **Techniques used:** Creating wrapped loops

Don't wrap the loop at the top of the teardrop bead too tightly, or you'll limit the movement of the earring. These focal beads are beautifully faceted, so you want them to swing as you move. They'll catch the light and dazzle passersby.

Directions

1. **Insert one piece of wire through one teardrop. Pull 1 inch of the wire through the hole. Cross the short end of the wire over the long end to make an "X," as shown in Figure 8-8.**

Figure 8-8: Cross the short end of the wire over the long end to create the triangle wrapped loop.

2. **Create a wrapped loop at the top of the teardrop by wrapping the shorter end of the wire around the longer end.**

   Remember to leave a little bit of room between the wire loop and the bead so the bead can swing as you walk or move your head.

3. **Slide a round bead onto the open end of wire. Begin a wrapped loop, but before closing the loop, slip on one ear hook. Complete the wrapped loop.**

4. **Repeat Steps 1 through 3 to complete a second earring.**

Chandelier Earrings

You get lots of wire-looping practice when you make your own chandelier earrings. This earring style became popular a while ago and has since become a classic. Use the wrapped loop method to attach lots of sparkling crystals to jewelry components made especially for chandelier earring designs. Then add an ear hook and, voilá, you're done. These chandelier earrings (see Figure 8-9) are made with royal blue teardrop-shaped crystals, brass chandelier components, and gold-filled ear hooks. Each earring has double dangle crystals, so they've got lots of sparkle, but you can still wear them comfortably all day long.

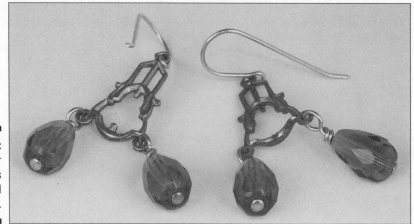

Figure 8-9:
Chandelier
earrings
make a bold
statement.

Materials and vital statistics

- ✔ **Beads:** 4 10x8mm cobalt blue teardrop crystals
- ✔ **Findings:**
  - 2 gold-filled ear hooks
  - 2 2-inch gold-colored head pins
  - 2 brass chandelier components
- ✔ **Tools:** Round-nose pliers, chain-nose pliers, wire cutters
- ✔ **Techniques used:** Creating a wrapped loop

The nose of the round-nose pliers are shaped like a round cone, so the tips have a smaller diameter than the base. Keep your wire loops, both wrapped or eye, evenly sized by consistently using the same spot on the round-nose pliers to make the loops. If you wrap the wire around the middle part of the nose the first time, use this same area on the next loop as well.

Any wire technique takes a good deal of practice to perfect. So, even if you know the basics of the wrapped loop technique but are still working on getting it exactly right, remember that practice makes perfect, or pretty darn close to it!

Directions

1. **Slip one teardrop bead onto a head pin so the wider end of the teardrop rests against the head of the pin.**

2. **With the round-nose pliers, make a wrapped loop at the top of the head pin, but before wrapping the loop closed, slip one side of a chandelier component onto the loop.**

3. **Wrap the loop closed with your chain-nose pliers, and trim off any excess head pin using your wire cutters.**

4. **Repeat Steps 1 through 3 for the second dangle on the earring, and then attach an ear hook to the top of the component.**

5. **Repeat Steps 1 through 4 for the second earring.**

Variation: Grande chandelier earrings

These grande chandelier earrings (see Figure 8-10) aren't for the faint-hearted or the wallflowers out there! These double hoop chandelier components require 24 4mm crystals per earring, plus one teardrop crystal to dangle from the center. Because the inside hoop of the earring is such a tight squeeze, use the eye loop technique to attach the crystal dangles.

Figure 8-10: Size does matter when it comes to dramatic earrings.

You can orient these chandelier earrings to face forward or to face to the side, whichever way is more comfortable for you to wear. To change the orientation of the earrings, play around with how you connect the ear hooks to the top of the earring component until you have the look you want.

Wrapped Loop Stitch Marker

The process for creating *stitch markers* (tools used by knitters to keep track of a pattern in a working knitting piece, shown in Figure 8-11) is similar to making earrings, but instead of topping them off with an ear wire, you add a round link. We recommend you use solid links rather than a split link or large jump ring so your finished project doesn't snag the yarn in the knitting project.

Figure 8-11: Make any in-process knitting project more beautiful with these simple stitch markers.

Materials and vital statistics

- ✔ **Beads:**
  - • 5 12mm flat square amber glass beads
  - • 10 3mm silver round beads
- ✔ **Findings:**
  - • 5 1½-inch silver head pins
  - • 5 16mm round silver links
- ✔ **Tools:** Round-nose pliers, wire cutters, chain-nose pliers
- ✔ **Techniques used:** Creating a wrapped loop

Because these beauties are sure to be used often by your favorite knitter, make sure to use your chain-nose pliers to press the sharp end of the wire flat to the piece. You don't want to leave any pokey parts to snag her in-progress knitted masterpiece.

Directions

1. **String one silver bead onto one head pin. Follow it with one amber bead and another silver bead.**

2. **Begin your wrapped loop.**

3. **Slip on a silver link before closing the loop.**

4. **Complete the wrapped loop.**

   Use your chain-nose pliers to press the sharp end of the wire as close to the piece as possible.

5. **Repeat Steps 1 through 4 to make four more stitch markers to complete the set.**

Wire-Wrapped Dangle Ring

Use many, many individual dangles to create this popular and spectacular special-occasion ring, shown in Figure 8-12. The adjustable ring blanks come with eight loops, but don't let that limit you. In our take on this design, we attach four dangles to each loop to completely fill your finger with sparkle. We chose beads from the same mix we used to make the easy wire-wrapped cuff bracelet later in this chapter (see Figure 8-17) because we wanted them to coordinate.

Materials and vital statistics

- ✔ **Beads:** 10 grams of mixed black, silver, and gray beads
- ✔ **Findings:**
  - • Adjustable eight-loop ring finding
  - • 32 1½-inch head pins
- ✔ **Tools:** Round-nose pliers, wire cutters, chain-nose pliers
- ✔ **Techniques used:** Creating wrapped loops

Your round-nose pliers get a workout when you create this unusual ring.

Figure 8-12:
Make the most of a ring finding by decking each loop out with tons o' dangles.

Directions

1. **Slide one or two beads on a head pin.**

If the bead is large, use one; if the beads are small, string on two.

2. **Begin a wrapped loop.**

3. **Before completing the wrap, slide the wire onto one loop of the ring finding.**

4. **Complete the wrapped loop.**

5. **Repeat Steps 1 through 4 with the remaining beads and head pins until all of the loops on the ring are filled to your liking.**

Variation: Sparkly crystal ring

Get a blindingly stunning effect by using 32 4mm bicone Swarovski AB crystals in place of the assorted beads. Place one crystal on each head pin. Attach four crystal head pin components to each loop, and you're ready for any formal occasion.

More-Is-Better Necklace

Get your creative juices flowing big time with this eclectic necklace (see Figure 8-13) as you use the wire-wrapping technique to connect your choice of sparkling beads and sections of chain. This design is called "more is better" because it's a great way to use all those extra beads you've been stashing away for just the right project. Including the clasp, the finished length of this necklace is about 22 inches, but of course, feel free to make it any length you want. This project is really more of a method than an exact science of jewelry design. So don't hold back. Remember — more, more, more!

Figure 8-13:
The more-is-better necklace is a great choice to show off several focal beads.

If you have some superfancy — as in expensive — beads that you've been hoarding because they're too good to use in just any old piece of jewelry, add a few here and there in this necklace. That way, you can finally show them off, but you can still keep a few for the bead-hoarder side of you.

Materials and vital statistics

✔ **Beads:** Variety of glass, crystal, and metal beads, all shapes and sizes

✔ **Findings:**

- Hook-and-eye clasp
- 16 inches of gold-colored thin link chain
- 24 inches of 22-gauge gold-filled wire

✔ **Tools:** Round-nose pliers, wire cutters, chain-nose pliers

✔ **Techniques used:** Creating a wrapped loop

Put away your ruler and don't worry about keeping your design symmetrical as you craft this necklace. The more eclectic the better. Because you aren't measuring every little thing as you construct this necklace, don't worry about measuring wire pieces either, even though we recommend that you have about 2 feet of gold-filled wire available for this project. Normally, it's best (as in more comfortable) to work with 8 to 6 inches of wire as you connect the bead sections to the chain sections.

Directions

1. Cut a piece of chain anywhere from 1 to 2 inches long, and attach wire to one end of it using the wrapped loop technique.

2. Take your choice of bead or beads and slide them onto the wire.

3. Start your next wrapped loop on the opposite side of the beads you just added, but before closing the loop, attach another 1- to 2-inch long piece of chain to the loop. Use the wire cutters to trim the excess wire.

4. Using the wrapped loop technique, attach another piece of wire to the chain you added in Step 3.

5. Repeat Steps 2 through 4 until the necklace is 21 to 22 inches long.

   Make sure to use a mixture of beads.

6. Use the wrapped loop technique to secure the hook part of the clasp to one end of the necklace and the eye part to the other end to finish your masterpiece.

Variation: More-is-better bracelet

Using the exact same method as the more-is-better necklace, make a bracelet that's about 7 to 7¼ inches long. Make sure to end each end of the bracelet with wrapped loop sections, and simply attach a spring ring clasp before closing one of the loops. The other loop can be used to connect to the clasp, working as a jump ring would.

Variation: More-is-better earrings

Of course, with the more-is-better earrings, you may want the beads to match instead of using random ones like you do when making the necklace and bracelet. But no worries, because this is very easy to do. Just select two of your favorite larger beads, like Venetian glass beads lined with gold foil. Add them to gold-colored head pins, add a textured metal disk bead, and attach all of that to about 1½ inches of gold-colored chain. Finish off the dangles with ear hooks, and you're ready to go!

Moss Agate Wrapped Loop Dangle Pendant

You can use wrapped loops to create hefty components and dainty features as well. In this pendant, shown in Figure 8-14, a single piece of wire is bent and wrapped to create a sturdy bail and a delicate spiral.

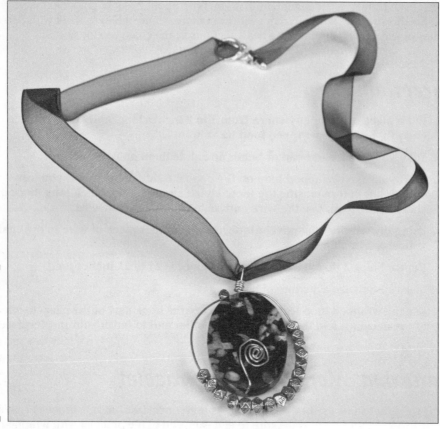

Figure 8-14:
Moss agate
and silver
create a
dynamic
contrast in
this one-of-
a-kind
pendant.

Materials and vital statistics

✔ **Beads:**

- 1 35x25mm flat oval moss agate pendant, top drilled
- 17 3mm silver spacer beads

✔ **Findings:** 12 inches of 22-gauge half-hard sterling silver wire

✔ **Tools:** Round-nose pliers, wire cutters, chain-nose pliers

✔ **Techniques used:** Creating wrapped loops, creating spirals

It may look tricky, but with a little time and patience, you can make your own wire wrapped pendant. Then add it to a simple link chain, or get extra creative and include it as a focal element in a beaded necklace design. The possibilities are endless.

Directions

1. **Slide the wire through the pendant. Pull approximately 2 inches of wire through the bottom hole.**

2. **Using your round-nose pliers, begin a spiral on the short end of the wire.**

Continue creating the spiral until it's roughly 10mm across.

If you need help making spirals with wire, check out *Jewelry Making & Beading For Dummies* (Wiley).

3. Bend the spiral up, and press it onto the flat surface of the pendant, using Figure 8-14 as your guide for placement.

4. Pull the long end of the wire taut, snugging the spiral against the pendant using your chain-nose pliers.

In this case, we recommend squeezing the pendant with the chain-nose pliers and intentionally roughing up the spiral a bit as you snug it against the pendant to give it the textured look you see in Figure 8-14.

5. Create a large wrapped loop with the open end of the wire by using the base of your round-nose pliers.

Make sure to situate the loop at the top of your pendant, where you want the pendant to hang. Don't trim the excess wire. This step creates your *bail*, the loop you pass the stringing material through when you wear a pendant.

When you make your bail, create the largest loop your pliers will allow, so you have flexibility when selecting the perfect stringing material for this unique pendant. Flip over to Chapter 3 to see how we strung this one up on gorgeous organza ribbon.

6. String the spacer beads onto the excess wire.

7. Gently curve the wire that's holding the beads along the natural shape of the pendant until you reach the wrapped loop you created in Step 5.

8. Wrap the excess wire around the loop, snugging it down with your chain-nose pliers as necessary.

Mod Wrapped Loop & Bead Bracelet

Wrapping and connecting are the two action words for this bracelet, featured in Figure 8-15. It's a great choice for honing your wrapping skills because the tight spaces between the components require quite a bit of precision. Wrapped loops are a great choice to connect components when you want to ensure they won't separate on you later, like eye loops might.

Figure 8-15: This mod-inspired Mod bracelet will become a wardrobe staple.

The different sizes of round beads in this design remind us of Mod design motifs. This just demonstrates how you can make something new that looks like it's been around forever (or at least since the 1960s).

Materials and vital statistics

- ✔ **Beads:**
  - 4 20mm lavender round shell loops
  - 4 6mm round rose quartz beads
  - 4 4mm blue-green fluorite round beads
  - 4 16mm round silver links
- ✔ **Findings:**
  - 1 silver toggle and bar clasp
  - 2 jump rings
  - 4 2½-inch pieces of 22-gauge half-hard sterling silver wire
- ✔ **Tools:** Round-nose pliers, wire cutters, chain-nose pliers, bent-nose pliers (optional)
- ✔ **Techniques used:** Creating wrapped loops, opening and closing jump rings

Finishing the wrapped loops between the pieces on this bracelet can be a little tight. In this case, the bent-nose pliers are the perfect tool to create a nice finished loop.

If you prefer, you can work with a single, longer piece of wire, instead of several 2½-inch pieces, as indicated in the materials list. You waste less wire, and it's easier on your fingers to wrap a longer piece of wire. The downside is that the longer piece of wire can be a little unwieldy if you're new to wire wrapping.

Directions

1. **Create a wrapped loop on the end of one piece of wire.**
2. **Slide the open end of the wire through the first hole in one shell loop.**
3. **With the wire in the center of the shell loop, slide on one rose quartz bead and one blue-green fluorite bead.**
4. **Thread the wire through the other side of the shell loop, in effect framing the round beads in the shell loop, as shown in Figure 8-16.**

Figure 8-16: Frame the rose quartz and blue-green fluorite beads with the lavender shell.

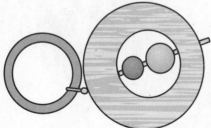

5. Begin your wrapped loop. Slip on one silver link before closing the loop. Complete the wrapped loop.

6. Using a new piece of wire, begin creating a wrapped loop. Before closing the loop, connect it to the silver link from Step 2. Complete the wrapped loop.

7. Repeat Steps 2 through 6 with the remaining beads and findings, creating a single chain of beads and wrapped loops.

8. Open one jump ring with two sets of pliers.

   For details on opening and closing jump rings, take a look at the appendix.

9. Slide the jump ring through the open wrapped loop on the beginning of the bracelet.

10. Slide the loop on the toggle clasp onto the jump ring. Close the jump ring with two sets of pliers.

11. Open the last jump ring.

12. Slide the last link attached to the other end of the bracelet onto the jump ring.

13. Slide the loop on the bar end of the clasp onto the jump ring. Close the jump ring.

Easy Wire-Wrapped Cuff Bracelet

When we say easy, we mean easy! The only tough part of creating this beautiful bracelet, pictured in Figure 8-17, is working with the 72-inch long piece of beading wire (that's 2 yards, if you'd rather think in small numbers and big dimensions). The wire can be a bit unwieldy in the beginning when you're stringing and wrapping the full length of it. In this case, the thin wire acts like a stringing material, and it virtually disappears inside the beads, so don't worry if you kink it a bit. As long as you can string your beads on it, you're home free.

Figure 8-17: A basic bracelet frame can become beautiful with assorted beads and wire.

Choose beads that complement each other so you can string them randomly to get this eclectic but coordinated effect. Select an already prepared bead mix to take the guesswork out of coordinating your beads.

Materials and vital statistics

- ✔ **Beads:** 25 grams of mixed black, silver, and gray beads
- ✔ **Findings:**
    - Cuff bracelet frame
    - 72 inches of 28-gauge silver beading wire
- ✔ **Tools:** Wire cutters
- ✔ **Techniques used:** Wrapping wire, stringing

As you string and wrap your way through this project, don't use pliers to twist the fine wire or you'll break it. Just use your fingers. Nothing is more frustrating than getting to the end of the project only to have to begin again. We speak from experience!

Directions

1. Wrap one end of the beading wire around the bracelet frame, leaving a 2-inch tail. Twist several times to secure.

2. Add an inch or so of beads, working them down the length of the wire.

3. Slide the beads over the tail to hide and secure it. Trim away any excess wire with your wire cutters.

4. Position the beads in between the top and bottom of the bracelet frame, and wrap the wire around the top and bottom of the frame.

   As you wrap the wire around the frame, make sure to pull the beading wire taut.

5. Wrap the wire around one edge of the frame twice, before moving to the next row of beads.

6. Continue sliding on beads and wrapping the wire around the frame until the bracelet frame is full.

7. Twist the end of the wire and weave the tail up through several beads to secure.

Part III
Putting Your Jewelry Skills to the Test

The 5th Wave · By Rich Tennant

"Well, it might be a little difficult, but I don't think being under house arrest means you can't have a creatively beaded ankle bracelet."

In this part . . .

Looking to jump to the next level in jewelry making? This part is a great stop on your journey. We include more-advanced and compelling projects here. You'll find the familiar organizational pattern here, with chapters dedicated to separate techniques, though with these projects, you're likely to find several techniques used in a single piece.

In addition to making gorgeous final pieces, this part guides you through creating one-of-a-kind components (findings, beads, and pendants, specifically) using different techniques. We dedicate complete chapters to forming wire jewelry components and to making beads and other things from polymer clay, for example. So we give you step-by-step instructions for creating the basic jewelry elements *and* for putting them together in stunning original designs.

This part is really for experienced jewelry makers. You definitely don't need to be an expert, but if you have no experience, we suggest you get a few basic projects under your belt (or draped around your neck) first. Tackle some projects in earlier chapter and work your way up. Definitely flip through these chapters, though, to see what's possible and to find tips to inspire your own designs.

Chapter 9

Stepping It Up: Advancing Your Bead-Stringing Skills

· ·

In This Chapter

▶ Connecting multiple bead units to add glamour and sparkle

▶ Stringing up inches and inches of beads

▶ Making multistrand masterpieces

· ·

As the title indicates, you tackle some tougher projects in this chapter, but in most cases, they're tougher only because they're longer. You can find the foundation for these projects in earlier chapters. But if you're feeling particularly crafty, feel free to start here and go back to those chapters later. The projects in earlier chapters give you great practice and can help you improve your skills in no time.

In this chapter, we give you some tips on creating dazzling multistrand bridal wear. You can try your hand at the latest in chunky, colorful beadware. You work on some complicated (but manageable) chandelier earrings using crystals and gemstones. And for the chapter's final project, you create a great necklace and earring set with an incredibly popular stone, onyx.

Bridal Party Bracelet

Is there any better reason to get all dressed up and sparkly than a wedding? We think not. This bracelet, shown in Figure 9-1, is a great addition to a bridesmaid's ensemble, or even a lowly wedding guest's attire. We love the classic combination of pearls and crystals. A dash of color with the peridot-colored crystal sliders makes this a more substantial, but feminine piece.

We used peridot (pale green) crystal sliders in this bracelet, but you can choose clear, blue, pink, or whatever color coordinates with your outfit.

Figure 9-1:
Use
two-hole
sliders
to unify
strands and
add sparkle.

Materials and vital statistics

✔ **Beads:**

- 5 12mm peridot Swarovski crystal two-strand sliders

- 12 6–7mm white potato freshwater pearls

- 30 6mm clear AB coin beads

✔ **Findings:**

- 1 two-hole silver tab clasp

- 4 sterling silver crimp tubes

- 2 9-inch pieces of 0.014-inch diameter nylon-coated stainless steel beading wire

✔ **Tools:** Crimping pliers, chain-nose pliers, wire cutters, binder clip

✔ **Techniques used:** Stringing, crimping

The most difficult part of this bracelet is working with the multiple strands. The binder clip helps you keep beads on one strand while you're working with another. Work slowly and keep your strands straight to make this sparkly accessory.

Directions

1. **String one crimp tube onto one length of wire. Slide the tail of the wire through one hole of the clasp. Feed the tail back down through the crimp tube, as shown in Figure 4-2 in Chapter 4. Using the two-phase crimp method, close the crimp.**

Keep your clasp closed while you create this piece. It keeps you from accidently connecting the clasp backwards or upside down. These clasps only connect one way, so you need to make sure you have everything connected properly, or it won't close.

2. **Repeat Step 1 with the remaining length of wire, feeding it through the second hole of the same clasp. After both lengths of wire are attached, your piece should look like the one in Figure 9-2.**

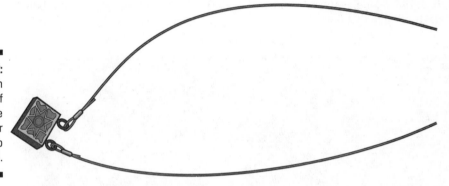

Figure 9-2:
Attach both lengths of wire to one side of your two-hole tab clasp.

3. **String the beads onto one piece of wire in the following order: 1 crystal, 1 pearl, 1 crystal. Repeat the pattern on the second piece of wire.**

When you string the beads, don't forget to cover up the tail of the wire with the crystals. The center hole of your pearl is likely too narrow to cover the tail, so trim it with the wire cutters if you need to, so it fits completely within the crystal.

4. **Feed one piece of wire through the top hole of the spacer. Feed the other piece of wire through the bottom hole of the spacer.**

5. **Repeat the pattern established in Steps 3 and 4 with the remaining beads and spacers.**

6. **Place a binder clip on one wire to hold the beads in place while you attach the other wire to the clasp.**

7. **Slide one crimp tube onto the open wire. Thread the wire through the corresponding hole of the open end of the clasp. Feed the wire back down through the crimp tube. Using the chain-nose pliers, pull the tail taut, as shown in Figure 4-3 in Chapter 4. Use the crimping pliers to close the crimp. Trim any excess wire with the wire cutters.**

8. **Repeat Step 7 with the other wire to complete the bracelet.**

Variation: Flower girl bracelet

You can quickly create a single-strand, coordinating bracelet for a flower girl using crystals and pearls. Substitute a single peridot crystal for each two-strand crystal connecter. Use a single piece of wire and the clasp of your choice, and string beads in this pattern — clear coin, pearl, clear coin, peridot crystal — until you reach your desired length, most likely 5½ to 6½ inches for most children.

46-inch I-Want-Candy Necklace

Acrylic beads are an incredibly hot trend in jewelry design right now and will be into the foreseeable future. Pick up any celebrity magazine and you can see lots of big, chunky, colorful beads. (And they're cheap too, so if the trend doesn't last so long, you're not blowing a fortune on it!) We spent less than $5 for these acrylic (yes, that means they're plastic) beads featured in the necklace in Figure 9-3. Acrylic is great for a project like this for two reasons: First, it's available in awesome colors, like pink, fuchsia, olive, lime, teal, and shades of orange. And it's lightweight, a great benefit for a megastrand like this one.

Figure 9-3:
Chunky pink acrylic beads make this clasp-free necklace look good enough to eat.

Materials and vital statistics

- **Beads:**
  - 2 ounces of jumbo mixed acrylic beads, assorted pinks
  - 20 grams of seed bead mix, pink, white, clear, lilac
- **Findings:** 2 yards of lilac no. 8 silk bead cord with needle attached
- **Tools:** Scissors, glue
- **Techniques used:** Stringing, knotting

Even though this necklace is fairly long, this tasty-looking delight should only take you about an hour to string. You can make it up in an afternoon and wear it to a party that night.

Directions

1. Unwrap the full length of bead cord from the card. Tie a stop bead at the end of the cord.

Check out Chapter 2 for details on using stop beads.

2. String on 1½ inches of the seed bead mix. String on one jumbo bead.

3. Repeat Step 2, varying the length of seed bead mix from 1½ to 2½ inches, until your strand reaches 46 inches, ending with a jumbo bead.

4. Thread the needle through the first section of seed beads you strung in Step 2 to close the necklace, as shown in Figure 9-4.

Figure 9-4: Feed the needle back through your first set of beads to tie off the end.

5. Untie the cord and remove the stop bead. Using the tail, tie a double overhand knot over the strand. Trim the knot with scissors. Apply a dab of glue to the knot.

6. Pull the needle end of the cord taut and tie a double overhand knot. Using the scissors, trim the knot. Apply a dab of glue. Allow the knots to dry before wearing.

Triple-Dangle Gemstone Earrings

Using threader findings is a great way to add a little variety to your earring wardrobe. The most basic *threaders,* like the ones we are using for our triple-dangle earrings in Figure 9-5, are basically a chain with an eye loop on one end and a short rigid wire on the other end that allows you to thread the finding through your pierced holes. The length holds the earring in your ear — no back required. We add multiple dangles to the eye loop to add more drama.

Figure 9-5:
Threader findings give you a head start on creating long, sexy strands.

Materials and vital statistics

✔ **Beads:**

- 2 12mm denim blue mountain jade faceted teardrops, top drilled
- 6 5mm blue mountain jade smooth round beads
- 6 5mm green mountain jade smooth round beads

✔ **Findings:**

- 2 sterling silver threader earring findings
- 4 1½-inch sterling silver head pins
- 2 3-inch pieces of 22-gauge sterling silver wire

✔ **Tools:** Round-nose pliers, chain-nose pliers, wire cutters

✔ **Techniques used:** Creating wrapped loops

Make the dangles first to make quick work of these not-so-complicated earrings. After you have them assembled, attach them to the threader findings for almost-instant glamour.

Directions

1. **Slide a blue round bead and then a green round bead onto a head pin. Using your round-nose pliers, create a wrapped loop, as pictured in Figure 9-6.**

   Repeat 3 times using the remaining head pins, creating 4 dangles total. Set the dangles aside.

Figure 9-6:
Make four
two-bead
dangles.

2. Slide one teardrop onto a 3-inch piece of wire. Bend the wire up around the top of the teardrop, leaving one tail longer than the other, as shown in Figure 9-7.

Figure 9-7:
Bend the
wire around
the top of
the teardrop
bead.

3. Use the short end of the wire to create a wrap around the longer end of wire, as shown in Figure 9-8.

Figure 9-8:
Create a
wrapped
loop above
the teardrop
bead.

4. Slide a green round bead onto the open end of the wire. Follow it with a blue round bead, as Figure 9-9 illustrates.

Figure 9-9:
Slide round
beads onto
the wire.

5. Using the widest part of your round-nose pliers, begin a large wrapped loop above the two round beads, as shown in Figure 9-10. Before closing the loop, slide on two of the dangles you made in Step 1 and the connecting loop of one threader earring finding. Close the loop and trim any excess wire.

6. Repeat Steps 2 through 5 to create the second earring.

Variation: Mega-strand gemstone earrings

For a highly textured version of these earrings, skip the large teardrops, and instead use multiple dangles of gemstone chips. The long line of the threader finding looks great with these small chunky strands.

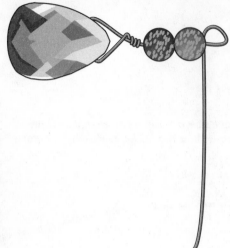

Figure 9-10:
Leave the loop open so you can slide on your dangles and threader finding.

Variation: Triple-strand crystal earrings

These earrings look great using a single color crystal (we like red). Vary the size and shape to get a gorgeous layered look with very little effort. The more faceted, the better, so look for rondelles, rounds, and tiny teardrops to make these earrings sparkle.

Jade and Crystal Chandelier Earrings

With 40 eye loops and 10 wrapped loops, these earrings, pictured in Figure 9-11, take a decent chunk of time, but they are so worth the effort. You pair jet black crystal coins with green mountain jade beads for a stunning combination.

Figure 9-11:
Chandelier earrings bring a touch of India to your wardrobe.

Materials and vital statistics

✔ **Beads:**

- 10 12mm green mountain jade faceted teardrops, top drilled
- 10 5mm green mountain jade smooth round beads
- 10 6mm black crystal faceted coin beads

✔ **Findings:**

- 20 ¾-inch pieces of 22-gauge sterling silver wire
- 10 2-inch pieces of 22-gauge sterling silver wire

  We've done the math for you: These 30 pieces of wire require a total of 35 inches of 22-gauge sterling silver wire. (If you think you'll create some "practice" pieces, plan on having a bit more wire on hand.)

- 2 round filigree sterling silver 5-hole chandelier earring findings
- 2 sterling silver ear hooks

✔ **Tools:** Round-nose pliers, wire cutters, chain-nose pliers

✔ **Techniques used:** Creating wrapped loops and eye loops

When you create the individual bead units that hang from the chandelier earring findings, you'll likely create some that are a wee bit longer and some that are shorter. That's the nature of handmade jewelry — no two pieces are exactly alike. To give your finished earrings the most professional look possible, attach the longest dangles to the center hole of the earring finding, working your way out to the shortest dangles. The arrangement of the holes on the earring finding helps create this staggered effect, but your placement of the dangles makes a huge difference.

Directions

1. **Slide one teardrop onto a 2-inch piece of wire, toward the middle of the wire. Bend both ends of the wire toward the top of the teardrop, as shown in Figure 9-12.**

Figure 9-12:
Bend both ends of the wire up toward the top of the teardrop.

For ease of wrapping, make one end of the wire slightly longer than the other.

2. **Using your fingers, bend the shorter end of the wire up around the top of the teardrop, and wrap the tail around the longer piece of wire, as shown in Figure 9-13.**

Use your chain-nose pliers, if necessary, to flatten the tail of the wrapped coil. You don't want to get scratched later.

Figure 9-13:
Wrap the shorter end of the wire around the longer end.

3. **Use your round-nose pliers to create a wrapped loop with the longer piece of wire. The two wraps should meet in the middle so they look like one single wrap, like the one in Figure 9-14.**

Use the wire cutters to trim away any excess wire, if necessary. Use the chain-nose pliers to flatten the tail of the coil.

Figure 9-14:
Use the longer end of the wire to create the top loop.

4. **Repeat Steps 1 through 3 nine times with the remaining long pieces of wire and teardrops.**

Set the 10 wrapped teardrops aside.

5. **Use the round-nose pliers to create an eye loop at the end of one ¾-inch piece of wire. Slide on one jet crystal coin. Use the round-nose pliers to create an eye loop on the open end of the wire, as shown in Figure 9-15.**

Repeat using the remaining 9 crystals. Set these 10 bead units aside.

Create coordinating earrings and a necklace with bold onyx beads and components. These feature handcrafted sterling silver elements for luxurious contrast. To make your own, take a look at Chapter 9.

Give the constellation crimp earrings and necklace from Chapter 4 a try when you're ready to perfect your crimping skills.

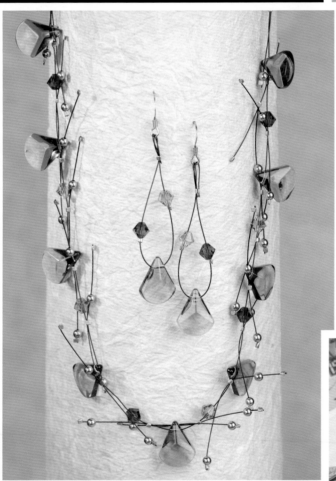

Add a pop of color to your jewelry wardrobe with this bright red netted necklace. Larger beads allow you to whip this up in no time, so you can make it and wear it in a matter of minutes. Turn to Chapter 11 for the instructions.

A boring laptop case gets a quick makeover with the addition of a beaded charm. Find instructions for this laptop charm that incorporates bead-stringing techniques in Chapter 14.

Hoop earrings are always a classic, but they still offer lots of versatility for the jewelry designer. Instructions for the silver filigree and crystal earrings and the gold wreath-style earrings are available in Chapter 8.

This bridal party bracelet becomes an instant classic with its crystal sliders and pearls. Check out Chapter 9 for details on this elegant but easy accessory.

Buttons aren't just for sewing. Pretty ones can make great focal pendants with the help of a little wire. In this necklace, you also have loads of wire-wrapped loops, lampwork beads, rose quartz gemstone beads, and glass accent beads. Find directions for this project in Chapter 14.

Create your own drama with these mountain jade and crystal chandelier earrings. Look for unique earring findings to personalize them. Turn to Chapter 9 for all the details.

Big pendants are a great way to make a bold statement. Buy a ceramic one (like the round one on the right) to create a quick stylish piece (see Chapter 5 for details), or make your own pendant with polymer clay (like the oval pendant on the left) by following the steps in Chapter 14.

Here, the convertible claspless necklace or bracelet is shown as a lariat. Take a look at the instructions in Chapter 4 to make one of your own and wear it how you like.

Brass jewelry components are great for creating superquick chandelier earrings. You'll find instructions for the blue crystal teardrop earrings in Chapter 8. That same chapter has instructions for the amazing gold-filled and red Venetian glass bead earrings. Finally, use bead-knotting techniques and bead tips to make the long snowflake obsidian and fluorite beaded earrings. The instructions are located in Chapter 5.

You don't need to stress when you lose an earring. You can use your collection of orphaned earrings to make this fun orphan earring charm bracelet project described in Chapter 14.

Let findings like head pins and bead caps help you create superfancy earring designs. Instructions for the pink pearl earrings and opal-colored crystal earrings are located in Chapter 8.

The I-want-candy necklace is long and chunky. Make your own trendy version by following the directions in Chapter 9.

These confetti napkin rings give you practice with working with multiple strands. Get the details in Chapter 3.

Get jiggy with wire and beads. You'll find instructions for the pearl and amethyst crystal double-strand bracelet as well as the double-strand onyx and cloisonné bead bracelet in Chapter 7. The steps for the two-strand black-and-white elastic crystal bracelet are detailed in Chapter 5. And the simple metallic bead bracelet is a great beginner project in Chapter 4.

You can discover all sorts of unique jewelry components at the hardware store, such as the metal washers used in this earring design. Add some copper wire and beads for an inexpensive pair of eye-catching earrings. You'll find instructions for these in Chapter 14.

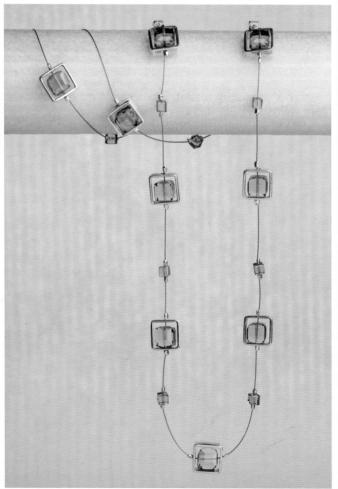

Less is definitely more when you're talking about this Swarovski crystal and sterling frame necklace. Take a look at Chapter 4 for the scoop on how to space these luxurious bead stations to create your own stunning piece.

Chunky glass nuggets and simple seed beads combine to create a bold and bright necklace. Get the instructions in Chapter 3.

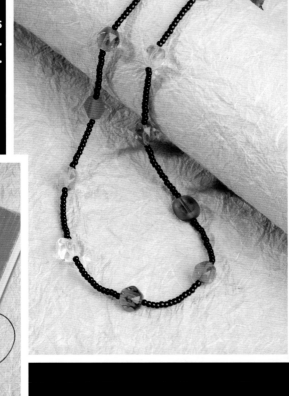

Embellish your books with beaded bookmarks. You use the peyote stitch and a fringe technique to craft the white and colorful crystal bookmark, which you can find instructions for in Chapter 6. Try your hand at tying your way to easy bookmarks using chandelier earring findings and silk bead cord or charms and waxed linen cord, using Chapter 3 as your guide.

The Mod-inspired wire-wrapped bracelet is simple and elegant. Dress it up or dress it down, but by all means, flip to Chapter 8 and get started.

The wooden bobble bracelet from Chapter 3 is a great way to accessorize for any casual occasion.

Get the scoop on creating adjustable knots in Chapter 3. While you're at it, make yourself one of these beautiful leather necklaces with a geometric pendant of your choice.

Earrings are the best jewelry items to make when you're practicing new techniques. Find the directions for the coin pearl and lime green beaded bead earrings in Chapter 11. For a little more glitz, head over to Chapter 8 for instructions on how to make chandelier earrings. For the gold-filed wire and iridescent green bead earrings, you'll need to use a jig, following the instructions in Chapter 7.

Have fun with a mixture of glass, crystal, and metal beads in all kinds of shapes and sizes when you construct this bead, wire, and chain necklace. You'll end up with an eclectic necklace design that you can wear with just about anything. Instructions for this necklace are located in Chapter 8.

Figure 9-15:
Create
crystal bead
units for
chandelier
earrings.

6. **Repeat Step 5, but instead of the crystals, use the round beads, as pictured in Figure 9-16.**

Repeat using the remaining 9 round beads.

Figure 9-16:
Small jade
bead units
coordinate
with the
faceted
teardrops
for a
dramatic
effect.

7. **Use your round-nose pliers to gently open one eye loop on a crystal bead unit. Slide the open loop through the wrapped loop of one teardrop bead unit. Use the round-nose pliers to close the eye loop, connecting the two bead units together, like the one in Figure 9-17.**

Figure 9-17:
Use your
round-nose
pliers to
open,
connect,
and then
close the
eye loop.

8. **Using your round-nose pliers, open the other eye loop of the crystal bead unit. Slide the open loop through the eye loop of one round bead unit. Use the round-nose pliers to close the connection, as shown in Figure 9-18.**

Repeat Steps 7 and 8 with the remaining bead units to create 10 dangles.

Figure 9-18:
Use your
round-nose
pliers to
open,
connect,
and then
close the
eye loop to
complete
the dangles.

9. Using your round-nose pliers, gently open the top eye loop of one dangle. Connect the open eye loop to one hole in the chandelier earring finding, as pictured in Figure 9-19.

Repeat using the 9 dangles.

Hang the longer dangles from the middle of the finding, moving to the shorter ones at the outside of the finding. You can always move dangles around if you find one hangs longer or shorter than you'd like after you get them on. Keep your pliers handy for adjustments later.

Figure 9-19:
Connect a
dangle
to the
chandelier
earring
finding.

10. Attach the ear wires to the chandelier findings to complete the earrings.

Before calling this project "done," take another look at all the eye loops to make sure they're properly closed. With so many connections, it's easy to miss a loose one. Double check now to make sure you don't lose a dangle later.

Variation: Grande chandelier earrings

If this pair of earrings isn't quite dramatic enough for you, you can make them even more spectacular by doubling the number of crystal and round bead units. Your grande dangles will consist of five bead units (from the bottom up: 1 teardrop, 1 crystal, 1 round, 1 crystal, 1 round) rather than the three in the original design. You also need another 15 inches (that's 50 inches total!) of sterling silver wire for this mega-masterpiece.

Onyx Multistrand Expander Necklace

Don't be put off by the length of the written instructions for this multistrand beauty shown in Figure 9-20. Think of it as making three separate necklaces, and then attaching them to a single clasp. See, that's not so bad.

Figure 9-20:
Onyx takes center stage in this gorgeous three-strand necklace.

We love onyx and silver together, but you can choose gold-filled or vermeil findings if that suits your taste better. Just substitute the metal you love for the silver or silver-plated items, and get beading!

Materials and vital statistics

✔ **Beads:**

- 3 40x40mm faceted onyx puffed squares
- 76 6mm faceted onyx rounds
- 88 8x5mm onyx smooth drums
- 12 12x8mm onyx diamonds
- 52 9x2mm silver-plated smooth tubes
- 4 8mm clear AB crystal cubes
- 5 6mm jet bicone crystals

✔ **Findings:**

- 3 pieces (20 inches, 34 inches, 44 inches) of 0.014-inch diameter black nylon-coated stainless steel beading wire
- 6 sterling silver crimp covers
- 24 2x2mm sterling silver crimp tubes
- 1 sterling silver 3-hole expander lobster claw clasp

✔ **Tools:** Crimping pliers, wire cutters, chain-nose pliers

✔ **Techniques used:** Stringing, crimping, using crimp covers

When we chose supplies for this necklace, we ordered one 16-inch strand of each of the different onyx beads. We had plenty of beads left over to make the onyx multistrand chandelier earrings as well. Two gorgeous accessories for (nearly) the price of one!

As you work on this project, take it one strand at a time. We've divided up the directions to help you focus on each piece individually.

Stringing the shortest length

1. **Attach the 20-inch piece of beading wire to the top loop of a 3-hole clasp finding with a crimp tube, using your crimping pliers, as shown in Figure 9-21.**

At this point it doesn't matter which side is the top of the clasp and which is the bottom. They look exactly the same. After you attach this first strand, though, make sure you stay consistent. This first hole is now officially the top one.

Figure 9-21:
Start your necklace with the choker strand connected at the top of the clasp.

2. **String beads onto the open end of the wire in this pattern: faceted round, smooth drum. Repeat this pattern 59 times for a total of 60 repetitions. Slip on one more faceted round.**

This strand measures approximately 13 inches. Don't be tempted to lengthen this strand unless you're absolutely sure that you need more length. Because we designed this necklace with a chain extender clasp, you can lengthen and shorten the finished necklace as you'd like. (In our case, the extender can give the necklace an extra 5 inches if needed.) If you shorten or lengthen individual strands during the creation phase, the necklace won't keep the same proportions.

3. Slide on a crimp tube. Slip the open end of the wire through the top hole of the other side of the clasp. Feed the tail back down through the crimp tube and several beads. Using your chain-nose pliers, pull the tail taut, as shown in Figure 4-3 in Chapter 4. Crimp the crimp tube. Use your wire cutters to trim away any excess wire. Cover the flattened tube with a crimp cover using the front jaw of your crimping pliers.

Tackling the longest length

1. Attach the 44-inch piece of wire to the bottom hole of the 3-hole clasp, using a crimp tube and your crimping pliers. Using the front jaw of your crimping pliers, cover the flattened crimp with a silver crimp cover, so it looks like Figure 9-22.

At this point, the center hole of the 3-hole clasp is empty. No worries; you attach something here in the next section. Be patient.

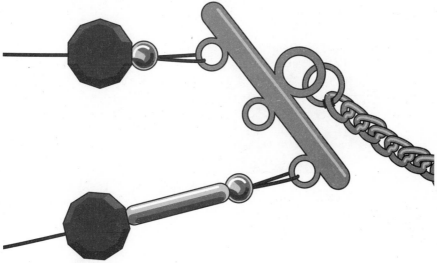

Figure 9-22:
Crimp covers create a consistent look between the strands of this necklace.

2. Slide one silver tube onto the open end of the wire. Use it to cover the tail of the crimped end of the wire.

3. String beads in this pattern: 1 coin, 1 tube, 1 drum, 1 tube, 1 drum, 1 tube, 1 coin, as shown in Figure 9-23.

4. String on these beads: 1 tube, 1 faceted round, 1 cube, 1 faceted round, 1 tube, as featured in Figure 9-24.

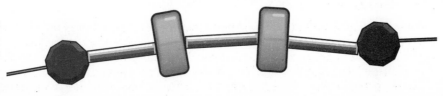

Figure 9-23:
Start your strand with this basic pattern.

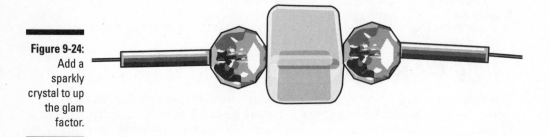

Figure 9-24:
Add a sparkly crystal to up the glam factor.

5. Repeat the pattern in Step 3.

6. String on these beads: 1 tube, 1 drum, 1 tube, 1 drum, 1 tube, 1 coin, 1 puffed faceted square, 1 coin, 1 tube, 1 drum, 1 tube, 1 drum, 1 tube. Figure 9-25 shows this sequence.

Figure 9-25:
Huge puffed squares define the piece.

7. Repeat Steps 3 and 4.

8. Repeat Steps 3 and 6.

9. Repeat Steps 3 and 4.

10. Repeat Steps 3 and 6.

11. Repeat Steps 3 and 4.

12. Repeat Step 3 and add one more tube bead.

13. Slide on a crimp tube. Slip the open end of the wire through the bottom hole of the other side of the clasp.

   Make sure to leave the center hole of the 3-hole clasp empty for now.

14. Slip the tail back through the crimp tube, and then down through several beads. Using the chain-nose pliers, pull the beading wire taut. Use the crimping pliers to flatten the crimp bead using the two-phase crimp method. Use the wire cutters to cut away any extra beading wire.

15. Using the front jaw of the crimping pliers, close a crimp cover over the flattened crimp.

Moving on to the middle strand

1. **Slide a crimp tube onto the 34-inch piece of beading wire. Slip the tail through the center hole of the 3-hole clasp and then back through the crimp tube. Use your crimp pliers to flatten the crimp bead.**

2. **Using the front jaw of the crimping pliers, close a crimp cover over the flattened crimp.**

3. **String beads onto the open end of this wire in this pattern: 1 crimp tube, 1 faceted round, 3 diamonds, 1 faceted round, 1 crimp tube. Figure 9-26 shows this pattern.**

   Don't close the crimp beads. You're just stringing at this point. You arrange and crimp them into place later on. Again, be patient!

Figure 9-26:
String your crimp tubes just like any other bead for now.

4. **String on beads in this pattern: 1 crimp tube, 1 bicone, 1 crimp tube.**

5. **Repeat Step 3, and then repeat Step 4 twice.**

6. **Repeat Steps 3 and 4.**

7. **Repeat Steps 3 and 4.**

8. **String on the last crimp tube. Feed the tail of the wire through the middle hole of the other side of the 3-hole clasp, and then back down through the crimp bead. Use the crimping pliers to flatten the crimp bead using the two-phase crimp method. Using the front jaw of your crimp pliers, close a crimp cover around the flattened crimp.**

9. **Lay the necklace flat. Arrange the bead units (a set of beads between two crimp beads) along the middle strand. Crimp the crimp beads into place to keep the bead units in position.**

   The space between the units can vary. We separated our units by 1 to 2½ inches along the length of the wire. Just put them where you like them.

Onyx Multistrand Chandelier Earrings

Just in case the necklace in the previous project isn't enough onyx for you, you can make these awesome coordinating earrings pictured in Figure 9-27. You use the same beads from the necklace and the most basic sterling silver 3-hole chandelier findings to provide a consistent look without being totally matchy-matchy.

Figure 9-27:
Use similar bead patterns to tie the necklace and earrings together.

Materials and vital statistics

✔ **Beads:**

- 8 6mm faceted onyx rounds
- 4 8x5mm onyx smooth drums
- 8 12x8mm onyx diamonds
- 10 9x2mm silver plated smooth tubes
- 4 6mm jet coin beads

✔ **Findings:**

- 6 3-inch lengths of 0.014-inch diameter black nylon-coated stainless steel beading wire
- 12 sterling silver crimp covers
- 12 2x2mm sterling silver crimp tubes
- 2 sterling silver 3-hole chandelier findings
- 2 sterling silver ear hooks

✔ **Tools:** Crimping pliers, wire cutters, chain-nose pliers

✔ **Techniques used:** Stringing, crimping, using crimp covers

Instead of using head pins or making loops to hold the beads on the dangles, crimp beads and covers do the work. They make these earrings quick to complete and professional looking.

Directions

1. Slide a crimp bead to the end of one open end of beading wire. Use the crimp pliers to move the bead to the end of the beading wire. Crimp the bead into place. Using the front jaw of the crimp pliers, close a crimp cover over the flattened crimp bead, as shown in Figure 9-28.

Figure 9-28:
The crimp covers act like head pins, holding the beads on a beautiful dangle.

2. String on beads in this order: 1 coin, 1 tube, 1 drum, 1 tube, 1 drum, 1 tube, 1 coin. (Refer to Figure 9-23 in the coordinating necklace project.)

3. Slide on a crimp bead. Loop the end of the beading wire through the center hole of one of the chandelier earring findings, and then feed the tail back down through the crimp bead and several other beads. Use the chain-nose pliers to pull the wire taut, as shown in Figure 9-29.

Figure 9-29:
Pull the wire taut between beads.

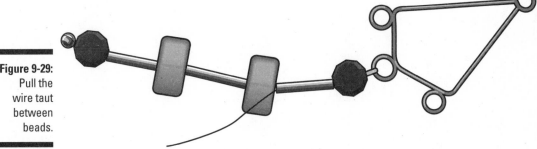

4. Using your crimping pliers, flatten the crimp bead. Use your wire cutters to trim away any extra tail. Use the front jaw of your crimping pliers to close the crimp cover around the flattened crimp.

5. Repeat Step 1. Then string on beads in this order: 1 faceted round, 1 diamond, 1 tube, 1 diamond, 1 faceted round. Figure 9-30 shows this pattern.

Figure 9-30:
Use this complementary pattern on the outside dangles of these earrings.

6. Repeat Steps 3 and 4, and then attach this strand to one of the outside holes of the chandelier finding.

7. Repeat Steps 5 and 6, attaching this strand to the remaining hole of the chandelier finding.

8. Use your chain-nose pliers to open the connector loop on the ear hook. Slip the top loop of the chandelier finding onto the connector. Close the connector with your chain-nose pliers.

9. Repeat Steps 1 through 8 to make the second earring.

Chapter 10

Fabricating Bead and Wire Components

*F*abrication, as far as jewelry making is concerned, includes the art of constructing items from scratch. Very often, fabrication in the jewelry world is practiced with metal, and in this chapter, we use metal in the form of wire to fabricate a number of components that will take your jewelry designs to the next level. How cool is it to be able to proclaim that you are the maker of a unique pendant or clasp? That's exactly what you'll be able to do when you complete the projects and variations in this chapter.

Along with the two tools on the end of your arms — your hands — you just need a minimal number of other tools to fabricate these projects. Most require your standard set of hand tools, such as wire cutters and round-nose and chain-nose pliers. Because wire is relatively soft, you can bend it pretty easily with your fingers as well. You're making real hand-crafted jewelry here! And then there are the beads. A number of the projects in this chapter use lampwork beads made by glass artist D.D. Hess (www.ddhess.com). *Lampwork* involves using a torch and rods of glass to form beautiful glass beads, and they are a wonderful element to combine with wire.

You'll notice that the techniques you use are very similar in each of the projects. Whether it's an ear hook or a hook-style clasp, they all start with some of the basic wire methods of looping. In fact, if you've already made some wire jewelry from this book or this book's predecessor, *Jewelry Making and Beading For Dummies* (Wiley), then you're already familiar with these techniques. If you're a total wire-wrapping newbie, head to Chapters 7 and 8 in this book for a few more basics before you jump into the projects below.

Pink Lampwork Bead and Wire Pendant

Many bead enthusiasts collect lampwork beads, and there's no better way to show off your wonderful collection than to turn a few of the pieces into pendants, like we did in Figure 10-1. Using the wrapped loop technique combined with half of an "S" scroll method, you can easily turn a simple bead into an eye-popping pendant with just a little wire and a few hand tools. Then slip the loop at the top of the bead onto your favorite silver chain, or better yet, combine it with other beads you string up, and use the pendant as the focal point of a beautiful beaded necklace.

Figure 10-1:
Add your completed lampwork bead pendant to a chain for an instant necklace.

If your wire looks a little tarnished, use a soft polishing cloth to shine it up before you start working with the wire. Most jewelry supply vendors sell them (one popular brand is Sunshine cloth), and you can also find them at discount stores that sell jewelry.

Materials and vital statistics

✔ **Beads:**

- 1 20mm pink lampwork bead

- 2 4mm daisy spacer beads

✔ **Findings:** 4 inches of 21-gauge dead-soft round sterling wire

✔ **Tools:** Round-nose pliers, chain-nose pliers, wire cutters

✔ **Techniques used:** Creating a wrapped loop and "S" scroll

Dead-soft wire is easier to work with if you have any hand issues, such as carpal tunnel syndrome or arthritis, and as long as it's not too thin, it will be plenty strong enough to handle most beads. Dead-soft wire, unlike half-hard and full-hard wire, has not been pulled through a *drawplate* (a metal block with holes in it), so it's very easy to manipulate and is intended for wire jewelry sculpting.

The lampwork bead is the star in this project, but the sterling daisy spacer beads add a nice touch and help balance the bead on the wire so it stays nice and straight.

Directions

1. Use your round-nose pliers to make a tiny loop on one end of the wire, and continue to wrap slowly until the coil becomes a little larger, like the one in Figure 10-2.

2. Hold the coil part with the chain-nose pliers, and use your fingers to continue coiling until the coil is approximately ¼ inch in diameter.

Figure 10-2:
Coil the end of the wire to help keep the lampwork bead in place.

3. Slide one daisy spacer, the lampwork bead, and another daisy spacer onto the wire.

4. Using round-nose pliers, create a wrapped loop at the top, as shown in Figure 10-3, and trim off any excess wire using the wire cutters.

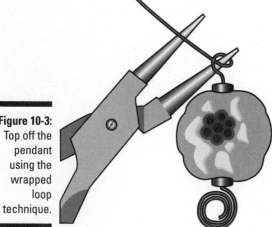

Figure 10-3:
Top off the pendant using the wrapped loop technique.

Triple Loop and Lampwork Pendant

Get looped — get triple looped, in fact — with the loop de loop technique when constructing this lampwork and crystal pendant. Finish it off by using your favorite technique and ours — wrapped loops. A purple lampwork bead and purple crystals accented with sterling daisy spacer beads really pop in this design in Figure 10-4, but of course, you can use this same method and switch the beads to any you prefer. Although this is a perfect pendant, you can also make two, add ear hooks (which you can make yourself by using the wire ear hooks pattern in this chapter), and voilá! You have a pair of earrings.

If you prefer a more uniform size to your loops, consider doing this same technique on a *wire jig*. A jig is a device with pegs in it, normally removable, that you can wrap the wire around to create different shapes. This allows for more uniform designs. You can find out more information on what a jig is and how to use it in Chapter 7.

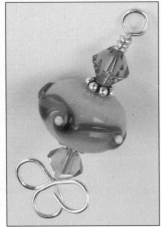

Figure 10-4: Give some sparkle to your lampwork bead by adding crystals on either side of it.

Materials and vital statistics

🗸 **Beads:**

- 2 4mm daisy spacer beads

- 2 6mm crystal beads

- 1 12mm lampwork bead

🗸 **Findings:** 4 inches of 21-gauge dead-soft round sterling wire

🗸 **Tools:** Round-nose pliers, chain-nose pliers, wire cutters

🗸 **Techniques used:** Creating loop de loops and wrapped loop

If you like to press your loops flat, try using a nylon-nose pair of pliers. You can press the wire in between the jaws of the pliers, and because the jaws are nylon, they won't scratch the metal. These pliers are handy for straightening bent wire as well.

Here's yet another way to create a pendant using wire and beads. This one combines two techniques: loop de loop and wrapped loop.

Directions

1. **Use your round-nose pliers to make 3 loop de loops, one right next to the other on the end of the wire.**

2. **Use the chain-nose pliers to bend the wire so it's straight up and positioned over the middle loop, as shown in Figure 10-5.**

3. **Slip on 1 crystal bead, 1 daisy spacer, 1 lampwork bead, 1 daisy spacer, and 1 crystal bead.**

4. **Using the round-nose pliers, create a wrapped loop at the top of the pendant, and trim off any excess wire using the wire cutters.**

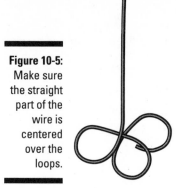

Figure 10-5: Make sure the straight part of the wire is centered over the loops.

Bead and Wire Hook-Style Clasp

The basic hook clasp is dressed up with a lampwork bead in Figure 10-6. And these aren't just any beads; these are tubular-shaped beads with tiny pink flowers and ribbons to help promote breast cancer awareness. Imagine this clasp accenting a necklace of pink gemstone quartz beads or crystals. This is another project that uses a lot of looping techniques, especially the eye loop and loop de loop.

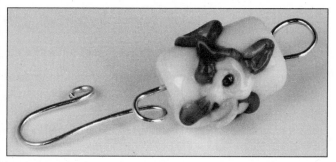

Figure 10-6: Lampwork beads are just some of the many types of beads you can add to a hook-style clasp.

Fancy clasps like these don't have to be positioned in the back of the necklace. By adding a bead to the hook, you combine form and function, so show it off by flipping your necklace around sometimes.

Materials and vital statistics

✓ **Beads:** 1 14mm tubular-shaped lampwork bead

✓ **Findings:** 3½ inches of 21-gauge dead-soft round sterling wire

✓ **Tools:** Round-nose pliers, wire cutters, chain-nose pliers

✓ **Techniques used:** Creating eye loops and loop de loops

Wire comes in different gauges. Because of its weight, 21-gauge tends to be one of the most versatile sizes, and it also fits through a large variety of beads. Generally speaking, 21-gauge wire is plenty strong enough for most beaded necklaces, as long as the beads aren't superheavy. For example, if you're going to make a necklace using a lot of 10mm hematite beads (a gemstone that is very heavy because it has iron ore in it), consider using a thicker wire like 20- or 18-gauge. Just be sure to double check that the wire still fits through the hole in the bead you plan to add to the clasp.

The loops used in this design have two purposes: They help secure the bead in place, and they provide a way to secure the clasp to your necklace design later.

Directions

1. **Use your round-nose pliers to make a large loop on one end of your wire, as shown in Figure 10-7.**

Figure 10-7:
Start
with one of
many loops
for this
looped-up
bead and
wire clasp.

2. **Slip the bead onto the wire, and push it down so it's up against the loop you just made.**

3. **On the end of the wire opposite the loop you made in Step 1, grasp the wire with round-nose pliers and use your fingers to loop de loop the wire around the nose of the pliers.**

Take a look at Figure 10-8 for help. Try to make the loop as close to the bead as possible to prevent the bead from sliding around.

Figure 10-8:
Make sure
the loop is
as close to
the bead as
possible.

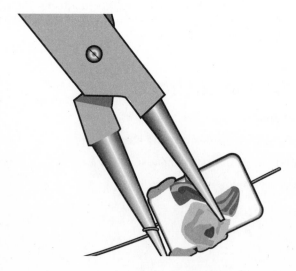

4. About ½ inch past the loop you created in Step 3, grasp the wire again with the round-nose pliers, and bend the wire around the nose of the pliers to create a hook, like the one shown in Figure 10-9.

Now, jewelry making isn't an exact science, so you'll want to ensure you have about another ½ inch of wire on the hook end of the clasp. If it's longer than this — and ours usually is because it's better to have too much wire than not enough — use the wire cutters to trim off any excess.

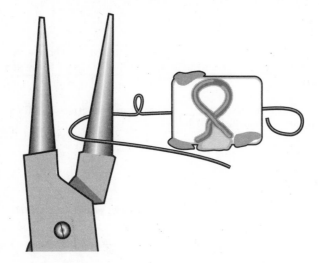

Figure 10-9: The hook part will connect to the other end of the necklace.

5. Using the round-nose pliers, finish the hook off with a tiny loop on the end, as shown in Figure 10-6, and use the chain-nose pliers as necessary to flatten or adjust any part of the wire clasp.

Wire Ear Hooks

Though there is nothing wrong with buying prefabricated earring hooks, it's very cool to be able to make your own. And, really, you'll be surprised at how easy they are to make. With a very small amount of wire and the handy loop technique, you can make these ear hooks very quickly. They are often referred to as *fish hooks* or *shepherd hooks* because of their shape. See them in Figure 10-10.

Figure 10-10: Fabricating your own earring hooks adds an extra design dimension to your finished jewelry piece.

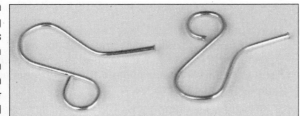

When you make matching earrings to go with a necklace that you intend to sell as a set, make an extra pair of earrings so that if they sell without the necklace, you already have a backup pair to make the set complete again.

Materials and vital statistics

- ✔ **Findings:** 2 1¾-inch pieces of 21-gauge half-hard round sterling wire
- ✔ **Tools:** Jeweler's file, round-nose pliers, chain-nose pliers
- ✔ **Techniques used:** Creating wire loops

When making ear hooks, 21- or 22-gauge is the best size of wire to use. The wire needs to be able to fit through the average person's ear hole, but it also needs to be strong enough to dangle an earring from.

It can be tricky to get your ear hooks to match, but with some practice, you'll soon get them matching pretty closely. Just take your time.

Directions

1. **File both ends of the wire to make sure it's smooth and won't scratch the wearer.**

File in one direction, like you would when filing your fingernails, instead of filing back and forth in a sawing motion.

2. **With the round-nose pliers, position the wire at about the middle of the nose and make a small loop on one end of the wire, like the one in Figure 10-11.**

This first loop is where you'll attach the dangly part of your earring.

Figure 10-11:
You'll attach the rest of your earring to the first loop of the ear hook.

3. **Measure about ¼ inch away from the loop down on your wire, and wrap the wire around the largest end of your round-nose pliers, as shown in Figure 10-12.**

The hook, at this point, doesn't look very round yet.

4. **To give your hook more of a rounded shape, take your round-nose pliers again, position the largest part of the nose in the same spot that you just wrapped the wire in Step 3, and gently bend the wire around the nose of the pliers at this point again. Because the wire is now around the larger part of the plier's nose, it will help make the hook rounder.**

This is a very small movement. You'll notice that the hook will look a little more round after this step.

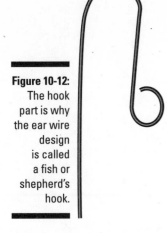

Figure 10-12:
The hook part is why the ear wire design is called a fish or shepherd's hook.

5. **Hold on to the end of the ear hook, and using your thumb and forefinger, gently bend the wire up a little. Use can also use chain-nose pliers instead of your fingers to bend the wire if you prefer.**

   This is a small bend, no larger than 25 degrees.

6. **Repeat Steps 1 through 5 to make another ear hook so you have a pair.**

Chapter 11

Bodacious Woven Bead Jewelry

● ●

In This Chapter

▶ Honing your brick stitching skills

▶ Making your own beads using the peyote stitch

▶ Weaving dazzling beaded jewelry designs

● ●

So, you've got the basic techniques down when it comes to a few bead-weaving stitches, but what's next? How do you bring it all together to make some bodacious beaded jewelry that you'll love to wear or give as gifts? This chapter has a few answers for you; here, you find some fairly simple projects that help you get in more weaving practice while you make some jewelry components as well as finished jewelry pieces. For example, make your own beads from tiny seed beads that you weave together. Then combine those with other beads to make some unique earrings that will have everyone amazed when you tell them you made some of the beads included in the design. Or how about making a pendant of woven seed beads that you can add to a beaded necklace for that stunning focal piece?

For some jewelry makers, bead weaving can seem to take a good deal of patience and time, but these projects are designed to give you quick results (in "seed bead" time, that is) while you hone your weaving skills. They also push you to be a little more creative as you consider how you can incorporate some of the beaded components into other jewelry pieces or you try to think outside the peyote box. Get ready to pull out those tiny magic beads and weave away.

Diamond Design Pendant

Diamonds are your best friends, especially if you can make them yourself, or at least if you can make yourself a diamond-shaped brick stitch pendant using cream-colored seed beads and aurora borealis enhanced crystals, as pictured in Figure 11-1. After you've completed the pendant, you can either keep it simple and add it to a silver chain, or use it as a focal piece and design a beaded necklace just to show off this pretty pendant.

If you're working with light-colored seed beads and can't find a thread to match them, stick with off-white. It's a general, all-purpose color to have on hand.

Figure 11-1:
Cream-
colored
seed beads
and crystal
make up
this woven
pendant.

Materials and vital statistics

✔ **Beads:**

- 8 4mm round Swarovski AB crystals
- 8 clear rainbow glass fringe beads
- 5 grams of size 11 cream-colored Japanese seed beads

✔ **Notions:** Off-white Silamide thread, size-12 beading needle

✔ **Tools:** Scissors

✔ **Techniques used:** Weaving ladder stitch and brick stitch, making fringe

Cream-colored beads provide a neutral shade that can be teamed up with all kinds of other beads, and the crystals give this pendant a little extra sparkle. The bottom of the pendant is finished off using the fringe technique. As with any brick stitch design, you first make a row of ladder stitched beads, and then start on the brick stitch portion of the design.

Directions

1. Use the scissors to cut about a yard of thread and thread it through the eye of your needle.

2. String 2 seed beads, and then insert the needle through the bottom of the first seed bead, as shown in Figure 11-2. Make sure to leave about a 6-inch tail of thread.

3. Pull the thread so both beads line up next to each other, and reinforce the stitch by bringing the needle back through the beads.

4. Continue the ladder stitch until you have connected 15 seed beads, as shown in Figure 11-3.

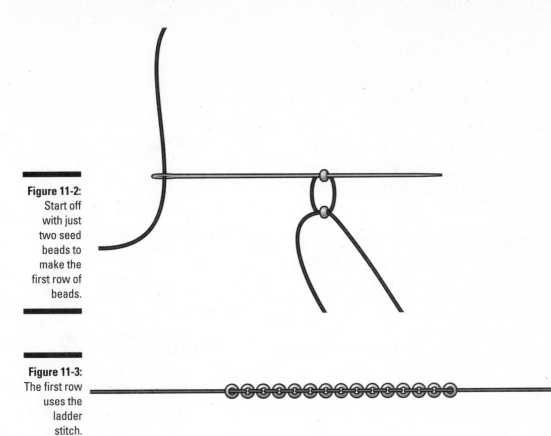

Figure 11-2:
Start off
with just
two seed
beads to
make the
first row of
beads.

Figure 11-3:
The first row
uses the
ladder
stitch.

5. To form the second row of beads string on a seed bead, and insert the needle under the thread that joins the first two beads in the ladder section (see Figure 11-4).

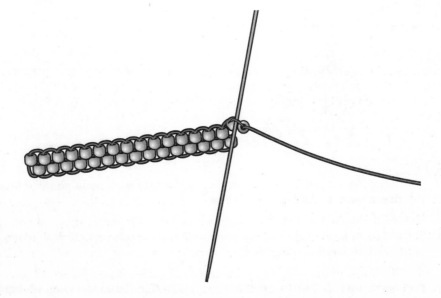

Figure 11-4:
This is the
beginning of
the brick
stitch.

6. Bring the needle up through the hole of the bead you added in Step 5, as shown in Figure 11-5, and pull the thread to snug the bead up against the top of the ladder section.

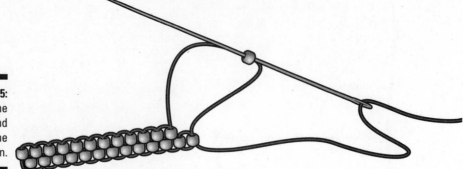

Figure 11-5:
Pull the
thread and
push the
bead down.

7. **Repeat Steps 5 and 6, moving back and forth weaving the beads until 2 beads are left at the top of the triangle that has formed.**

Most bead-weaving projects require you to add new pieces of thread because your first working thread may not be long enough to complete the entire piece. Refer to Chapter 2 for a refresher on attaching threads and finishing off threads.

8. **String on 4 seed beads, and insert the needle down through the next bead, as shown in Figure 11-6. Pull the thread so you have a loop of beads at the top of the triangle.**

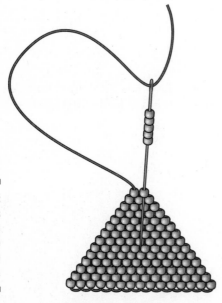

Figure 11-6:
Use beads
to make a
bail at the
top of the
pendant.

9. **Reinforce the loop of beads by snaking the needle back through the 4 beads a few times, knot, and tie off the thread.**

10. **Snake the needle through the beads just woven so it's coming out of one end of the first row (see Figure 11-7), and continue the brick stitch. Stop when your last row has 8 beads woven on to it.**

11. **Add 8 strands of fringe in the following bead patterns (see Figure 11-8), remembering to bring the needle back up through the beads after adding the teardrop, and then inserting the needle down into the next bead on the last**

row of beads before starting the next fringe strand:

Fringe strand 1: 5 seed beads, 1 4mm crystal, 3 seed beads, 1 teardrop

Fringe strand 2: 5 seed beads, 1 4mm crystal, 4 seed beads, 1 teardrop

Fringe strand 3: 5 seed beads, 1 4mm crystal, 5 seed beads, 1 teardrop

Fringe strand 4: 5 seed beads, 1 4mm crystal, 6 seed beads, 1 teardrop

Fringe strand 5: 5 seed beads, 1 4mm crystal, 6 seed beads, 1 teardrop

Fringe strand 6: 5 seed beads, 1 4mm crystal, 5 seed beads, 1 teardrop

Fringe strand 7: 5 seed beads, 1 4mm crystal, 4 seed beads, 1 teardrop

Fringe strand 8: 5 seed beads, 1 4mm crystal, 3 seed beads, 1 teardrop

12. Complete the pendant by weaving and trimming off any excess thread.

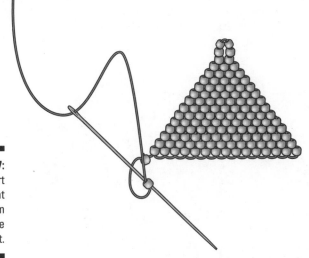

Figure 11-7:
Start
weaving at
the bottom
of the
pendant.

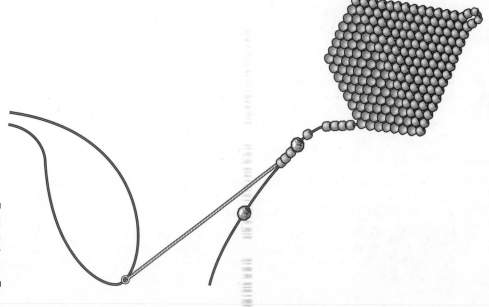

Figure 11-8:
Now it is
time for
some fringe!

Variation: Diamond design with a dangle

Follow these same pendant directions, but instead of stopping after the 15th row of beads, continue to weave until your pendant is pointed at the end for a true diamond shape. Then add one large crystal teardrop bead as a dangle accent at the point you've created. This variation can be made with cream-colored beads as well or any other colors you're partial to.

Free-Form Peyote Bracelet

Extra-creative souls are easily drawn to the free-form peyote stitch. You can't do this stitch wrong because the technique is loosely based on the more traditional flat peyote stitch in which you string on a seed bead, skip a bead, and insert your needle into the next seed bead. But, with free-form, it's just that — you're free to use any size, color, and shape of bead, and you skip one, two, or even three beads. This bracelet project (see Figure 11-9) was designed around the lampwork flower bead and is definitely a method rather than an exact how-to, which is the nature of free-form peyote. So get ready to throw the rule book out the window.

Figure 11-9:
Feel free to be creative while weaving this free-form peyote bracelet.

Focusing on one element, such as a lampwork bead like the one shown in Figure 11-10, is a good way to create a theme for any free-form jewelry pieces you make. For example, the bead has a flower on it, so I decided to use a nature theme to help select the other beads used to make this bracelet.

Figure 11-10:
The lampwork bead used in this bracelet design was created by glass artist D.D. Hess.

Materials and vital statistics

✔ **Beads:**

- 1 20x15mm side-drilled lampwork bead
- 2 6mm clear crystal Czech beads

  Various amounts of the following beads:
- Dark rose luster size 11 seed beads
- Cream size 11 seed beads
- Clear fuchsia-lined size 11 seed beads
- Pearl salmon Delicas
- Leaf beads
- Crystals in pinks, greens, and clear
- Light pink size 6 seed beads

✔ **Notions:** Off-white Silamide thread, size-12 beading needle, 1 foot of ½-inch wide pink ribbon with pink hearts pattern

✔ **Tools:** Scissors

✔ **Techniques used:** Weaving peyote

There's no way to do this project wrong because this is free-form, so you don't have to make a bracelet that looks like a carbon copy of this one. More than likely, you'll need to add new thread and finish off existing thread pieces as you work through your free-form design. Refer to Chapter 2 if you need some help.

Stringing the base strand

1. **Use the scissors to cut about a yard of thread and thread it through the eye of your needle.**

   If you're comfortable with a longer piece of thread, it's okay to make it longer; however, more than likely, you'll need to add thread as you weave this bracelet.

2. **Place all of your beads in front of you in small piles so you can access them at random.**

   As you work, you want to create an eclectic mixture of beads.

3. **Insert the needle through a random assortment of seed beads until you have approximately 3 inches of beads on your thread. String on 1 Czech crystal bead, the lampwork bead, and the other Czech crystal bead. Then string on about another 3 inches of seed beads, again in random order, similar to what is pictured in Figure 11-11.**

Figure 11-11:
String beads in random order on your working thread.

4. Following the peyote technique and working in the opposite direction you just came from on the strand, pick up a bead onto the thread, skip a bead on the strand you just created, and insert your needle through the next bead.

5. Repeat Step 4 using random colors of seed beads.

When you get to the lampwork bead, insert the needle through it and continue to work down the beads on the other side of the lampwork bead in the same fashion.

6. Repeat Step 4, moving up and down the strand of beads one or two more times until you have a piece that looks similar (remember, it won't look exact) to the piece pictured in Figure 11-12.

At this point, you're creating a few base rows of beads so you can start attaching larger beads and use more free-form techniques. You can make this base as wide as you'd like.

Figure 11-12:
A few rows of peyote create a base to begin some real free-form fun.

Building a series of bridges

1. Now you can get a little more crazy (or creative) with peyote by adding on larger beads and making little bridges of beads, like those pictured in Figure 11-13. A *bridge* means that you string on a number of beads, and then you skip a number of beads (not just 1 like traditional peyote), and you insert the needle into a bead that's farther down on the bead base you created. The result is a sort of bridge that skips over beads.

Figure 11-13 shows a bridge being attached on the other side of the lampwork bead. You'll notice some leaf beads have also been added in a few places as well.

Figure 11-13:
Make a bridge of beads to cross over the lampwork bead.

2. After you're on the other side of the lampwork bead, continue to string on random beads in different colors and shapes, and make more bead bridges if you want, until you reach the end of the base, as shown in Figure 11-14.

Figure 11-14:
Keep going crazy with beads all the way down to the end of the base.

3. Continue to work back and forth down the base using this free-form technique until the bracelet is almost ½ inch wide.

4. Weave in and trim off all excess threads.

Finishing with the ribbon

1. Locate the middle of the ribbon and position the peyote piece so the middle of the ribbon is aligned with the middle of the peyote piece, which in this case happens to be where the lampwork bead is located (see Figure 11-15).

Figure 11-15:
Match the middle of the peyote piece and the ribbon to each other.

2. Add more thread (about 24 inches) to your needle, and make an overhand knot on the end of the thread.

3. Insert the needle up through the ribbon and right behind one side of the lampwork bead, thread it through the lampwork bead, and back down on the other side of the lampwork bead. Repeat this a few times.

This step ensures that the lampwork bead is securely anchored to the ribbon, which will make it easier for you to stitch the peyote piece to the ribbon.

4. Knot and trim off the excess thread.

5. Repeat Step 2, and starting on one end of the peyote piece, stitch it to the ribbon, moving the needle up through the ribbon and down through the peyote piece. Work from one end to the other as pictured in Figure 11-16.

Figure 11-16:
Stitch the ribbon to the peyote piece.

6. **When you get to the end, knot and trim off the excess thread.**

The ribbon works as a decorative fiber clasp. To wear the bracelet, place the peyote section on the top of your wrist, and tie the ribbon ends into a bow.

Variation: Free-form peyote pendant

For another free-form challenge, consider using the same technique where you work your bead weaving around one focal bead, but this time, create a pendant instead of a bracelet. Use seed beads to make a loop at the top to create your bail. After you complete your pendant masterpiece, string up some matching beads on beading wire and include the pendant in the center.

Peyote Beaded Bead Earrings

The technique used to make these beaded beads, which are incorporated into these peyote beaded bead earrings (shown in Figure 11-17), is deceptively simple. It really is just plain old even-count flat peyote like you've done before, and yes, you can make your own beads with this stitch. After you understand the technique, you'll be able to whip up these beads in mere minutes. White mother-of-pearl dangles and bright green Delicas create a bright and cheerful earring design in this project that introduces you to the beaded bead.

Figure 11-17:
You need four beaded beads for this pair of earrings.

Materials and vital statistics

✔ **Beads:**

- 5 grams of opaque rainbow yellow-green Delicas
- 2 10mm coin pearl beads
- 4 6.5mm silver daisy spacer beads

✔ **Notions:** Off-white Silamide thread, size-12 beading needle

✔ **Other:** 2 26mm mother-of-pearl dangle components

✔ **Findings:**

- 2 sterling silver ear hooks
- 2 4-inch pieces of 24-gauge dead-soft wire

✔ **Tools:** Scissors, round-nose pliers, wire cutters, chain-nose pliers

✔ **Techniques used:** Weaving flat peyote, creating wrapped loops

Make sure to keep the tension on the tight side as you weave peyote. This helps keep the finished weave consistent. After you've got the hang of this technique, you can use these beads on any of your stringing designs.

Crafting the beaded beads

1. Use the scissors to cut about a yard of thread and thread it through the eye of your needle.

2. Add a stop bead (designed to hold your beads in place while you weave; see Chapter 2) by stringing on a bead and inserting the needle back through the bottom of the bead.

3. Thread on 6 Delica beads, as shown in Figure 11-18.

Figure 11-18: Just six beads are needed to start.

4. Pick up another bead with your needle, skip the bead previously strung on the thread, and insert the needle through the next bead on the thread, as illustrated in Figure 11-19.

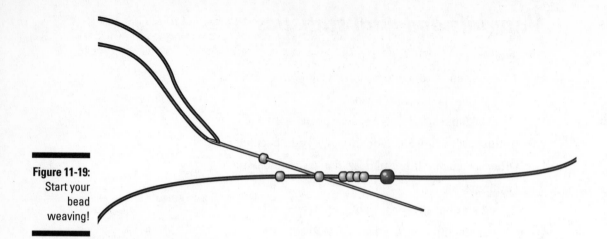

Figure 11-19:
Start your
bead
weaving!

5. Continue this process — pick up a bead, skip a bead, insert the needle through the next bead — moving back and forth until you have a total of 5 beads on either end of the little square, like the one shown in Figure 11-20.

If you ask ten bead weavers how to count rows of beads in peyote, you'll more than likely get ten different answers. Some bead weavers count rows by zigzagging up and down from one bead to the next. Some count down in one direction and back across in the opposite direction. Whichever method you use to count rows, make sure you have the same number of beads on both sides of the piece when making a piece of flat even-count peyote that you plan to sew up the sides on (thus creating a tube shape of some kind). Otherwise, when you try to fit the beads together before stitching, they won't fit. So, always double check the straight edges of the peyote piece to make sure you have the same number.

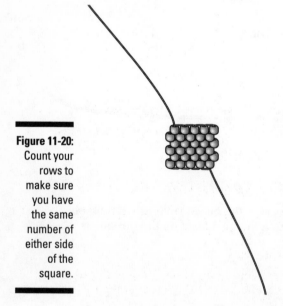

Figure 11-20:
Count your
rows to
make sure
you have
the same
number of
either side
of the
square.

6. Fold the little square of beads you just wove in half. The sides should fit together like a zipper, so that where a bead sticks out on one side, an indent exists for it on the other side.

7. Begin to sew the two sides together, thus creating a tube of beads, by inserting the needle through the beads that look like zipper teeth (they'll be sticking out), as shown in Figure 11-21. Zigzag back and forth as you sew up these beads to form the tube, as shown in Figure 11-22.

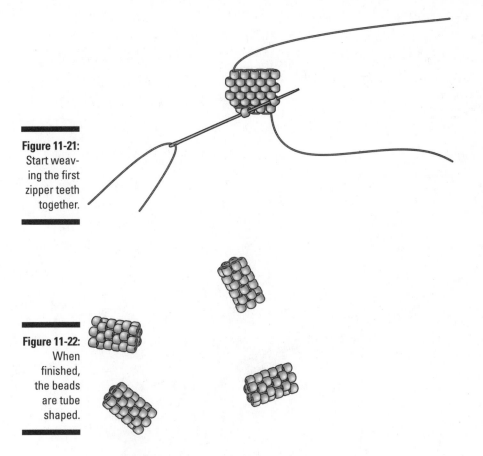

Figure 11-21: Start weaving the first zipper teeth together.

Figure 11-22: When finished, the beads are tube shaped.

8. Weave in any remaining threads.

9. Repeat Steps 1 through 8 three more times so you have 4 beaded beads.

Now, be totally impressed with yourself because you can weave your own beads.

Putting all the components together

1. Use the round-nose pliers and wire to start a wrapped loop, and connect it to one of the mother-of-pearl components, as shown in Figure 11-23.

2. Use the chain-nose pliers to close the wrapped loop.

3. Using the wire cutters, trim off any excess wire, and thread 1 beaded bead, 1 daisy spacer, 1 coin bead, 1 daisy spacer, and 1 beaded bead onto the wire (see Figure 11-24).

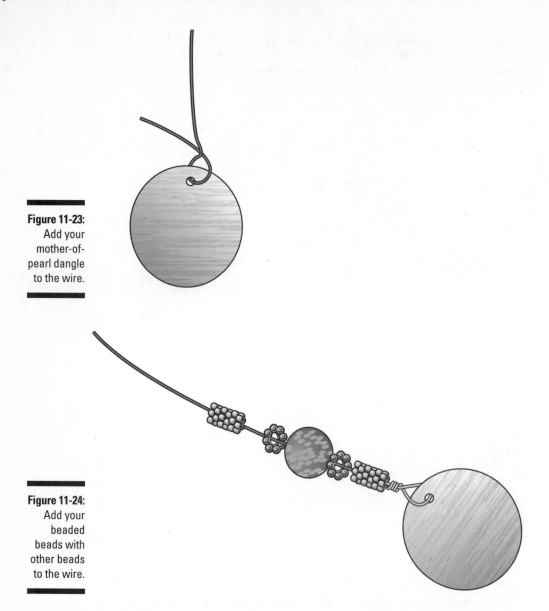

Figure 11-23:
Add your
mother-of-
pearl dangle
to the wire.

Figure 11-24:
Add your
beaded
beads with
other beads
to the wire.

  4. Finish the top by making another wrapped loop, and then attach an ear hook.

  5. Repeat Steps 1 through 4 for the other earring so you have a matching pair.

Variation: Peyote beaded bead bracelet

After you make a pair of beaded bead earrings and you discover that these little beads
really aren't that time consuming to make, you can attempt a larger project, like using
them to string up a bracelet. Make more beaded beads with yellow-green Delicas, and
instead of using the mother-of-pearl dangles, alternate the beaded beads with 6mm
mother-of-pearl round beads accented on either side with daisy spacer beads. Now
you have a matching set.

Red-Hot Net Necklace

The bright red beads used in the net stitch necklace look very similar to those little red-hot cinnamon candy pieces many of us loved as a kid. In fact, anyone with a sweet tooth probably still likes these, but now you can use them as eye candy and have a zero-calorie treat to wear in this red-hot net necklace, pictured in Figure 11-25. These particular beads often tend to be less than uniform in shape, but the fabulous color makes up for this many times over, resulting in a classic but more relaxed look to your finished jewelry piece. Finish off the necklace with a hook-and-eye clasp, which you can either make yourself or purchase.

Figure 11-25: The beads in this necklace look like red-hot candies you loved as a kid.

Not all seed beads are teeny tiny. Larger seed beads, like size 6, are about the same size as a 4mm gemstone bead. So one way to make faster projects when bead weaving is to use larger beads.

Materials and vital statistics

✔ **Beads:**

- 20 grams of ruby red silver-lined size 6 seed beads

- 1 size 11 seed bead of any color

✔ **Notions:** Off-white Silamide thread, 2 size-12 beading needles

✔ **Findings:**

- 2 gold-filled bead tips

- 1 gold-filled hook-and-eye clasp

✔ **Tools:** Scissors, jeweler's cement, pin cushion, ruler, corsage pin, chain-nose pliers

✔ **Techniques used:** Weaving net stitch

Netting is one of the fastest beading stitches available for bead weavers, and with larger beads, it goes even more quickly. For this necklace design, you create a base row with one thread that's doubled and finished off with bead tips, and then you use a second needle and thread to add your bead swags. Though you can make swags all the way down your base row, for this design, we just added a few in the middle of the base row.

Anchoring the necklace

1. **Use the scissors to cut about a yard of thread and insert it through the eye of one needle. Repeat this for the second needle.**

2. **For one needle, pull the thread so it's a double thickness. This will be used for your base row of beads.**

3. **Holding the ends of the threads that are in both needles (which should be three because one needle's thread is doubled), tie two overhand knots, one on top of the other. String the size 11 seed bead onto both needles and all threads, and then push it down so it rests up against the knots.**

4. **Insert both needles back through the bottom of the seed bead, and push the bead up against the knots.**

5. **Insert the needles through the hole in one of the bead tips, and pull the threads so the knots and seed bead rest inside one of the shells of the bead tip.**

   Flip back to Figure 6-35 in Chapter 6 if you need help with this step.

6. **Use the scissors to trim off the excess threads, and add a small drop of jeweler's cement inside the bead tip.**

7. **Use the chain-nose pliers to close the bead tip around the seed bead and knot.**

Stringing the main strand

1. **Now you're ready to start adding beads to the doubled thread. Pull the other single thread aside so it's not in your way as you work.**

   Make sure to secure the needle safely, such as in a pin cushion.

2. **On the doubled thread, thread on the size 6 seed beads until you have a strand that's about 15 inches long.**

   Because these beads tend not to be uniform, rather than count the beads, use a ruler to measure your progress.

3. **To attach another bead tip to the other end of the doubled thread, insert the needle through a bead tip (making sure the opening of the bead tip is facing away from the beads) and one seed bead. Push the seed bead down into the opening of the bead tip, and tie two overhand knots with the doubled threads. Then use the same process as described in Steps 6 and 7 in the preceding section to secure the bead tip.**

   You may find it helpful to insert a corsage pin (which is pretty thick) into the knots, and then pull on the doubled thread as you use the pin to push the knots into the bead tip.

Supplementing with swags and finishing

1. Take the working thread and snake the needle down about 5½ inches (again use the ruler for this) on the base row you made in the previous section so you're an inch or so from the middle of the strand.

2. String on 7 beads, then count over 6 beads, and snake the needle through the 6th bead, as shown in Figure 11-26.

Figure 11-26:
Snake the working thread through the beads.

3. Repeat Step 2 two more times so you have three swags of beads (see Figure 11-27) in the middle of the base row.

Figure 11-27:
Make three swags of beads.

4. To secure the thread, snake the working thread all the way to the end of the base row, and make an overhand knot just past the last seed bead on the base row.

5. Thread the needle back through some of the beads on the base row, and tie another overhand knot on the base row.

6. Snake the needle down through the base row of beads for a few more inches, and use the scissors to trim off the thread.

7. Attach a hook-and-eye clasp to both bead tips, as illustrated in Figure 11-28.

You can either use a prefabricated clasp you've purchased or use the instructions from our first book, Jewelry Making & Beading for Dummies (Wiley), to make your own.

Figure 11-28:
Add a
hook-and-
eye clasp to
finish the
necklace.

Variation: Netting anklet

With all these earrings, bracelets, and necklaces, you still have some other body parts to adorn. Don't forget about your ankles. Stick with some of the larger size 6 seed beads in the color of your choice. Purple or blue would be an excellent color choice for this design. Follow the same instructions as described for the main project, but shorten the strand to about 10 inches in length. Then create beaded scallops using the same method, but weave them around the entire strand rather than just in the center.

Chapter 12

Piecing It Together with Polymer Clay

● ●

In This Chapter

▶ Adding texture and design to clay with rubber stamps

▶ Rolling your own beads

▶ Imitating gemstones with polymer clay

● ●

*P*olymer clay is an incredibly versatile medium. You can form it into many shapes, wrap it around objects, knead particles into it, and on and on. You can make your own beads and components using all kinds of tools and cutters. Or you can keep it simple and use the two original tools, your hands. Because you can use so many different techniques to work polymer clay into beautiful jewelry pieces, we can only cover a few in this book. Think of this chapter as an introduction to this enormously deep crafting category that has countless books dedicated to it.

A quick general reminder about working with polymer clay: Any tools — such as cutters, baking sheets, and the like — you use with polymer clay should be dedicated solely to this medium. The tools don't have to be designed especially for clay, but after you use them with clay, don't use them for anything else. Even though the clay is a nontoxic product, you don't want to ingest it accidentally. You can't use this clay for food-safe dishes or pots.

Always bake your clay in a well-ventilated area. If the clay heats at a higher-than-recommended temperature, it can give off toxic fumes. Many ovens spike and cool to regulate their temperature as part of their normal operating process, so proper ventilation is essential.

Funky Flower Initial Pendant

Coauthor Heather's friend Beki first showed her a version of these pendants (pictured in Figure 12-1), and she loved them immediately. Right away she went out and bought tons (okay, many, many ounces) of clay and made all kinds of charms and pendants for her friends. The girls in Heather's Girl Scout troop even got in on the action. They started out making pendants with their own initials, and then of course they had to make some for non-troop friends, their moms, aunts, and neighbor's cousins.

These pendants are one of the most addictive craft projects we've run across, so be warned. After you start making them, you'll be hooked. And don't forget that we're not responsible for financial damages incurred based on calling in sick to stay home and craft while catching up on missed episodes of *American Idol*, *Ugly Betty*, or *Grey's Anatomy*.

Figure 12-1:
Create these custom pendants in a few easy steps.

New skill: Creating rubber stamp impressions on flat polymer clay components

One of our favorite (and easy) ways to use polymer clay to create jewelry components is by using rubber stamps. If you've been in a craft store lately, no doubt you've seen the explosion in the paper-crafting area. Mixed in with all the scrapbooking and card-making fun are entire aisles dedicated to rubber stamps. In most cases, people use these items to stamp ink images onto paper and other surfaces. But you can also use them without ink to add impressions and texture to polymer clay beads and components.

Here's the basic process for creating stamped impressions on clay:

1. **Condition the clay. Work it with your hands until it's warmed up and pliable.**

    The clay is conditioned when it can stretch a bit without breaking.

2. **Use a clay roller (or *brayer*) to roll the clay to desired thickness.**

    A clay roller is a small rolling pin designed to roll clay. It's usually 5 to 6 inches long without handles.

    In general, for making pendants and flat components (which is pretty much anything except beads), we roll the clay to about an ⅛ inch thickness.

3. **Mist a clean rubber stamp lightly with water. Press the stamp into the clay, pressing harder if you want a bolder impression, lighter if you want a more subtle one. Remove the stamp to reveal the impression.**

    If you're an experienced rubber stamper (one who's used to working with ink and paper, that is), you may be surprised to know that it's perfectly fine to rock the stamp a bit if you need to ensure a firm impression. (This is a no-no with ink because you may touch the stamp edge onto your surface, ruining the image in the process.) Don't lift the stamp, though, and then try to place it back in the same spot, or you're sure to create an unintentional shadow that looks sloppy.

Materials and vital statistics

🖊 **Materials:**

- ½ ounce white polymer clay

- Acrylic craft paint (We used pink, teal, copper and black.)

- Polymer clay glaze

- Card stock or recycled file folder

- Parchment paper

🖊 **Findings:** 5-inch piece of 22-gauge sterling silver wire (You need one piece of wire for each charm you make.)

🖊 **Tools:** Clay roller or brayer, 1¼-inch flower-shaped cutter, initial rubber stamps, bamboo skewer, baking sheet exclusively for polymer clay, paintbrush, round-nose pliers, chain-nose pliers, wire cutters

🖊 **Techniques used:** Stamping clay, baking clay, wire wrapping

Make these pendants as unique as the friends you're sure to give them to. Craft a whole alphabet and keep them ready to give as quick gifts. With the listed materials, you can make one pendant. But the clay is often sold in larger quantities at a better per ounce price, so feel free to stock up. Remember, you need a 5-inch piece of wire for each pendant.

Directions

1. **Preheat the oven to the temperature specified by the clay manufacturer, typically 275°F or 300°F. (We preheat ours to 275°F.)**

2. **Condition the clay by working it with your hands until it's warmed up and pliable. Lay the clay down on a piece of card stock. Using a clay roller, roll it to a uniform thickness of approximately ⅛ inch.**

We recommend that you roll the clay to a uniform thickness here, but being the budding jewelry designer that you are, you may have a perfectly good reason for wanting to roll this clay unevenly. If so, go for it! If you don't like the look later, you can always smash it up and roll it out again. This action sends a message to the other wanna-be pendants that you mean business, so they typically behave themselves while you stamp and paint them.

3. **Using the cutter, cut a flower from the clay. Remove the excess clay around the flower and save it to make another pendant later.**

If you've ever made sugar cookies, you have the skills to make this pendant. For this design, Heather used a fondant cutter she purchased in the cake-decorating section of her craft store. But, after you've used the cutter for clay, don't use it for food.

4. **Stamp an initial in the middle of the flower.**

See the "New skill: Creating rubber stamp impressions on flat polymer clay components" section earlier in this chapter for help.

If you're not thrilled with the first impression you create, don't scrap your pendant yet. Flip the clay over and try again. With every cutout, you get two chances to get it right.

4. Use a bamboo skewer to pierce a hole in the top petal of your flower pendant, using Figure 12-1 as your guide for placement.

5. Lift the card stock and gently pull it away from the pendant, being careful not to distort the piece. Lay the pendant on a piece of parchment paper on a cookie sheet. Bake your pendant based on the instructions listed on your clay for an item that's ⅛ inch thick. We baked ours for about 15 minutes.

If you're baking many pendants at one time, you may need to increase the baking time just a bit. The first time we made these, we made them as part of a large group, trying to cure roughly 60 or so charms at once. They took quite a while to cure, so allow yourself some extra time, or better yet, cook them in reasonable batches (like whatever fits on a single cookie sheet).

6. Allow the cured clay to cool completely. Paint the charm however you like. Allow it to dry completely before moving on to Step 7.

We painted the "H" charm in Figure 12-1 with copper paint. After it dried completely, we applied a coat of black paint to the whole charm, allowing it to set up for about 1 minute. Then, using a dry paper towel, we wiped off the black paint. Some of the black paint remained in the impression, giving the charm an antiqued look. For the "R" charm, we layered on pink and then teal, allowing the paint to dry for only a minute or so. We rubbed the wet paint with a dry paper towel to reveal the original white finish of the clay underneath on the high spots of the impression. Experiment with different painting techniques to get effects you like.

7. After the paint has dried completely, apply a coat of polymer clay glaze. Allow the glaze to dry completely, preferably overnight, before moving on to the next step.

8. Using the round-nose pliers, create a ¼-inch-wide spiral on one end of the wire, as shown in Figure 12-2.

Figure 12-2: Wrap a wire spiral with the round-nose pliers.

If you need help making spirals with wire, take a look at *Jewelry Making & Beading For Dummies* (Wiley).

9. Bend the spiral at a 90-degree angle with your chain-nose pliers. Slide the pendant onto the wire so the spiral rests against the front of the pendant.

The long tail of the wire is now on the back side of the pendant.

10. Wrap the long tail of the wire around the widest part of the round-nose pliers to create a bail, as shown in Figure 12-3.

11. Wrap the remaining tail back around the wire, as shown in Figure 12-4, to finish the bail. Trim away any excess wire with the wire cutters.

12. Repeat Steps 8 through 11 with any remaining pendants and wire pieces.

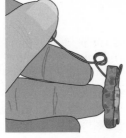

Figure 12-3:
Make a bail
for your
pendant.

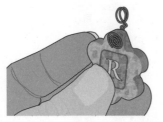

Figure 12-4:
Finish the
bail by
wrapping
the tail
around the
wire.

Textured "Pottery" Necklace

You combine a couple of different clay techniques in this earthy, pottery-inspired neck-lace, shown in Figure 12-5. First, you discover how to roll your own beads using a cool hand tool, known as a bead roller (check it out in Figure 12-6). Then you texture your newly rolled beads with a rubber stamp to give them the look of intricately carved pot-tery. Using the same rubber stamp, you make a fun large pendant to coordinate with these fancy beads. Finally, you put them all together in this casual, but striking design.

Figure 12-5:
Use rubber
stamps and
a bead
roller to
create the
components
of this
beautiful
necklace.

New skill: Using a bead roller

A *bead roller,* shown in Figure 12-6, is a handy tool for creating consistently sized clay beads. It's basically two interlocking plastic trays with differently shaped channels that slide back and forth. This sliding motion quickly forms uniformly sized and shaped beads.

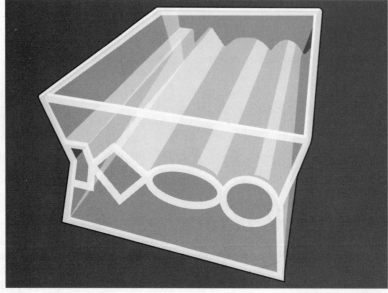

Figure 12-6:
Use a bead
roller to
quickly
make lots of
uniform
beads.

After you get the hang of using the bead roller, you can make mountains of beads in no time. Most bead rollers come with basic instructions, but here's our version to help you get the most out of your new tool.

1. **Condition your clay by working it with your hands until it's warmed up and pliable. Press the clay into the measuring ring, completely filling the ring, as pictured in Figure 12-7. Using the eraser end of a pencil or a clay-making tool, push the clay out of the measuring ring.**

The key to getting consistently sized beads is to use the same amount of clay each time. So the manufacturer of your bead roller included a handy measuring tool, called a *measuring ring,* shown in Figure 12-7, to make sure you use the right amount.

Make sure you get all the clay out of the measuring tool, scraping it out with a spatula, the tip of a paintbrush, or whatever you need to use to get the job done. If you don't get all the clay out, the bead size will be off, and the bead won't hold its perfect shape when you form it in Step 3. Too much clay and the bead won't roll smoothly, but instead will kind of limp along like a flat tire. Too little clay and your bead will have a definite divot somewhere!

2. **Roll the measured clay into a general ball shape. Place it into the rolling channel on the roller base, using Figure 12-8 as a guide. Place the roller top on the base and slide the alignment bar into the channel.**

3. **Gently slide the roller top and roller bottom in opposite directions, applying gentle pressure as the bead forms. It only takes a few slides to make the beads. Remove the top to reveal your gorgeous new beads, like the ones in Figure 12-9.**

Rolling the oval beads seems to be a little tougher than making round beads. If you have trouble getting the ovals to roll properly, mist the channel with a bit of water (or wipe it down with a damp paper towel) in between beads. The moisture keeps the clay from sticking and helps smooth out the beads.

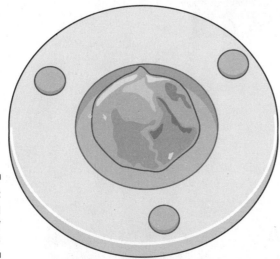

Figure 12-7:
Fill the ring completely with clay.

4. **Allow the beads to sit for at least half an hour. Pierce the beads with a large gauge wire or bamboo skewer.**

Letting the beads sit before you pierce them helps them retain their shape. They harden up just a little and distort much less if you let them rest. If you do dimple one (like the one in Figure 12-10a), gently smooth the dimple back into place with your finger and a tiny bit of water, as shown in Figure 12-10b.

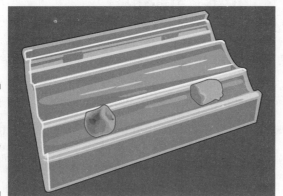

Figure 12-8:
Drop measured balls of clay into the channel.

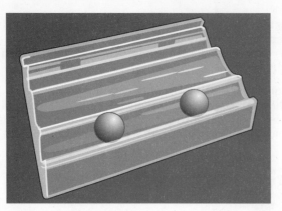

Figure 12-9:
Slide the top and bottom of the bead roller together to create uniform beads.

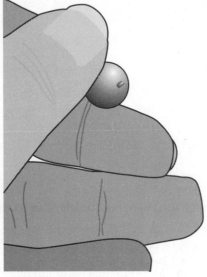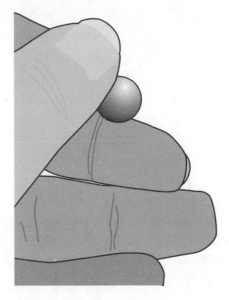

Figure 12-10:
If you create a divot when you pierce the bead, smooth it out before curing the clay.

New skill: Creating rubber stamp impressions on beads

You can use rubber stamps to create impressions on beads. Instead of pressing the stamp onto rolled-out clay, you roll the beads over the rubber stamp.

Here's the basic process for creating stamped impressions on beads:

1. **Condition the clay by working it with your hands until it's warmed up and pliable.**

2. **Use a bead roller to create beads the size and shape needed for your project.**

   See the preceding "New skill: Using a bead roller" section for the skinny on how to do this.

3. **Allow the beads to sit for at least half an hour. Gently slide a bead onto a piece of large gauge wire, being careful not to alter the shape of the bead, as shown in Figure 12-11.**

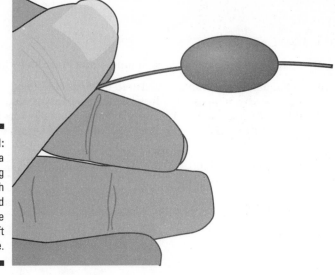

Figure 12-11:
Create a
mini-rolling
pin with
your bead
and a large
gauge craft
wire.

4. **Mist a clean rubber stamp lightly with water. Hold both ends of the wire, and using the bead as sort of a mini-rolling pin, roll the bead gently over the rubber stamp to create the impression, as pictured in Figure 12-12.**

Figure 12-12:
Roll the
uncured
bead over
the rubber
stamp to
create an
impression.

Materials and vital statistics

✔ **Materials:**

- 1 ounce Sculpey III polymer clay Pottery #1655
- Acrylic craft paint, black
- Polymer clay glaze
- Parchment paper
- 18 11mm black faceted bicone glass beads

✔ **Findings:**

- 2 silver crimp beads

- 1 silver toggle and bar clasp

- 24 inches of 0.014-inch diameter black-coated stainless steel beading wire

✔ **Tools:** Bead roller with an 8x16mm oval channel, textured clay rubber stamp sheet (We used Circles & Spirals by Sculpey), bamboo skewer, polyester quilt batting, accordion-folded file folder baking rack, baking sheet exclusively for polymer clay, paper towels, paintbrush, spare craft wire, chain-nose pliers, crimping pliers

✔ **Techniques used:** Stamping flat components, rolling clay beads, stamping clay beads, baking clay, tying knots, wire wrapping

You make all the components for this necklace by hand, so the project does take some time. Work through the steps, though, and you'll get a huge payoff in this unique necklace.

Directions

1. **Condition the clay by working it with your hands until it's warmed up and pliable. Using the bead roller, create 16 8x16mm oval beads.**

If you need help using the bead roller, check out the "New skill: Using a bead roller" section earlier in this chapter.

Although you need only 16 beads to complete the necklace, we suggest that you make a few extras so you have some spares. This way, if a few don't turn out the way you want (or one breaks), you don't have to start all over to make one or two beads.

2. **Gently slide a bead onto a piece of large gauge wire. Select a section of the textured sheet that will fit on your bead. Roll the bead over the textured sheet to create the impression.**

Take a look at the section "New skill: Creating rubber stamp impressions on beads" earlier in this chapter for details on completing this step.

3. **Remove the bead gently from the wire, being careful not to distort the bead or the stamped impression. Lay the stamped bead in a channel in an accordion-folded bead rack, as shown Figure 12-13.**

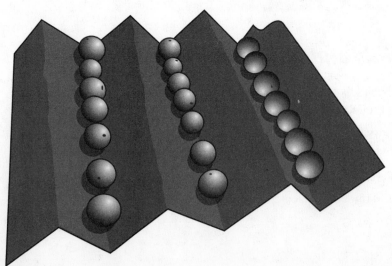

Figure 12-13:
Accordion fold a recycled file folder to make a baking rack for your beads.

4. Repeat Steps 2 and 3 until you have a total of 16 beads (or a few more if you want to have some extras just in case something happens to one of the beads).

5. Preheat the oven to 275°F.

6. Roll the remaining clay to ⅛ inch thickness. Select a larger section of the textured stamp that appeals to you for the coordinating pendant. Use the image to create an impression in the clay, like the one we made in Figure 12-14.

   If you need help stamping the image, check out the section "New skill: Creating rubber stamp impressions on flat polymer clay components" earlier in this chapter.

Figure 12-14:
Press the textured sheet into the flattened clay to make an impression for the pendant.

7. Using a clay-working tool or bamboo skewer, cut out the stamped image. (We made ours roughly 3-x-2 inches.) Use a bamboo skewer to pierce a hole for hanging the pendant. Use your fingers to smooth any rough edges on the pendant, so it looks like the one in Figure 12-15. Place the pendant on a piece of polyester quilt batting on a cookie sheet.

Figure 12-15:
Cut out the impression and gently smooth the edges of the clay.

8. Bake the beads and pendant at 275°F for 25 minutes. Allow the components to cool completely.

9. Using a paper towel, dab black paint onto the beads and pendant. Rub the paint into the impressions, removing excess paint as you go, as shown in Figure 12-16. Allow the paint to dry completely.

   The paint stays in the indentations in the impressions to highlight the design.

Figure 12-16: Rub black paint into the impression to highlight the pattern.

10. Apply polymer clay glaze to the beads and pendant. Allow them to dry, preferably overnight, before continuing with the next step.

> To speed along the glazing and drying process, coauthor Heather strings her beads on a piece of spare craft wire after they're painted, but before they're glazed. Then she hangs the strand and glazes the beads. This way, she can glaze the entire bead at once (rather than glazing one side, waiting for it to dry, turning it over, glazing the other side, and waiting for it to dry). It saves her half the wait time.

11. Feed both ends of the tail of the beading wire through the hole in the pendant from the back to the front. Tie a lark's head knot to the secure the pendant to the wire.

> Take a look at the appendix for information on tying knots.

12. String the beads on one length of the wire in this order: glass, clay. Repeat seven times (for a total of eight pairs). Top off the strand with another glass bead.

13. String on one crimp bead. Slide on the connector loop of one side of the toggle clasp. Feed the tail back down through the crimp bead, and down through several other beads. Using the chain-nose pliers, pull the wire taut. Crimp the bead into place with the crimping pliers. Trim the excess wire with the wire cutters.

> Go to Chapter 2 for more information on crimping.

14. Repeat Steps 12 and 13 to complete the necklace.

Faux Jade Maori Twist Necklace

The Maori are people indigenous to New Zealand. They have a long history in creating beautiful carved masterpieces from bone, stone, and other materials. We created this necklace in Figure 12-17 as an homage to the traditional images they use to celebrate life. This symbol, called Double Twist, crisscrosses to represent two people following the many paths of life and love. They may move apart throughout life, but they always come back together, blending to become one.

New skill: Making faux jade with polymer clay

Even though clay comes in so many colors, you may find that you want to create your own custom colors for the ultimate in unique, handcrafted jewelry. Making your own "gemstones" is one of those times. Clay is a terrific medium to use to make imitation stones like jade or rose quartz. (For more information on rose quartz, check out the section "New skill: Making faux rose quartz clay" later in this chapter.)

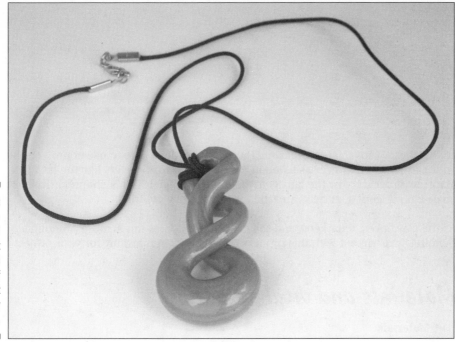

Figure 12-17:
This Maori-inspired pendant represents one of the oldest eternity symbols.

To make jade from polymer clay, follow these steps:

1. **Pinch off a ¾-inch ball of translucent clay from a 2-ounce package. Separately condition this clay, a ¼-inch ball of green clay, a ¼-inch ball of gold metallic clay, and a ⅛-inch ball of bright yellow clay. Then thoroughly combine the colors. Divide the mixture into small, medium, and large balls. Set aside.**

2. **Condition the remainder of a 2-ounce package of translucent clay. Divide it into three equally sized pieces.**

3. **Combine one green ball with one translucent ball. Thoroughly combine the colors. Repeat with the remaining green and translucent balls.**

   The color differences between these mixtures shouldn't seem drastic. This step creates a subtle marbling effect in the finished pieces.

4. **Roll each mixture into a snake. Stack the snakes together in a pyramid, as shown in Figure 12-18.**

Figure 12-18:
Stack snakes of varying shades together.

5. **Twist the snakes together to begin mixing the colors, as shown in Figure 12-19. Mix as much or as little until your clay looks as marbled as you want it.**

   If you're looking to create jade that looks more aged, you can mix in some black embossing powder at this stage.

Figure 12-19:
Twist the snakes together to blend the colors.

Follow these steps to create *uncured* (not yet hard) faux jade to use in projects. Shape your clay as you like it (or as listed in the directions for projects like the faux jade Maori twist necklace or the faux gemstone bracelet later in this chapter). To finish the piece bake it, cool it, glaze it, and then allow it to dry overnight.

As the clay bakes, it darkens, and the marbling becomes much more pronounced. Definitely experiment with this process to get the right marbling for your project.

Materials and vital statistics

✔ **Materials:**

- ½ ounce uncured faux jade polymer clay (See the section "New skill: Making faux jade with polymer clay" earlier in this chapter for instructions on making this)

- Polymer clay glaze

✔ **Findings:**

- 26 inches of 1mm black silk pendant cord

- 1 gold lobster clasp with tab and jump rings attached

- 2 gold cord ends

✔ **Tools:** Polyester quilt batting, baking sheet exclusively for polymer clay, paintbrush, round-nose pliers, chain-nose pliers, wire cutters

✔ **Techniques used:** Working with clay, stringing

These instructions make enough clay to make the pendant in this project plus the beads you need for the faux gemstone bracelet later in this chapter.

Directions

1. **Preheat the oven to the temperature specified by the clay manufacturer, typically 275°F or 300°F.**

2. **Condition the clay by working it with your hands until it's warmed up and pliable. Roll it into a thick snake, roughly 1 inch in diameter, as shown in Figure 12-20.**

Figure 12-20:
Make a fat
clay snake.

3. **Begin to work the snake, so it tapers drastically on the ends but remains fat in the center.**

It should look like the snake ate a big lunch that lodged right in the middle of his belly. Check out Figure 12-21 for an example.

Figure 12-21:
Morph your
fat snake
into a skinny
snake that
ate a big
lunch.

TIP

To get the drastic but smooth difference in diameter for this snake, coauthor Heather makes a "V" with her index and middle fingers about ¾ inch apart. She places her fingers on the center of the snake and starts rolling. As she rolls the snake, she gently spreads her fingers apart as wide as she can, gently applying pressure to taper the snake as she goes. Eventually, as the snake lengthens, she has to use both hands to keep tapering.

4. **Cross the left end of the snake over the right one. Make sure the fattest part of the snake is situated in the bottom curve, as shown in Figure 12-22.**

Figure 12-22:
Fold the left
tail over the
right one to
form the
bottom loop
of the
pendant.

5. **Continue the twist, so the top end wraps under the bottom one, making a figure eight, as shown in Figure 12-23a.**

6. **Create one more smaller loop at the top, and connect the ends of the clay, as shown in Figure 12-23b.**

Figure 12-23:
Continue
the twist
to make
a figure
eight and
make one
more loop
at the top.

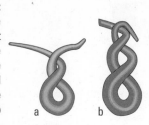

a   b

7. **Gently use your fingers to smooth out the seam where you connected the pieces. If you need to, use the end of a paintbrush, pencil, or other round object to round out the top loop after the seam is gone.**

    This loop is the bail for the pendant, so make sure it's large enough to hold the stringing material you choose.

    You can use a paintbrush with a dab of water to help smooth this seam out, as pictured in Figure 12-24.

Figure 12-24:
Use a damp
paintbrush
to help
smooth out
any seams.

8. **Place the pendant on the quilt batting. Bake the pendant in a preheated oven for the specified time for a ½-inch piece.**

    Heather baked hers at 275°F for 30 minutes.

    Baking the pendant on the batting keeps the round parts round without developing flat shiny spots.

9. **Allow the pendant to cool completely. Apply the glaze to give the piece the shine of natural jade. Let it dry completely, overnight if possible.**

10. **Wrap the bead cord through the top hole of the pendant three or four times. Insert the cord into the two cord end findings, and using your chain-nose pliers, flatten the cord ends.**

11. **Use the chain-nose pliers to open the jump ring connected to the clasp. Slide on the loop of one of the cord ends. Close the jump ring. Repeat with the other half of the clasp and the remaining cord end.**

Faux Gemstone Bracelet

Create chunky jade and rose quartz round beads from polymer clay to make this classic preppy stretch bracelet, shown in Figure 12-25. Alternating colors of uniformly sized beads are a great way to show off your style.

Figure 12-25:
Make this double-strand stretch bracelet with your own custom clay beads.

New skill: Making faux rose quartz clay

Creating rose quartz from polymer clay is similar to making faux jade, but the process involves a few extra steps to give the quartz its shimmering, veined appearance.

To make pink quartz from polymer clay, follow these steps:

1. **Condition 2 ounces of translucent polymer clay by working it with your hands until it's warmed up and pliable. Flatten the clay into a pancake and drop on a ¼-inch-wide ball of conditioned red clay, as shown in Figure 12-26.**

Figure 12-26:
Add a bit of red clay to the translucent clay.

2. **Twist, knead, and roll the clays together until the colors are fairly well blended but you can still see some color distinctions. Add ⅛ teaspoon of silver embossing powder, as shown in Figure 12-27, to create the shimmer.**

3. **Continue kneading the clay, dispersing the powder throughout the mixture to complete the color.**

Let this clay rest 7 to 8 minutes before using it. The clay is extremely pliable, almost sticky, after so much kneading. It holds its shape much better if you let it set for a bit.

Figure 12-27:
Use silver embossing powder to add shimmer in the finished stone.

4. **Shape the clay into the desired shapes, beads, or components. Bake the required time, depending on the clay used and thickness of the shapes.**

   Most clays cure at around 275°F for 15 minutes per ¼ inch of thickness.

   This clay darkens quite a bit during the *curing,* or hardening, in the oven, so don't be shocked when you take it out of the oven. It starts out almost a soft ballet pink and then works its way up to a light translucent salmon.

5. **Remove the cured pieces from the oven, and immediately immerse them in ice water. Allow them to cool in the water for a few minutes.**

   This step gives the beads the uneven pebbling of real stone.

6. **Remove the pieces from the water and allow them to dry completely. After the pieces are dry, paint them with a high-gloss glaze designed for polymer clay to give them a polished stone-like finish. Allow the glaze to dry completely, preferably overnight, before using the clay pieces.**

These instructions make enough clay to make about 60 11mm round beads. Follow the steps under the section "New Skill: Using a bead roller" earlier in this chapter to turn this clay into gorgeous beads.

Materials and vital statistics

✔ **Materials:**

- 1 ounce uncured faux jade clay (See the section "New skill: Making faux jade with polymer clay" earlier in this chapter for instructions)

- 1 ounce uncured faux rose quartz clay (See the section "New skill: Making faux rose quartz clay" earlier in this chapter to create this)

✔ **Findings:** 2 12-inch strands of 0.5mm diameter clear stretchy bead cord

✔ **Tools:** Bead roller with channel to create 11mm round beads, 3 inches of 20-gauge craft wire, accordion-folded file folder baking rack, baking sheet exclusively for polymer clay, paintbrush, scissors, glue

✔ **Techniques used:** Rolling clay beads, baking clay, using stretchy cord, knotting

This bracelet is a great project to hone your bead-making skills. After rolling nearly 40 beads (more if you make some spares), you'll be a round bead expert.

Directions

1. Condition the jade clay. Using the bead roller, create 18 11mm round beads.

If you need details on rolling clay beads, take a look at the section "New skill: Using a bead roller" earlier in this chapter. Set the rolled beads aside.

It's a good idea to make several spare beads just in case some don't turn out the way you'd like.

2. Repeat Step 1, this time making 18 11mm beads with the rose quartz clay.

3. Preheat the oven to the temperature specified by the clay manufacturer, typically 275°F or 300°F.

4. Using the craft wire, gently pierce holes in the beads. Place the file folder baking rack on a cookie sheet, and place the pierced beads in the channels of the baking rack.

5. Bake the beads in a preheated oven for 20 minutes. Remove the beads from the oven. Immediately place the rose quartz beads in a bowl of ice water to cool for several minutes. Remove the beads from the bath and allow them to dry thoroughly before moving to Step 6.

This step helps the finished beads look more like the real stone.

6. Apply polymer clay glaze to the beads. Allow the glaze to dry completely, overnight if possible.

7. String the beads on one piece of stretchy cord in this pattern: pink, green. Repeat the pattern eight more times, using 18 beads total.

8. Holding both strands together, tie an overhand knot, pulling the cord taut as you go. Apply glue to the knot.

If you need help tying this knot, check out the appendix.

9. Repeat Steps 7 and 8 with the remaining strand of stretchy cord and beads. Let the knot dry 10 minutes or so before moving to the next step.

10. Tie the tails from both bracelets together, using a double overhand knot to connect them. Apply glue to the knot, and allow it to dry thoroughly. Then trim the tails.

Part IV
Mixing It Up: Incorporating Multiple Techniques and Materials

The 5th Wave   By Rich Tennant

"You're right — I probably <u>will</u> be the only one on the dirt track circuit to own a beaded carburetor cozy."

In this part . . .

Think of this part as sort of the "nontraditional projects" part. In one chapter, we take standard jewelry and beading techniques and make non-jewelry accessories with them. String and wire wrap a pair of sparkling flip-flops, or crimp and string your own decorative ornaments. This chapter is really just a starting point, to help you think of ways to beautify your life (or home, bedroom, or, um, feet) with beads in ways you may not have thought of.

The second chapter in this part is dedicated to making jewelry with nontraditional materials, using traditional techniques. We incorporate a glass tag into a whimsical necklace and turn felt into a funky flower pin. We also help you figure out what to do with leftover items, like those darn orphan earrings (earrings that have lost their twin). Soon you'll start seeing jewelry pieces that may be lying in a desk drawer or in the workshop.

Chapter 13

Creating Non-Jewelry Beading Projects

· ·

In This Chapter

▶ Creating sparkling ornaments and fan pulls

▶ Embellishing flip-flops for every outfit

· ·

*B*eading isn't just for jewelry. You can apply beading and jewelry-making techniques, like wire wrapping and crimping, to all sorts of home accents to jazz up any room of the house. You can also create non-jewelry accessories, like the awesome flip-flops in this chapter. Start looking around your home for other items that need a little customization, and you're sure to find a use for your quickly improving beading skills.

Swarovski Crystal Snowflake Ornament

You already know that wire-wrapping skills allow you to create beautiful custom jewelry. But they also come in handy to create custom decorations and ornaments for your home. This ornament, shown in Figure 13-1, is made of beautiful, shimmery Swarovski crystals and sterling silver wire. Create one for every window and hang them at different lengths to dress up your home for the holiday season.

Figure 13-1: Create these custom pendants in a few easy steps.

Materials and vital statistics

✔ **Beads:**

- 36 3mm Swarovski crystal AB bicones
- 12 6mm Swarovski crystal AB bicones
- 18 4mm Swarovski crystal Montana AB rounds

✔ **Findings:**

- 3 4½-inch pieces of 22-gauge sterling silver wire
- Hanging material of your choice

✔ **Tools:** Round-nose pliers, wire cutters, chain-nose pliers (optional)

✔ **Techniques used:** Stringing, making eye loops

You can create these versatile ornaments in a variety of colors. They take about half an hour each, so you can decorate your whole house in no time.

Directions

1. **Holding the three pieces of wire together in the middle, spread the ends out like the spokes of a wheel. Bend the wires around each other, connecting them in the middle, so they resemble Figure 13-2a.**

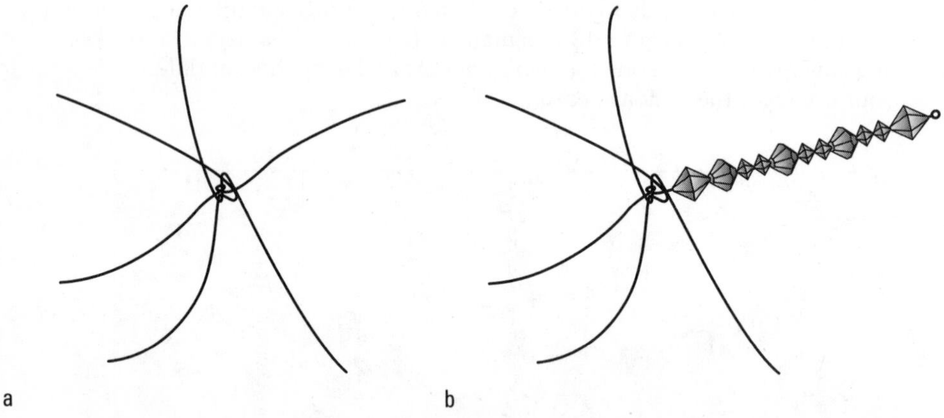

Figure 13-2:
Wrap your
wires
so they
resemble
the spokes
of a wheel.

a   b

Your spokes may feel a little flimsy at this point. That's okay. Feel free to use the chain-nose pliers to mash and press the center where the wires meet to make the ornament a bit sturdier.

2. **String beads on one spoke in this order: 1 large crystal bicone, 1 Montana round, 2 small crystal bicones, 1 Montana round, 2 small crystal bicones, 1 Montana round, 2 small crystal bicones, 1 large crystal bicone.**

3. **Using your round-nose pliers, make a loop at the end of the wire to secure the beads in place. If you need to, trim any excess wire with the wire cutters.**

Your spoke should look like the one in Figure 13-2b.

4. **Repeat Steps 2 and 3 to use all the beads and wire.**

5. **Hang your ornament from a ribbon, a piece of yarn, or whatever stringing material works for you to decorate your windows or holiday tree.**

Cosmic Crystal Beaded Fan Pull

Tired of standing on your bed or a chair to adjust the speed of your ceiling fan? Customize your own fan pull and make it whatever length you need to fit your room. You use a chandelier earring finding as the base for this cosmic crystal fan pull, shown in Figure 13-3, stringing up several inches of sparkling crystals.

Figure 13-3:
Pink and purple crystals give this fan pull a hip, sparkly look.

Materials and vital statistics

✔ **Beads:**

- 1 6mm Swarovski light rose bicone
- 11 6mm Swarovski crystal AB bicones
- 2 6mm Swarovski light amethyst bicones
- 6 6mm Swarovski amethyst bicones
- 2 6mm Swarovski crystal AB cubes
- 1 20mm Swarovski Violet Cosmic freeform faceted diamond pendant
- 2 12x7mm faceted crystal teardrops, top drilled

✔ **Findings:**

- 1 silver chandelier earring finding with a large top hole
- 6 silver crimp tubes
- 3 4-inch pieces of 0.014-inch diameter silver stainless steel beading wire
- 10 inches of ball chain

✔ **Tools:** Crimping pliers, chain-nose pliers, wire cutters

✔ **Techniques used:** Stringing, making eye loops

Use your earring-making and crimping skills to create this sparkling room accessory. If the bead colors we chose don't match your décor, feel free to pick ones that better coordinate with your room.

Directions

1. **Slide one crimp tube onto one piece of beading wire. Follow it with the violet pendant. Slip the tail of the wire back down through the crimp bead. Using the crimping pliers, crimp the bead into place using the two-phase crimp method. (For more on crimping, see Chapter 2.)**

This strand creates the center dangle and focal point for your fan pull.

2. **String the following bicone beads onto the open end of the wire, covering the tail near the crimped end as you go: 1 crystal AB bicone, 1 amethyst, 2 crystal AB bicones, 1 amethyst, 1 crystal AB bicone, 1 light rose, 1 crystal AB bicone.**

3. **Slide on a crimp tube. Loop the tail of the beading wire through the middle loop of the bottom of the chandelier finding. Feed the tail down through the crimp tube and a few crystals. Using the chain-nose pliers, pull the wire taut. Secure the crimp bead with the crimping pliers. Trim away any excess wire with the wire cutters, or tuck it down through the other crystal.**

Check out Figure 4-3 in Chapter 4 for help with pulling the wire taut before crimping, and then cutting the wire flush and creating a professional finish to your crimped strands.

4. **Repeat Step 1, using a faceted teardrop instead of the violet pendant.**

Make sure you don't pull the wire really tight before crimping your teardrop. You need to allow enough room for the point of the teardrop to swing freely.

5. **Slide on crystals in this order: 1 amethyst bicone, 1 crystal AB cube, 1 crystal AB bicone, 1 light amethyst bicone, 1 crystal AB bicone, 1 amethyst bicone, 1 crystal AB bicone.**

6. **Repeat Step 3, attaching this strand to one of the outside bottom loops of the chandelier finding.**

7. **Repeat Steps 4 through 6 to complete the final strand.**

For best results, before crimping your last strand to the chandelier finding in Step 6, do your best to make sure the two outside strands are roughly the same length. After you feed the tail back through the crimp bead and a couple of crystals, hold the tail with the chain-nose pliers to adjust the length of the strand before crimping it into place.

8. **Attach the ball chain through the top loop of the chandelier finding. Use your chain nose pliers to give it a gentle squeeze to push the ball through the hole. Using the wire cutters, you can cut the ball chain to the desired length.**

Preppy Beaded Flip-Flops

Flip-flops aren't just for the beach these days. Beads, sequins, and feathers can adorn these simple shoes to make them something special. These fun beaded flip-flops, pictured in Figure 13-4, have become a year-round staple in coauthor Heather's wardrobe since she moved to the warm and sunny Southeast last year. This particular color combination (hot pink and lime green) is classic, straight out of the preppy handbook.

Figure 13-4:
Creating these one-of-a-kind flip-flops is easy, and just takes a little perseverance.

Materials and vital statistics

- ✔ **Beads:** 50 grams of seed and bugle beads in assorted pinks
- ✔ **Findings:**

    - Approximately 5 yards of 28-gauge gold beading wire
    - ½-inch wide Art Accentz Terrifically Tacky embellishment tape

        This tape is a specially designed double-sided tape. In our experience, it works better with beads than other tape does. Initially, it's fairly sticky, but overnight, the bond becomes stronger as the adhesive cures. Look for it at craft stores.

- ✔ **Other:** Lime green flip-flops
- ✔ **Tools:** Scissors
- ✔ **Techniques used:** Stringing, using double-sided tape

This project takes some time, roughly three or four hours, so settle in and get ready to wrap your flip-flops. If you need to break this project into shorter segments, you can, but remember to tape only what you can wrap in a single sitting.

Directions

1. **Cut the double-sided tape with scissors to fit one half of the toe strap of one of the flip-flops, as shown in Figure 13-5.**

    The tape is double sided. It has a red-tinted protective film on one side of the tape to keep it from sticking to itself. Trim and adjust the tape and set it into place before you remove the protective film.

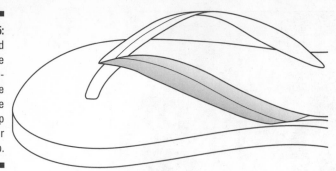

Figure 13-5:
Adjust and trim the double-sided tape to fit half the toe strap on your flip-flop.

2. Remove the protective film to reveal the second sticky side.

3. Using the scissors, cut a roughly 2-foot length of wire. Imagine the whole toe strap to be a "V," with the top of the "V" about midway between the heel and toe of the flip-flop, and the point of the "V" as the toe divider. Measuring from the top of the "V," place about an inch of the wire on the tape, pointing toward the point of the "V." Wrap the long end of the wire around the toe strap to secure the end of the wire in place.

4. String on ½ inch of beads, roughly 3 or 4 depending on the size. Slide the beads together, leaving no gaps. Adjust them so they fit across the width of the top of the toe strap, flat and flush. Situate the beads on the toe strap close to the edge, covering the tail. Wrap the wire around the underside of the toe strap.

5. Repeat Step 4, lining up the newly strung beads with the previous row.

As you bead up the toe strap, press the strung beads into contact with the tape.

6. Continue stringing beads on top of the toe strap, wrapping empty wire on only the underside of the toe strap. When you have approximately 6 inches of wire left, cut a new 2-foot piece of wire. Tuck one end of the new wire under the rows of already strung beads, as shown in Figure 13-6.

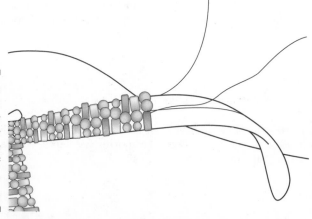

Figure 13-6:
Tuck the tail of the new wire under the last few rows of beads to secure it.

7. Continue wrapping the first piece of wire, covering the tail of the second piece of wire, until only an inch or so of the first piece remains. Press the tail down onto the tape. Pick up the second piece of wire and begin stringing beads as described in Step 4, covering the tail of the first piece as you go, as shown in Figure 13-7.

After you cover the tail, press the beaded rows down firmly to get good contact with the adhesive on the tape.

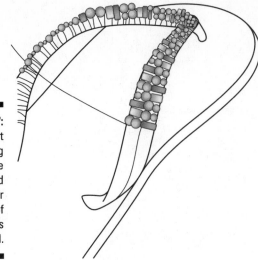

Figure 13-7:
Start beading with the new strand and cover the tail of the previous strand.

8. **After you've completely beaded the first half of the toe strap, cover the other half of the toe strap with tape, as described in Steps 1 and 2.**

   For best results, don't end or begin using a piece of wire around the toe divider (or point of the "V"). Cut a piece that's long enough to allow you to seamlessly move from one side of the divider to the other.

9. **Continue beading the other half of the toe strap until you've completely covered the toe strap. When you come to the end of the toe strap, wrap the tail of the wire around the beaded strands several times, tucking it between beads as necessary. Snip the end with scissors. Press the beads and wire firmly onto the adhesive to get a strong bond.**

10. **Repeat Steps 1 through 9 to embellish the second flip-flop. Allow the flip-flops to sit for 24 hours if possible to create the strongest bond.**

Chapter 14

Using Nontraditional Materials

Most of the projects in this book focus on jewelry making using traditional materials such as beads and wire. Of course, there isn't anything wrong with that. In fact, beads and wire are some of the most versatile materials for jewelry making. You just can't go wrong using them. However, for those who are ready to spread their jewelry-making wings and think outside the jewelry box, you can experiment with all kinds of possibilities to create jewelry with that little something extra. You can choose from nontraditional materials such as buttons, hardware, office supplies, fiber, glass, and more for your jewelry construction.

In this chapter, you use some basic jewelry fundamentals and techniques and combine them with traditional and nontraditional supplies to fashion fun jewelry designs. Though the materials and designs may be a little off-the-wall, many of the techniques stay true to what you've already mastered, including wire-wrapping and bead-stringing methods. If you're a little unsure of where to find some of the unusual materials used in the projects in this chapter, flip over to Chapter 16 for some excellent tips on locating offbeat materials.

Materials aren't the only nontraditional elements in this chapter. Along with a mixture of materials — often referred to as *mixed media* — you also make pieces that have a mixture of uses, such as adorning a laptop case, dangling from a purse strap, or jazzing up a humdrum ID badge. No law says that jewelry is only to be worn on your body. Jewelry is a wonderful accessory that can add a fashion statement to items normally considered as primarily utilitarian. You can be both functional and fashionable at the same time.

Felt Flower Pin

Felt is a fun fiber to incorporate into your jewelry designs, and this pin (see Figure 14-1) is one of those no-brainer projects that you can make in only a few minutes. The longest part of the entire process is waiting for the glue to dry. Add one to the lapel of your overcoat or blazer; attach one to your favorite hat to give it an updated look; or pin it onto the handle of your purse. Flowers are forever "in" as fashion statements. You can buy these felt flowers, available in a variety of colors, from vendors, such as Ornametea (www.ornamentea.com), that specialize in mixed-media supplies and fiber supplies. Buy them by the dozen because you'll want to make a lot of these.

For this project, we use glue to attach the pin back to the felt flower. However, if you think you may want to use the flower for something else later on, try using a needle and thread instead of glue. Sew the flower onto the pin back, and you can simply cut the threads off later. You'll have your felt flower to do with as you please.

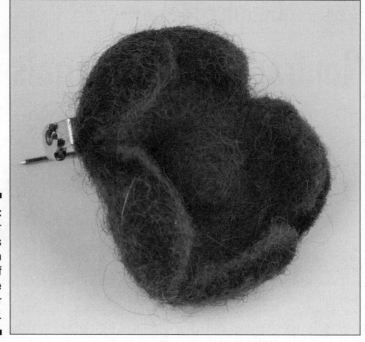

Figure 14-1:
A felt flower pin looks snazzy on the lapel of your favorite coat or blazer.

Materials and vital statistics

- ✔ **Other:** 1 felt flower, tacky glue
- ✔ **Findings:** 1 pin back
- ✔ **Techniques used:** Attaching with glue

Tacky glue is a very versatile type of glue because you can use it with all kinds of materials, such as metal, fabric, wood, and more. It's inexpensive as well, so any crafter or jewelry maker should be sure to have a bottle of this on hand at all times. Just about any craft store carries tacky glue, so check for it on the glue and adhesive aisle.

Don't blink or you'll miss how supereasy this flower pin is to make. It'll probably take you longer to read the instructions than to actually make the pin.

Directions

1. **Using the pointed applicator at the top of the glue bottle, squeeze some tacky glue onto the metal part of the pin back.**

See Figure 14-2 to see what the pin back looks like before it's attached to the flower.

Figure 14-2:
The pin back is made of base metal.

2. **Press the pin back up against the top, back part of the felt flower.**

3. **Allow the glue to dry according to the manufacturer's directions.**

   If you live in a humid climate, you may want to let it dry overnight.

Mixed-Up Charm Bracelet

The eye loop technique is perfect for finishing off the ends of this memory wire bracelet (pictured in Figure 14-3). Plus the eye loops provide a few spots to add some cool dangle elements. The rest of the bracelet is a hodgepodge of mixed materials, including all kinds of stone beads, metal beads, glass beads, and charms. The result is a memory wire bracelet that goes with just about everything you wear. These also make great gifts because memory wire is a one-size-fits-all material.

Figure 14-3:
This memory wire bracelet has everything on it but the kitchen sink.

If you pull on memory wire too much while working with it, you'll stretch it out, and after it's stretched out, it won't go back to its original size. As long as you don't over-work the wire by pulling on it as you string the beads, you'll be fine.

Materials and vital statistics

✔ **Beads:**

- 16 inches of temporarily strung 10mm multistone beads
- Miscellaneous crystal, glass, and metal beads

✔ **Findings:**

- 4 to 6 charms with attached jump rings

- 6 silver-plated bell dangles

- 2 head pins

✔ **Tools:** Memory wire shears, round-nose pliers, chain-nose pliers, wire cutters

✔ **Techniques used:** Creating eye loops and wrapped loops, stringing

You can damage your wire cutters if you use them to cut memory wire. Either use shears made for cutting memory wire or a heavy-duty pair of wire cutters that you don't normally use for your silver or gold-filled wire. If you plan to use a lot of memory wire in your jewelry work, it's worth the cost to purchase shears. They make cutting the wire supereasy on your hands, and you'll save your cutters from possible permanent damage.

You can't go wrong when making this bracelet because there's really no set pattern for the beadwork. Just turn off the symmetrical side of your brain and mix up the design as much as possible. The more you mix, the better it will look.

Directions

1. Using memory wire shears, cut about 3 loops of memory wire bracelet.

2. Make an eye loop on one end of the memory wire using the round-nose pliers, as illustrated in Figure 14-4.

Memory wire can be difficult to work with, so if your loop is difficult to close, use the chain-nose pliers to close it up some more.

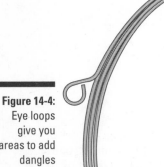

Figure 14-4:
Eye loops give you areas to add dangles later.

3. In no particular order, start stringing away with stone, glass, crystal, and metal beads, bells (stringing two together so they hit against each other), and charms.

4. When you've added as many beads and charms as you'd like, finish the other end of the memory wire with another eye loop, just like you did in Step 2.

5. To finish off the bracelet, take two head pins and two beads of your choice, and using the wrapped loop technique (see Chapter 2), make two dangles as shown in Figure 14-5. Add these to each end of your bracelet. Cut off the excess head pins as necessary using the wire cutters.

Figure 14-5:
Make
dangles for
each end of
the bracelet.

Variation: Mixed-up charm necklace

Use the same idea with this mixed-up charm necklace as you did with the memory
wire bracelet — mix, mix, mix it up. Instead of using memory wire that is bracelet size,
just switch to the size used for necklaces. This size wraps around your neck and creates a choker look for the necklace, but you don't need any clasp. You'll also need lots
more beads and charms to fill it up, but otherwise, the methodology and techniques
are the same as making the bracelet — same techniques, just a different size.

Variation: Mixed-up charm ring

You'll need to scale down the size of your beads and charms for this ring project, but
just like the mixed-up charm bracelet and necklace, you do the same thing: Use an
eclectic assortment of beads and charms, and thread them onto ring-size memory
wire. Look for small beads that are no larger than 4mm and lots of small charms and
dangles. Wear this as a ring, or make an assortment of them and use them as fun accessories for your wine glasses.

Orphan Earring Charm Bracelet

Don't you just hate it when you lose an earring? Bummer! But hey, maybe not. In fact,
you may start looking for orphan earrings to adopt after you use this simple charm
bracelet method to create one-of-a-kind jewelry. But you don't have to stick with
single earrings.

For this project (pictured in Figure 14-6), coauthor Tammy used old clip-on earrings
and cut off the screw parts to make them into earring charms. Some earrings she only
had one of, and some she had pairs of, but either way, they aren't exactly her style,
unless she finds a time machine and goes back to the 1950s. She's collected most of
them over the years, stumbling upon one here or there. A few of them came from her
mother and grandmother, so now Tammy can wear these little jewelry memories, but
instead of torturing her ears with their screw-back earring designs, she can dangle
them from her wrist.

Figure 14-6:
This charm bracelet is made up of old rhinestone clip-on earrings and crystal dangles.

Check out thrift stores and flea markets for rhinestone clip-on earrings. They're perfect for recycling into charms. Also let friends and family know that you're on the lookout for old screw-on earrings, and ask them to save them for you if they ever decide to clean out a basement for that all-important garage sale.

Materials and vital statistics

- ✔ **Beads:** 9 4mm fire-polished AB red crystal beads
- ✔ **Findings:**
  - • 1 7-inch link chain with connected clasp
  - • 9 1-inch pieces of 21-gauge half-hard silver wire
  - • 8 5mm jump rings
- ✔ **Other:** 8 clip-on earrings
- ✔ **Tools:** Heavy-duty wire cutters, round-nose pliers, chain-nose pliers
- ✔ **Techniques used:** Creating eye loops and "S" scrolls

Some of the screw posts on the earrings may be difficult to cut off with your average pair of wire cutters. Be careful not to damage the cutters you normally use for your precious metal wire. It's better to use an old heavy-duty pair of cutters for this sort of thing. Check in your garage for some old cutters that your better half uses for fishing. No one will even know you used them, and you can tuck them back into the tackle box before anyone's the wiser.

Although this project uses eight old earrings and nine crystal beads, you can add as many as you like. You may even want to use up some of your leftover crystal beads for this bracelet design.

Directions

1. Start by using the heavy-duty wire cutters to cut off the screw part of the earrings, making sure to leave as much of the metal part that's attached to the screws (the *shank*) as you can.

2. Use the round-nose pliers to curl the shank into an eye loop. Then use the chain-nose pliers to attach a jump ring to the loop as shown in Figure 14-7.

Don't worry about closing up the rings just yet. You'll see why pretty soon. Repeat this step for each earring.

Figure 14-7: Curl the back shank of each earring and attach a jump ring.

3. Set out the chain and determine where you'll attach each earring onto the chain.

You may want to move these around until you get the configuration you want (see Figure 14-8 for an example).

Figure 14-8: Move the earrings around to figure out where you plan to attach them.

4. Using the chain-nose pliers, open the jump rings as needed, attach the jump rings of each earring to a link in the chain, and then make sure to close each jump ring up so it's securely attached to the chain link.

5. With about an inch of wire and the round-nose pliers, make half of an "S" scroll on the end of the wire, slip on a crystal bead, and make an eye loop at the top, as shown in Figure 14-9.

Repeat this step for all nine crystal beads.

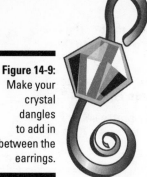

Figure 14-9:
Make your crystal dangles to add in between the earrings.

6. Finish your bracelet by using the chain-nose pliers to attach each crystal dangle made in Step 5 to links in between each earring.

Don't worry about counting links and being perfect. Just eyeball it because your earrings aren't all the same size.

Variation: Orphan earring pendant

Using the same techniques of eye loops and "S" scrolls, again connect a collection of earrings and crystal dangles to a 30mm jump ring that is soldered closed. Rings are very popular these days, so many jewelry vendors sell just rings, both soldered and unsoldered. The dangles and earrings will fall in the middle of the large ring, and there you go — a cool pendant. Add the pendant to a long ribbon or a sterling chain by inserting the ribbon or chain through the jump ring and securing the ends. What's nice about this pendant design is that you can switch out the chain or neck piece very easily and wear it a number of different ways.

Laptop Charms

Laptops are now part of many people's daily arsenal of technological toys that we must carry around. Students use them, and so do those who must bring work home from the office. But just because you have to lug around that laptop doesn't mean you can't do it in style. Simple bead-stringing techniques, like those used to make the laptop charm pictured in Figure 14-10, can make your laptop case a little more stylish and take some of the drudgery out of carrying your laptop around wherever you go. After you see how this is done, you may have one of those "Duh, why didn't I think of that" moments.

If you want to make a laptop wardrobe, consider making charms for major holidays like Valentine's Day, St. Patrick's Day, and so on. That way you have a theme to get you started. Also, if you have tough-to-buy-for techno-friends, a personalized laptop wardrobe is something they'll enjoy.

Figure 14-10:
A laptop charm gives your laptop case some instant style.

Materials and vital statistics

✔ **Beads:**

- 2 15mm pink lampwork heart beads
- 4 4mm red crystal beads
- 9 6mm clear AB crystal beads
- 10 6.5mm sterling daisy spacer beads

✔ **Findings:**

- 1 sterling heart toggle clasp
- 2 2x2mm crimp beads
- 8 inches of 0.014-inch diameter nylon-coated stainless steel beading wire

✔ **Tools:** Crimping pliers, wire cutters

✔ **Techniques used:** Creating crimps

If you're concerned about the strength of your crimps holding, flatten the crimp beads a little more with a pair of chain-nose pliers after using the crimping pliers to close them. Be careful not to break the beads that are right next to the crimp bead when you do this.

This laptop charm design is like creating a mini-bracelet for your laptop case. The completed charm should be about 5 inches long. To attach it to your laptop, just wrap it around one of the handles and secure the toggle clasp.

Directions

1. Insert the beading wire through a crimp bead and the loop on one side of the clasp, and use the crimping pliers to secure the crimp bead to the beading wire.

2. Thread your beads in the following order, making sure to cover the doubled-up portion of beading wire and ensuring that the hearts are oriented so the narrow ends point toward each other:

3 each of alternating clear crystals and daisy spacers

1 red crystal, 1 heart, and 1 red crystal

> 4 daisy spacers alternating with 3 clear crystals
>
> 1 red crystal, 1 heart, and 1 red crystal
>
> 3 each of alternating clear crystals and daisy spacers

3. **Repeat Step 1, but this time secure the other side of the toggle onto the end of the beading wire. Use the wire cutters to trim off the excess beading wire as needed.**

Variation: Purse charm

Using this same idea — meaning that you're basically making a mini-bracelet — instead of using bead-stringing techniques and beading wire, use 22-gauge gold-filled wire and 6mm purple crystals to make a bead-and-wire chain using the wrapped loop technique. With a jump ring, attach a butterfly charm to the end of the bead-and-wire chain at the same time that you attach the clasp.

Hardware Earrings

A trip to the hardware store doesn't have to be geared toward just those home-improvement projects. You can improve on your jewelry designing as well. Hardware takes on a new meaning when you team it up with wire-wrapping techniques and some colorful beads. These dangle earrings, pictured in Figure 14-11, combine simple metal washers with copper wire, stainless steel ear hooks, and ceramic beads for a fun and easy-to-make earring project. You can find washers at any hardware store, and you can find copper wire at most of them as well. The different colors of metal along with the colored beads make these whimsical earrings pop.

Figure 14-11:
Copper wire is supereasy to wrap around these washers.

The hardware store can be a great place to shop for inexpensive jewelry components. Look for items with holes so you can use those along with wire to connect to other components as well as beads.

Materials and vital statistics

- ✔ **Beads:** 2 5mm red-and-black ceramic beads
- ✔ **Findings:**
  - • 2 ear hooks, stainless steel
  - • 7 inches of 24-gauge copper wire

✔ **Other:** 2 ¾-inch metal washers

✔ **Tools:** Chain-nose pliers, wire cutters, round-nose pliers

✔ **Techniques used:** Creating a wrapped loop

Some metals, such as copper, darken over time. For some designs, this effect is nice and gives the piece a *patina* (a change in color). However, if you prefer to keep the copper bright, you can polish it with a polishing cloth, just like you would silver jewelry.

The wrapped loop technique comes through for you again in this fun earring design. If you need a refresher on the how-tos of this technique, flip back to Chapter 2.

Directions

1. **Insert about 3½ inches of wire through the hole in one of the washers, use the chain-nose pliers to bend the wire around the washer, and make a wrapped loop at the top of the washer as shown in Figure 14-12. Use the wire cutters to trim off the excess wire.**

Figure 14-12: Make the first wrapped loop to connect the wire to the washer.

2. **Insert one bead onto the wire, and make another wrapped loop above the bead using the chain-nose pliers and round-nose pliers, as shown in Figure 14-13. Trim off the excess wire with the wire cutters.**

3. **Use the chain-nose pliers to open the loop on an ear hook, slip the loop of the component you just made onto this loop, and close it with the chain-nose pliers.**

4. **Repeat Steps 1 through 3 to make the second earring.**

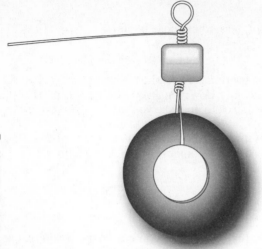

Figure 14-13:
Make a second wrapped loop so you can attach an ear hook.

Variation: O ring earrings

You can find O rings (also referred to as gaskets) in the plumbing section of hardware and home-improvement stores. They come in a lot of different sizes and a few different colors. For this project, you need two O rings, about the same diameter as a quarter, in your favorite color (though black is probably the easiest one to locate). Using your chain-nose pliers, open the loops on two ear hooks and slip an O ring onto each hook. Close the loops. Ta-da! You have some instant hoop earrings. Make an assortment of these earrings by using larger O rings in different colors.

Glass Tag Necklace

Glass tags are superpopular with the mixed-media crowd these days. Artists use these in altered books, as ornaments, for gift tags, as home décor items, in scrapbooks, to stamp on, and yes, of course, with jewelry making as well. The tags come in an array of colors (clear, yellow, blue, red, pink, orange, and green) as well as shapes (round, square, rectangular, and heart-shaped). Just think of these as little blank canvases of glass for you to decorate however you please.

This glass tag necklace, pictured in Figure 14-14, combines several crafting techniques, such as knotting, painting, and stamping. The mix of materials includes ribbon, paint, and glass. After you try out the techniques in this project, you'll probably come up with many more ways to use these glass tags in other jewelry designs. Smaller tags can be turned into earrings. Different types of stamps create a different jewelry theme. Change the color of the paint as well, and, well, you get the idea — experiment!

One technique you use in the project is *embossing,* which is related to stamping more so than jewelry making. This method allows the image you stamp to raise a little off the surface after the elements are heated. You'll need a few specialized materials and tools, including pigment ink (which dries slowly), embossing powder, and a heat gun. You've probably seen embossing done on paper, but it can be done on just about any surface, and in this project, you'll do it on glass.

You can buy glass tags through online stamping and scrapbook vendors, or look in the stamping or scrapbook aisles of your local craft store for them. They're pretty inexpensive — only a few dollars apiece — but you may want to try to purchase them by the dozen to get a price break.

Figure 14-14:
A glass tag becomes a miniature work of art.

Materials and vital statistics

✓ **Other:**

- 2-x-1½-inch yellow glass tag
- 30 inches of ¼ inch-wide rainbow ribbon
- Black pigment ink pad
- Clear embossing powder
- "Wish" stamp
- Water-based sealant
- Red and purple acrylic paint
- Scrap paper
- Cotton swab
- Paper towels

✓ **Tools:** Heat gun, small paint brush, foam brush, scissors

✓ **Techniques used:** Tying a lark's head knot, tying an overhand knot

It's important to seal the paint and pigment ink on the glass so it won't chip or get scratched off over time. Mod-Podge is a water-based sealant that is popular with crafters. If you've ever done any decoupage, you're probably familiar with this sealant.

Even if you've never done any rubber stamping before, you'll be able to handle this project. If your ink smears before you emboss it on the glass, just wipe it off with a wet paper towel and start over. You may want to practice your stamping on scrap paper before you tackle the glass.

Directions

1. **Press your stamp against the ink pad, and press the stamp onto the glass.**

Be sure to not rock the stamp but to just press down firmly and pull up. Otherwise, the ink may smear.

2. **Sprinkle embossing powder over the glass tag so you completely cover the word that you stamped in Step 1.**

   You may want to do this over a paper towel or piece of scrap paper because it's kind of messy.

   Though you don't have to emboss superquickly because the ink dries slowly, you also don't want to wait overnight or any extended length of time because the ink should be nice and wet when you begin to heat it up.

3. **Turn the glass tag over and dump the loose powder onto a piece of scrap paper.**

   You want to get as much of the powder off the pendant without smearing your stamped word. Tap the pendant to help get the excess powder off, and if necessary, use a cotton swab to remove the powder that's not part of the image.

4. **Return the powder on your scrap paper to the container of powder because it's reusable. Set the glass tag on top of the scrap paper.**

5. **Use the heat gun to heat-set the embossing powder onto the pigment ink.**

   Hold the heat gun a few inches away from the glass and move it in small circles as you heat up the embossing powder. Be careful not to touch the glass because it will get hot from the heat gun. When you see that the stamped word on the glass has risen, the embossing is complete.

6. **After the glass has cooled, use a small paint brush to paint a few simple flowers onto the glass.**

   Dip the tip of the paint brush into the red paint and make some long dabs onto the glass to make flower petals. Use the purple paint to finish the flowers with a dot in the middle of the petals. Allow the paint to dry before continuing.

7. **Using the foam brush and sealant, brush a few thin coats of the sealant over the glass.**

   Allow each coat to dry before adding the next one. Allow the last coat to dry completely before continuing. At this point, the glass tag pendant is finished.

8. **Fold the ribbon in half, insert the two ends of the ribbon through the hole at the top of the glass tag, and pull the doubled ribbon through the hole just a little bit.**

9. **Secure the ribbon onto the glass tag using a lark's head knot.**

   Take the two ends you pulled through the hole in Step 8, and insert them through the loop of ribbon you created by doubling it up. Pull the ends to tighten the knot around the tag.

10. **Take both ends of the ribbon and secure them using an overhand knot (see the appendix for instructions). With scissors, trim the ends of the ribbon so they're even.**

Red Crystal ID Badge Necklace

Identification badges, also known as ID badges, are part of our lives these days. Your badge usually is placed in some icky plastic cover, and that cover is attached to some other icky cord or chain. But enough is enough! It's time for an office revolt and for you to just say no to boring badges! There's no reason your ID badge can't be functional and fashionable at the same time. Use your bead crimping and stringing skills to make some fabulous badge lanyards that do double duty as necklaces outside of the office. Not only will you look and feel much better with your snazzed-up badge, but you'll be the envy of your entire office. Figure 14-15 shows the lanyard attached to an ID badge, but take off the badge, double up the lanyard, connect the lanyard to the jump ring, and you have a beautiful double-strand necklace.

Figure 14-15:
You can wear your ID badge attached to the lanyard during the day at work.

When you show up at work with this crystal ID badge necklace, be prepared because your co-workers (at least the ladies) will want one just like it. So you may want to make a few extras and have them stashed away in your purse for a possible quick sale. These also make perfect gifts for your fellow cubicle-mates.

Materials and vital statistics

✔ **Beads:** 3 strands of temporarily strung 4mm AB fire-polished red crystal beads

✔ **Findings:**

- 2 8mm jump rings
- 4 2x2mm crimp beads
- 1 swivel clip lanyard
- 1 plastic card holder
- 2 22-inch pieces of 0.014-inch diameter nylon-coated stainless steel beading wire

✔ **Tools:** Round-nose pliers, crimping pliers, scissors, wire cutters, chain-nose pliers

✔ **Techniques used:** Creating crimps, stringing

When figuring out how long your ID necklace should be, consider the types of shirts you wear. If you wear shirts with collars, you'll want it extra long so the lanyard will fit over the collar easily. The one in this project is 40 inches long. Obviously, this takes a good deal of beads, so consider buying them by the mass versus by the strand. You'll usually get a break on the cost of each strand when you buy them that way, and you'll end up with lots of extra beads to make more necklaces later.

This ID badge necklace is very versatile, so plan on making a few by using different types of beads to create different looks. Solid-colored necklaces will help stretch out your jewelry wardrobe, or you can make one with mixed colors so it goes with lots of different outfits.

Directions

1. **Begin by attaching a crimp bead to one end of one of the pieces of beading wire. Insert the nose of your round-nose pliers through the wire as you insert it back into the crimp bead and close the crimp bead using the crimping pliers.**

This gives you a nice loop of beading wire before you close the crimping bead with your crimping pliers.

2. **Take one of the three strands of beads and remove the beads from the temporary thread by cutting the thread with scissors.**

Do this with just one strand, not all three of them. You'll see why in a second.

3. **Take a second strand of temporarily strung beads, and insert one end of the beading wire through the beads. Snake it through the entire strand, as illustrated in Figure 14-16, and then use the scissors to cut the temporary thread and pull it out.**

Voilá! You have all of those beads on your beading wire lickety-split.

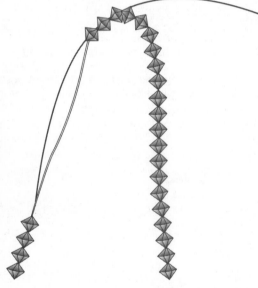

Figure 14-16:
Keep the beads on the temporary thread and snake the beading wire through the beads.

4. **On this same wire, using the beads you removed from the thread in Step 2, string 15 more beads, and then finish the end with another crimp bead as described in Step 1.**

5. **Using the second piece of beading wire, repeat Steps 1, 3, and 4 to create a second strand, and use the wire cutters to trim off the excess beading wire as needed.**

6. **Use the chain-nose pliers to open one jump ring, and slip on one end of one of the beads strands, the lanyard clip, and one end of the second bead strand. See Figure 14-17 to see how this is done.**

7. **Repeat Step 6 with the other two ends of the beading strands.**

Figure 14-17:
Connect your bead strands and lanyard to a jump ring.

Button Pendant with Beaded Chain

Flower power is going strong in this flower-button-turned-pendant project (see Figure 14-18). You use several wire techniques to turn the button into a pendant and then finish it off with a bead-and-wire chain and hand-fabricated hook. In fact, this project uses a lot of wire because the entire necklace is constructed using wire-wrapping techniques. So for now, you can set all that beading thread aside. And if you're still a little green to wire wrapping, you may want to practice first with some copper wire before attempting this intermediate-level project.

Lampwork beads, accented with tiny pink flowers, are combined with pale pink, 3-D diamond-shaped lampwork beads, rose quartz beads, and smaller pink glass beads. The pink color and flower lampwork beads create a feminine feel. You may get the urge to drink a cup of tea and read a romance novel after you finish your masterpiece.

For unusual buttons, check out vintage clothing stores. The buttons are often worth more than the clothing they're sewn on to. In fact, try to avoid cutting the shanks off of your buttons when you incorporate them into jewelry because doing so devalues antique and vintage buttons.

Figure 14-18:
Flowers are the theme for this necklace featuring a flower button pendant.

Materials and vital statistics

- ✔ **Beads:**
  - • 4 15mm flower lampwork beads
  - • 4 12mm 3D diamond-shaped pink lampwork beads
  - • 10 8mm rose quartz beads
  - • 20 4mm dark pink glass beads
- ✔ **Findings:** 5 feet of 22-gauge gold-filled round wire
- ✔ **Other:** 1 20mm gold-tone flower button
- ✔ **Tools:** Round-nose pliers, tacky glue or E6000 glue, chain-nose pliers, wire cutters
- ✔ **Techniques used:** Creating a wrapped loop, "S" scroll, and wire hook

Buttons aren't necessarily cheap. In fact, if you've ever done any sewing, you know that already. By the time you buy all your notions — buttons, thread, ribbon, and trims — they often cost you more than the material needed for the garment you plan to make. However, many hobby and sewing centers often have sale coupons in the weekend newspaper, so keep an eye out for sales like these when you're ready to invest in some nice buttons for your jewelry needs.

The finished necklace is about 22 inches long. You make the pendant first, and then create the bead-and-wire chain. Feel free to shorten or lengthen the chain to suit your own taste.

Directions

1. **Start with about 3½ inches of wire, and using the round-nose pliers and the "S" scroll technique, curl both ends of the wire toward each other. Leave about an inch or so of straight wire in between the two scrolls, as shown in Figure 14-19.**

Figure 14-19:
Make large curls on both ends of the wire.

2. **Grasp the center part of the straight wire with the round-nose pliers, and use your fingers to bend the wire in half so the curls are on the outside.**

   The wire should looks like the piece in Figure 14-20. You've just created the button's *bail.*

3. **Glue the scrolling part of the wire component onto the back of the button. Check out Figure 14-21.**

   Now you've turned your button into a pendant. Wait for the glue to dry before continuing.

Figure 14-20:
Bend the wire in half to create a bail for the button.

Figure 14-21:
The wire component you made turns the button into a pendant.

4. **With the round-nose and chain-nose pliers and using the wrapped loop technique, connect your first piece of wire onto the bail, slip on 1 dark pink bead, 1 rose quartz bead, another dark pink bead, and make another wrapped loop on the other end of the wire. Use the wire cutters to trim the wire for each bead-and-wire section as necessary.**

   We call this section a "rose quartz station."

5. **For the next bead-and-wire section, repeat Step 4, but instead string 1 dark pink bead, 1 lampwork flower bead, and another dark pink bead. Before wrapping the second wrapped loop closed, slip it onto the rose quartz station you made in Step 4.**

   We call this section a "flower bead station." At this point, you should have in place your button pendant, one rose quartz station, and one flower bead station.

6. **Repeat Step 4.**

7. **For the next bead-and-wire section, repeat Step 4, but instead string 1 dark pink bead, 1 diamond-shaped lampwork bead, and another dark pink bead.**

   We call this section a "diamond bead station."

8. **Continue repeating Steps 4, 5, 6, and 7 until you have an alternating pattern of bead stations in this order: rose quartz station, flower bead station, rose quartz station, diamond bead station, rose quartz station, flower bead station, rose quartz station, and diamond bead station. End the strand with a rose quartz station.**

   See Figure 14-22 for an idea of what your bead stations should look like.

Figure 14-22:
Make the
necklace
straps out
of beads
and wire.

9. Repeat Steps 4 through 8 for the other side of the necklace.

10. Use the wire cutters to trim the wire for each bead-and-wire section as necessary.

11. To make the clasp, take about 4 inches of wire, and use the round-nose pliers and the wire hook technique to make a hook on one end of the wire (see Chapter 10 if you need help making a hook). Use the wrapped loop technique to secure the other end of the wire to one side of the bead-and-wire strand.

Because you ended the other side of the necklace with a wrapped loop, you can connect the hook to this loop to secure the necklace around your neck, as shown in Figure 14-23.

Figure 14-23:
Add a wire
hook for the
clasp on the
necklace.

Part V
The Part of Tens

The 5th Wave
By Rich Tennant

"For such an obnoxious person, she makes a lovely charm bracelet."

In this part . . .

The Part of Tens is a quick stop, but it can be a super-handy resource as you progress in jewelry design. We've put together three detailed lists to help you with various parts of your newest pastime. First, we help you take care of your newest jewelry creations with tips for caring for or storing your pieces. Next, we give you our best bets for places to find unlikely jewelry making supplies (which comes in very handy after you've been inspired by the awesome projects in Part IV!). Finally, we help you avoid common mistakes that many new jewelry designers and beaders run into. Don't miss this chapter to save yourself time, money, and heartache.

And if you're looking to brush up on some skills or you need to quickly find a specific technique, look no further than the appendix that comes directly after the Part of Tens chapters. We include many of the most common techniques you need, complete with illustrations, to help you get on track and keep your projects going. If you need something you can't find here, check out *Jewelry Making & Beading For Dummies* (Wiley).

Chapter 15

Ten Tips for Storing and Caring for Your Jewelry Creations

After you make your beautiful handcrafted jewelry, you should take one more important step in the process of becoming a jewelry aficionado: knowing how to keep your jewelry looking forever fabulous. This chapter provides you with ten tips for properly storing your jewelry, as well as how to keep it clean and in ready-to-wear shape at all times. You find out how and where you should store your finished jewelry pieces, as well as ideas for cleaning and maintaining your jewelry creations so you can enjoy them for many years. When you start making jewelry for other people you may want to pass along a few of these tips to them as well.

Use Polishing Cloths

One of the most economic items you'll ever purchase to help keep your jewelry looking fabulous is a simple *polishing cloth*. These are available from jewelry supply vendors, but you can also find them at most discount stores for around $5 each. These supersoft cloths are chemically treated. Simply rub the cloth along your silver or other metals, and with a little elbow grease and time, your metal jewelry will look shiny and new. Invest in a few of these. Keep one in your jewelry toolbox and another near your jewelry storage area for quick swipes when you're racing out the door but need to clean a piece before you wear it.

Know What to Store Flat and What to Hang

Depending on the design of the jewelry item, how it's constructed, and how it's meant to be worn, you need to store jewelry pieces two different ways:

✔ **Hanging:** For some items, such as chains and most earrings, you want to hang them. This way, they don't get tangled up when you aren't wearing them. Nothing can drive you crazier than to have to pull a knot out of a piece of chain or to unkink a pair of dangling chandelier-style earrings.

✔ **Storing flat:** Some jewelry pieces last much longer if they're stored flat because they can stretch. These include bracelets and necklaces strung on mediums such as elastic cord, nylon, or silk. The weight of the beads on the stringing material can, over time, stretch the piece and distort it. So try to find a shallow drawer to store these types of pieces in.

A jewelry armoire provides a way to hang some pieces and store others flat. So if you're a jewelry junkie, it may be worth it to invest in one. Most discount and department stores carry them these days. The cost varies depending on the size, but $100 is a ballpark range for smaller armoires.

Keep Sets Together

Though many items in this book can be mixed and matched, when you go through the trouble of making a complete jewelry set — matching necklace, bracelet, and earrings — it's worth the extra trouble to keep the pieces together when you store them in your jewelry box. Many jewelry armoires these days come with shallow drawers that are sectioned off. This can help you keep sets organized so they're together and easy to find when you have that perfect outfit to show off the particular bead in your jewelry set. If sets are split up in your jewelry box, it can be difficult to find all the pieces when you need them.

Inspect Your Knots

Tying knots between beads keeps your beads from hitting against each other and possibly cracking or breaking. Knots are also handy when a necklace may break, because they keep you from losing all your beads (or marbles, as the case may be). But it's important that you are aware of your knots. What shape are they in?

Most jewelry pieces, like your classic strand of pearls, which is worn regularly throughout the year, should be restrung and reknotted annually. If you don't have time to do this (or if you forget), try to check your knots now and then to see how they're doing. If they become loose or frayed, it's time to restring and reknot your piece.

Be Gentle on Your Soft Stones

Be extra careful with stones that are considered soft. These stones are normally porous and can crack and break more easily than stones that aren't porous. Some examples of softer stones are turquoise, pearl (yes, not a stone, but in the gemstone family), opals, and malachite. Pearls, one of the softest beads you'll probably use, should be stored in a soft pouch to keep them from getting scratched. Harder stones that you don't have to worry about so much include gemstones such as hematite (an iron ore), diamonds (of course), onyx (which is used in a few of the projects in this book), and jade.

You should never soak softer stones in any kind of cleaning liquid or tumble them in a polisher. Softer stones are fine to use for jewelry, but you generally don't want to throw them around too much because you can damage them.

If the findings of your softer stone beaded pieces, such as the metal clasps or wire sections, need to be cleaned, you have a few options. First and easiest is to clean these areas with a soft polishing cloth (see the "Use Polishing Cloths" section earlier in this chapter). Another option is to purchase an ionic cleaner. These handy little machines are safe to use on many jewelry components and beaded items because they clean in just seconds. They use a combination of electricity and cleaning solution. You simply connect the metal area of the jewelry piece to a clip in the ionic machine, set this in the solution inside the machine, and push a button. Seconds later, you pull out your jewelry, rinse it briefly, and let it dry thoroughly. You'll be amazed at how clean it is.

Shade Your Jewelry from the Sun

Just like your skin, the sun can damage your jewelry, especially gemstone jewelry. Although your beaded amethyst necklace or citrine dangle earrings may look wonderful hanging in a display window so the sun streams down to reveal how gorgeous they are, you're signing a death warrant for your beads when you do this. The sun will suck the color right out of your stones. Some of this is because many stones are treated — color enhanced, you might say — through dyeing and heat treating. So, by being exposed to ultraviolet light over a period of time, the beads' color eventually fades.

Tone Down the Tarnish

All metals eventually tarnish at some point, but sterling silver especially seems to have this problem more so than other metals. To help keep the tarnishing to a minimum, you can use a couple of tricks.

- ✔ **When you aren't wearing your metal jewelry, store it in airtight containers.** This can be as simple as a plastic sandwich bag. By keeping the metal away from oxygen, you slow down the oxidizing process.

- ✔ **Check out products that combat tarnish.** You can store your silver jewelry in jewelry boxes and armoires that have chemically treated linings. Tarnish strips are also a great product to store with your jewelry. These strips are inexpensive, and you can drop one inside an airtight container with your jewelry. They work by eliminating the gases from sulfur.

Take Off Your Bling When You Exercise

Jewelry is an important accessory, but it's not necessary to wear it 24/7. Although exercising regularly is good for your body, it's not so good for your jewelry, so remember to remove your rings and other baubles before hitting the gym. High-impact sports and other forms of exercise can cause you to accidentally chip, scratch, or crack your beaded jewelry. For those who enjoy a dip in the pool, strong chemicals such as chlorine can damage many stones as well as metals. If you feel totally naked without some jewelry on, limit your adornments to small post or hoop earrings and maybe that must-wear ring.

Keep It Clean

After you start to get a pretty fair collection of jewelry — and as a jewelry maker, that will happen as you slowly become addicted to this wonderful craft — remember to periodically clean your jewelry collection. This accomplishes a few different things. First of all, and most importantly, your jewelry will always be ready to wear when you want to wear it. Nothing is more irritating than rushing around getting ready to go to work and planning to wear a particular piece of jewelry, only to discover it's so tarnished that you'd be ashamed to be seen with it on. Secondly, if you keep your jewelry clean and well cared for, it will last much longer.

For metal jewelry, such as silver or gold, you can make your own homemade cleaning solution using a recipe often referred to in jewelry circles as Super Cleaner. This cleaner is for jewelry that's all metal. Don't use this with any pieces strung on beading wire, silk, or other types of stringing medium, because extended soaking can damage the stringing material.

You use household chemicals to make this solution, but these are, well, chemicals, so keep the kids and pets out of this, work in a well-ventilated area when mixing and using the cleaner, and follow the manufacturers' warnings.

Okay, on to the cleaning solution:

1. **In an 8-ounce container (like a pickle jar), combine**

   1 inch of cleaning detergent (Top Job or Mr. Clean are recommended)

   1 inch of dishwashing liquid

   1 inch of ammonia

   Fill the rest of the container with water. Shake well.

2. **Heat the solution in the microwave (remove the metal lid first), or put it in an old pot (one you don't use for food and never will after this) and simmer it on the stovetop.**

   The solution should be heated to just below the boiling point.

3. **Remove the cleaning solution from the heat source. Place your jewelry (silver or gold) into the solution and let it sit for about 10 minutes.**

4. **Remove the jewelry from the solution, rinse it well with water, and dry it with a paper towel.**

   Put on your sunglasses because these babies will be super clean now!

Over time, the solution will evaporate, but you can continue to reheat and use it over and over again until it's gone.

Make Yourself Pretty, Then Add Shine

We're bombarded by chemicals today, and that doesn't just refer to the prepackaged foods we eat. Most of us on a regular basis cover ourselves in creams, spray ourselves with perfumes and hairsprays, and decorate our faces with an assortment of makeup. So go ahead and use your special mix of beauty products, but remember to dab them on before you put your jewelry on rather than after. Your jewelry and your shoes should be the last items you put on before you walk out the door.

Chapter 16

Ten Places to Peruse for Offbeat Jewelry-Making Materials

In This Chapter

▶ Checking out nontraditional sources for beading materials

▶ Considering unusual items to incorporate into your jewelry

*J*ewelry makers are really lucky these days because you can find readily available beading and jewelry-making supplies all over the place: on the Web, at craft stores, and even at some discount stores. Beads, especially, have become so popular that they're pretty easy to find these days, no matter where you live. But this can be a double-edged sword as well because everyone has access to the same or very similar jewelry-making supplies. What if you want to try something different? What if you want to make your jewelry stand out from that of the average craft store shopper?

This chapter lists ten ideas for locating nontraditional jewelry materials and brainstorms different ways to incorporate them into your jewelry designs. After you read this chapter and your creative juices start flowing, you'll probably be able to add to this list.

Hunt through Hardware Stores

Large or small hardware stores are full of possibilities for the jewelry designer. Consider just a few possibilities:

- Chain
- Fan pulls
- Nails
- Nylon string
- Rope
- Screws
- Washers
- Wire

The list goes on as you stroll down aisle after aisle of hardware goodies.

Look for items that you can attach to other things. Washers have holes in them, and copper wire, usually intended for wiring a light switch, is perfect for wrapping and connecting items together.

Scout Out Scrapbook Shops

Scrapbooking is hugely popular right now, even more so than jewelry making (believe it or not!). As a result, little scrapbook shops have popped up here and there. They offer all kinds of unique items for the crafter, from pretty paper to little embellishments, many of which can also be transformed into jewelry items.

For example, small die cuts normally pasted onto a scrapbook page can instead be glued onto pin or post earring findings. Scrapbooking stores sell ribbon by the spool or by the inch that you can use as the base for a necklace or bracelet. Check out special scrapbooking touches that go beyond paper, such as plastic eyelets, metal or rhinestone brads, and charming charms, that you can use to make unique jewelry.

Instead of gluing fabric flower accents on a scrapbook page about your garden, pick a bunch of brightly colored flower accents, cut a piece of ribbon or elastic long enough for a necklace, grab a handful of beads and spacers, and you've got all the makings for a one-of-a-kind Hawaiian lei.

Stroll around Your Block, through the Park, or on the Beach

Go for a walk in your neighborhood and get some exercise while you scout for natural elements to add to your jewelry creations. Or look for items while you're on vacation that you can bring home with you and use to make your own souvenirs (just don't take any plants, leaves, or other native species from prohibited areas). Here are just a couple of ideas:

- ✔ A leaf can be rolled into polymer clay to make a leaf impression. Then cut and fire the clay, and you have a leaf charm. (See Chapter 12 for more on working with polymer clay.)

- ✔ Small stones can be glued onto bails for supereasy pendants.

- ✔ Pretty seashells can be strung onto wire or nylon string for a nautical necklace. Sometimes you can even find shells that already have a hole in them, making them an instant pendant. Otherwise, you can attach the shell to a bail or try to drill a hole through it (practice first on a couple of extra shells). The necklace pictured in Figure 16-1 was made with a shell that already had a hole at the top, a piece of linen cord, and a few crystals to give the necklace some sparkle.

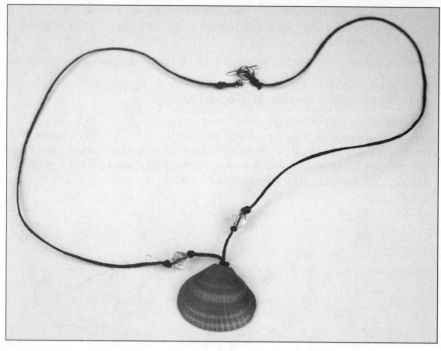

Figure 16-1: Shells with holes make instant jewelry possibilities.

Rummage through Garage Sales, Thrift Stores, and Auction Listings

Someone else's trash can be your treasure if you like to hit neighborhood garage sales or local secondhand shops, like the Salvation Army or Goodwill. These are excellent places to load up on old jewelry that you can take apart and make something old into something new. Use wire and other beads to connect the mismatched jewelry items you've found.

And don't restrict your findings (no pun intended) to old jewelry. Think about ways you can deconstruct other items:

✔ Check out buttons on old shirts and dresses.

✔ Look through kids' games for board game pieces, Army men, and so on (see the next section).

✔ Snatch up home décor items such as beaded lampshades, those beaded curtains people used to hang in doorways, and assorted small knickknacks.

✔ Dismantle an old typewriter (or computer keyboard), and use the keys to make wordy jewelry:

• Make a lapel pin that bears your initials.

• Wear a pair of N-O earrings on a day you're feeling grumpy, or make an H-I pair for those days when you're feeling friendly.

- String together a necklace that conveys your worldview: "PEACE," "LOVE," "BEADING." (Obviously, you'll need more than one set of keys if you have to repeat letters.)

✔ Use old scarves as stringing material for extra-large lampwork or crystal beads.

✔ Take apart small hair accessories, like those worn by little girls, and glue pin backs to them for some whimsical broaches.

✔ Turn smaller components from outdated computer parts into fun fashions for the office. Take apart the electronics and use the memory chips, wires, and whatever else you can salvage to make a modern-day statement. Just make sure that none of the items will harm the wearer. Figure 16-2 shows a RAM and bead necklace design, which is strung on purple hemp and accented with purple lampwork beads.

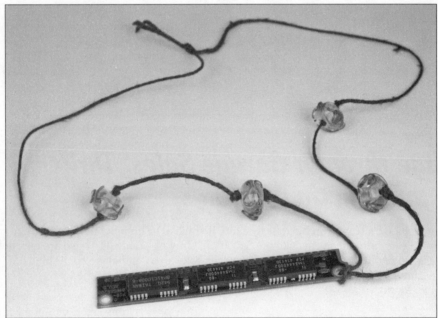

Figure 16-2:
Recycle
computer
parts into
fun fashion.

Another place to find deals on vintage jewelry pieces that you can take apart and recycle is eBay. A lot of estate sale auctions appear on this Web site, so you can buy lots (meaning groupings) of jewelry. And "lots" also means "a lot," because you usually have to buy a bunch of pieces for one flat fee. You may not get an exact choice of each piece because you bid to buy all of it, but you may find at least one big-time treasure in there. You just never know.

Track Down Tiny Toys from the Toy Box

Little toy soldiers and small plastic toys from a gumball machine can become funky and spunky charms. Just wrap some wire around them, adding a wrapped loop someplace as you wrap the wire, and then connect the loop you've made to a chain for a quick necklace.

Search a Stash of Fabric Scraps

Appeal to your favorite seamstress for access to her scrap fabric stash. Some ideas:

- ✔ Use little pieces of ribbon to make perfect cording for attaching a fun pendant.

- ✔ Cover a tiny bit of lace with glue and allow it to dry. The lace will become stiff, and you can divide it in half and create a pair of post earrings.

- ✔ Add a bail to a piece of stiffened lace and make it into a pendant to hang from the ribbon you found.

Browse through the Button Box

If you've ever sewn, you probably have a button box around because you hate to throw out a perfectly good button. If you don't sew, find someone who does. Maybe she'll be kind enough to let you take a few from her collection. Buttons make nice, quick pendants with the addition of a bail glued to the back. Or, glue posts to the back instead for earrings if you can manage to find two matching buttons.

You can also use buttons to create a treasure necklace or bracelet. With a ribbon as the base, sew on buttons up and down on both sides. Make sure to leave about 6 inches of ribbon on each end, and use these ribbon lengths to attach the piece to your wrist or tie it around your neck.

Raid the Office Supplies Cabinet

Paper clips aren't just for keeping your boring paperwork together. Attach ear hooks to two paper clips for a pair of quirky earrings. Don't forget, too, that paper clips come in all kinds of colors these days, so you don't have to use the old silver-colored ones. Make them extra dangly by connecting a few together before adding the ear hooks. Speaking of color, rubber bands are also available in bright shades of red, blue, and green. Use a slip knot to attach a bunch together for an extra-stretchy necklace or bracelet.

Many office supply stores also carry pretty stationery papers. Pick some up, cut out geometric shapes, and laminate them. Then punch a hole at the top and attach ear hooks, or use them as charms for a lightweight bracelet or necklace.

Recycle Your Junk Mail

Save those colorful fliers you find in your mailbox every day. Cut them into 1-inch-wide strips and then coat them with some glue diluted with water. Wrap the strips around a plastic straw and let them dry. Depending on how humid it is where you live, this could take up to 24 hours before they're completely dry. When you slide the dried paper off the straw, you have some cool and colorful beads! String these up with other beads, like crystal or gemstone beads, or use them solo with some hemp cord. This is a great project for kids because it's fun to rip up the paper pieces and get gooey with the glue. Plus, they can make a lot of jewelry for practically nothing and give the pieces as gifts to friends and family.

Dig around for Deals at the Dollar Store

Next time you drive by one of those dollar stores, drop in. You just never know what you'll find. They always have an assortment of the weird as well as the practical when it comes to the merchandise available. And, of course, because everything is only a dollar, you can let your creativity go crazy. Even if your jewelry experiment doesn't work, you've only invested a buck or two, so no big deal.

Chapter 17

Ten Mistakes to Avoid When Expanding Your Jewelry Hobby

In This Chapter

▶ Buying the right tools and supplies for the right price

▶ Figuring out findings

▶ Schmoozing with fellow jewelry makers

*N*ot long after you made your first piece or two of jewelry, you probably started thinking of ways to expand your new hobby. Perhaps you thought about how this could become more than just a hobby someday. Maybe you could make jewelry for profit as well as pleasure. These thoughts are typical of anyone who has made even just a little jewelry. But before you get too deep into this creative craft, it's a good idea to be aware of some of the mistakes to avoid.

This chapter lists ten pitfalls to steer clear of as you expand your jewelry hobby and hone your beading skills. As with any artistic endeavor, you should keep in mind some do's and don'ts before you get too far into your jewelry adventure.

Buying Only from Retail Outlets

Most of us start out by buying our supplies locally, either at a bead shop (if you're lucky enough to have one in your area) or at one of the large chain craft stores. This is exactly where the new beader should start shopping. You need only a small number of supplies to get started, so it makes sense.

However, when you want to grow your inventory of supplies and tools, these retail outlets aren't going to cut it any longer. Besides the fact that retail costs more than wholesale purchases, you're also limited by selection. If you want to make superdistinctive, fabulous jewelry, you don't want to use supplies that any Tina, Dina, or Harriet can purchase at the same craft store. By locating multiple wholesale suppliers and attending wholesale jewelry and bead shows, you can save money and also select from a larger array of unique supplies.

Most jewelry supply vendors, wholesale and retail, have Web sites these days and are easily located through search engines like Google. You can also find lots of vendor links and bead show links at `jewelrymaking.about.com`. Though many vendors give quantity discounts no matter whether you're a "real" business or not (such as `www.firemountaingems.com`), some wholesalers require that you have a tax identification certificate and won't sell to you without one. This certificate can bring you bargains, but it can also bring you legal headaches if you don't plan to seriously pursue jewelry making as a business.

If you do plan to start a jewelry business and need some serious price cuts and a serious amount of supplies, then wholesale jewelry shows are the way to go. A larger jewelry show promoter, Gem and Lapidary Wholesalers (www.glwshows.com) has shows throughout the United States. They require that you register with them and send them a copy of your tax certificate before you can attend a show, but after you're registered, you'll get notices of shows in your area.

Ordering Small Amounts of Supplies Too Often

To build your jewelry inventory, you need to start thinking in terms of volume. You'll need larger quantities of beads and findings, and that will lead you to shop at wholesale suppliers where you can get more beads for your buck (see the preceding section). Buying a dozen ear hooks means you can make six pairs of earrings, but stocking up on a gross of ear hooks means you can make 72 pairs of earrings. If you plan to sell your jewelry at a craft show, for example, six pairs of earrings obviously aren't going to be enough.

Instead of buying small amounts of supplies every week or two weeks, wait and start a list of what you need. Then purchase supplies in volume but less often, such as quarterly. Some vendor sites, like Fire Mountain Gems & Beads (www.firemountaingems.com), allow you to keep items in your cart for a long period of time, so this is one way to start your list.

Buying Cheap Tools

Your tools are essential to your jewelry-making successes. It's easy to get blinded by the other supplies you need to buy, like wire and beads, and forget that you need tools to put all those supplies together to make your jewelry. Quality tools help you create a quality jewelry product. Cheap tools usually mean just that — cheap — as in yucky to use. They're bulky and cumbersome to work with comfortably; they may not have a spring handle, so they fatigue your hands while you work; and they break after using them just a few times. If you're serious about your jewelry, get some serious tools.

Picking Out Beads by Price Only

Quality is an issue for beads as well as tools. Although there isn't necessarily a direct correlation between price and quality — cheap beads bad, expensive beads good — you should consider additional elements besides price when purchasing your beads:

- A quality formed bead should be symmetrical. For example, if the bead is round, it should be the same diameter all the way around.
- Bead holes should be drilled straight through, not crooked.
- There shouldn't be any cracks around the holes.

Don't solely consider price when purchasing beads if you want to make a quality piece of jewelry that others will appreciate and possibly want to purchase from you.

Forgetting About Findings

Those little sparkly beads can easily distract you from the fact that you need findings as well. And, in fact, the right findings can create a hot fashion statement. So, just as you spend time considering the right bead purchase, put a good amount of time and effort into thinking over your findings inventory as well. You'll need a large quantity of jump rings, ear hooks, bead tips, crimp beads, and clasps if you plan to build up your inventory. Buy a lot of the basics, but then splurge a little on a few unusual findings that can help you develop a signature style.

Not Sharing Information with Fellow Jewelry Makers

After spending time mastering your jewelry-making craft and searching for just the right jewelry supply vendors, you may be tempted to carefully guard your knowledge like you would some deep, dark family secret. You worked hard to refine your skills and to find your suppliers. Why should you help anyone else? Gasp, they may steal your wonderful ideas! But that's the wrong way to think if you plan to become part of the jewelry art community.

Sharing your knowledge, talent, and skills is not only personally rewarding, but you'll be surprised at how much you, in turn, will learn from other knowledgeable jewelry makers who are willing to talk about their skills and techniques. What goes around really does come around.

Using the Wrong Tool for the Job

Jewelry making involves a number of specialized tools, and there's a reason for this. The right tool results in a quality piece of jewelry. For example, round-nose pliers help you create rounded loops and curls in your wire. And there really is no substitute. You just can't get nice round loops by trying to do the same thing with, for example, a pair of chain-nose pliers.

Although there's nothing wrong with experimenting, be aware of what a specific tool is used for and why. This can really make a difference in your end results.

Forgetting that Practice Makes Perfect

It's amazing how many jewelry makers come down on themselves for the occasional, or even frequent, mistake. This is especially true when they're figuring out a new technique or trying to remember a familiar one that they haven't used in a while.

You're not a machine, so you won't make perfect jewelry every single time. If you want to sell perfect jewelry, then buy machine-made, cookie-cutter boring jewelry and sell that instead. As you practice, you'll perfect your technique. It's just a matter of time. So take it easy on yourself and allow yourself to make mistakes because, unfortunately, mistakes are part of the learning and perfecting process.

Not Following Directions

When you want to practice a new technique or create a jewelry design by following a set of instructions (like the ones in this book, of course), make sure you read the instructions carefully, as well as follow the pictures. The text and images are meant to work together to help you achieve the same results as the finished project. If you simply try to follow along with the pictures and ignore the text nearby, you may miss some crucial information. It's best to move back and forth between the two. Read a little of the text, and then review the images to get a better understanding of what you just read.

Following Directions

On the flip side of the previous section, just as an experienced cook may not follow a recipe word for word, many experienced jewelry makers will tweak a set of project instructions. They do this on purpose to change the results of the finished jewelry piece they're crafting.

Deviating from the instructions is a great way to discover how to design your own jewelry. Jewelry design is all about experimentation, and a pre-established jewelry project is a good place to start. If you prefer to follow the instructions to the letter, there isn't anything wrong with that, but by trying something a little different, you may end up with a totally different jewelry piece. So sometimes it's a good idea not to follow the directions too closely.

Appendix

Jewelry and Beading Techniques

Even though you're an experienced jewelry maker, you may find that you need a quick refresher on how to complete a specific task that you don't do every single day. This appendix is just the stop for you. Here we show you several knots to help you on your quest to complete your jewelry designs. We help you master the fundamentals, like using jump rings and attaching clasps. And we do it all with handy figures for you to refer to as needed.

If you're looking for the how-tos of bead-weaving stitches, working with crimps, or wrapping wire into loops, check out Chapter 2.

Adjustable Knot

An *adjustable knot* allows you to change the length of a piece of jewelry. It consists of two figure-eight knots made from the ends of a single piece of cord. Each knot is tied around the strand of the opposite end of the cord. Here's how you make one:

1. **Lay both ends of ends of the cord parallel to each other, but pointing in opposite directions.**

2. **Holding one end stationary, tie the other strand around the first strand like a figure-eight, as shown in Figure A-1a and b.**

Figure A-1: Tying an adjustable knot.

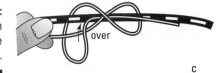

3. **Slip the tail of the figure-eight strand up between the stationary strand and the figure-eight strand, as shown in Figure A-1c.**

4. **Pull the knot tight, as shown in Figure A-1d. Use scissors to trim any excess cord from the open end of the knot.**

Don't cut the long end of the cord; you need it to make your next knot.

5. **Repeat Steps 2 through 4 with the other strand to make the second knot.**

6. **Pull the knots apart to make the necklace shorter, or slide them together to make the piece longer.**

Overhand Knot

The most simple of all knots, the *overhand knot* is used in many beading techniques. You probably know how to make one already, but may knot, er, I mean, not call it that. To make an overhand knot, follow these steps:

1. Make a simple loop at the end of your thread, as shown in Figure A-2a.

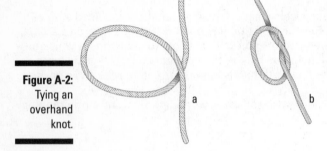

Figure A-2:
Tying an overhand knot.

a   b

2. Bring one end of your thread under and then up through the loop, as shown in Figure A-2b.

3. Pull the thread to tighten the knot.

In many jewelry-making techniques, you can insert a needle in the loop before you tighten it in Step 3. The needle lets you slide the knot to position it perfectly.

Double Overhand Knot

Similar to the overhand knot, the *double overhand knot* provides a bulkier knot. It's great for holding larger-holed beads and components right where you want them. To make a double overhand knot, follow these steps:

1. Make a simple loop at the end of your thread, as shown in Figure A-2a in the overhand knot directions.

2. Bring one end of your thread under and then up through the loop, as shown in Figure A-2b in the overhand knot directions.

3. Bring the end of the thread under and through the loop once more, as shown in Figure A-3.

4. Pull the thread to tighten the knot.

Figure A-3:
Creating a double over-hand knot.

Square Knot

Square knots get their name from the square-ish shape you make with the thread before you tighten it. You can use these knots in macramé designs, bead-weaving projects, and more. To make your own square knot, follow these directions:

1. **Cross both strands and twist them over each other one time, as shown in Figure A-4a.**

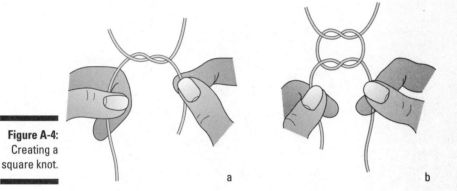

Figure A-4:
Creating a square knot.

a   b

2. **Turn the ends back toward the middle, crossing them over each other, and then twisting again. This step creates the square, as shown in Figure A-4b.**

3. **Pull the threads to tighten the knot.**

Lark's Head Knot

A *lark's head knot* (sometimes called an *anchor knot*) is commonly used for attaching a bead or component that you want to lay flat. Typically you tie the knot in the middle of your stringing material, instead of at the end. Here's how to create a lark's head knot:

1. **Fold your stringing material in half, and then thread the folded end through the center hole of bead, as shown in Figure A-5a.**

Figure A-5:
Use a lark's head knot to attach large beads, doughnuts, and components.

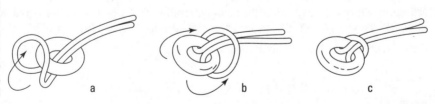

a   b   c

2. **Continue to pull the folded end through the center, creating a loop. Feed the open ends of the stringing material through the loop, as shown in Figure A-5b.**

3. **Pull the ends tight to complete the knot, as shown in Figure A-5c.**

Slip Knot

A *slip knot* is most commonly used as a temporary knot in jewelry making. You use it when you want to secure something but want to be able to take it out later. Here's how to make a slip knot:

1. **Tie an overhand knot (refer back to Figure A-2), but before pulling the knot tight, pull the main thread back through the knot, as shown in Figure A-6.**

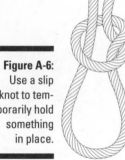

Figure A-6:
Use a slip knot to temporarily hold something in place.

2. **Pull the knot tightly to finish the knot.**

3. **When you're ready to undo the knot, simply hold the knot with one hand and tug the long strand with the other.**

Attaching a Clasp to a Bead Tip

Bead tips are essential when you string your beads with silk or nylon bead cord but want to finish the piece with a metal clasp. By following a few simple steps, you can quickly use these findings (both cup style and clamshell style bead tips) correctly, resulting in a professionally finished jewelry piece.

1. **Insert the tip of your round- or chain-nose pliers into the loop of the bead tip.**

2. **Gently twist your wrist to open the loop.**

3. **Slip on the connector piece of the clasp. Using your round-nose pliers, gently grasp the loop and pull it back into the closed position, as shown in Figure A-7a.**

Figure A-7:
Use your pliers to gently close the loop.

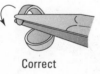 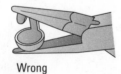

Correct   Wrong

a   b

Don't use your pliers to mash or pinch the bead tip (like Figure A-7b). You'll bend the bead tip, leaving your project looking amateurish.

Opening and Closing Jump Rings

Jump rings are incredibly useful in jewelry making, but you must open and close them the right way to keep your pieces looking professional. If you use a lot of jump rings, you can invest in a jump ring tool. We typically just use two sets of pliers with smooth jaws (like chain-nose pliers or round-nose pliers) for this delicate task. Here's how:

1. **Hold the jump ring with two sets of pliers. Situate the pliers so the opening of the jump ring sits between them, as shown in Figure A-8.**

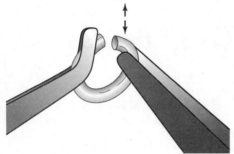

Figure A-8:
Use two sets of pliers to twist open and close a jump ring.

2. **Gently twist the two sets of pliers in opposite directions to open the jump ring.**

3. **Repeat Steps 1 and 2, but twist in the opposite direction, to close the jump ring. Make sure to line up the ends to ensure an almost seamless look.**

Never pry the ends of the jump ring straight apart, or you'll warp its shape. The result looks more like an oval than a nice round jump ring. No matter how good you are, you can't unwarp it.

Attaching a Clasp with Crimp Beads (Beginning a Strand)

After you've mastered the art of the crimp (see Chapter 2), you can use it in many different ways. One of the most common uses is attaching clasps to finish a jewelry piece.

1. **String a crimp bead onto your cord. Slide on one half of the clasp, as shown in Figure A-9a.**

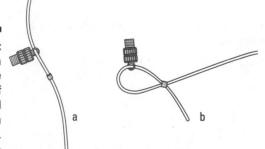

Figure A-9:
Attaching a clasp to the beginning of a strand with a crimp.

a   b   c

2. Fold the beading wire back over itself, and slide the tail back through the crimp tube, as shown in Figure A-9b. Tighten up the loop, and position the crimp bead where you ◆ant it, leaving just a bit of room for the clasp to move.

3. Using your crimping pliers, close the crimp using the two-phase crimp method (see Chapter 2) to secure the clasp. (See Figure A-9c.)

Your strand is now ready to string. As you're stringing, use your beads to cover the tail of your beading wire. Snug the beads up next to the crimp bead and allow the wire tail to slide inside as many beads as necessary to cover it. This keeps the pesky tail from poking you when you wear the piece.

Attaching a Clasp with Crimp Beads (Ending a Strand)

Using a crimp to attach the other half of a clasp to the final end of your strand is almost as easy as stringing the one at the beginning (see the preceding section), with one exception. Before you crimp the last bead into place, you want to remove any extra slack from the wire. Here's how you do it:

1. String a crimp bead onto your cord. Slide on the second half of the clasp, as shown in Figure A-9a earlier in this appendix.

2. Fold the beading wire back over itself, and slide the tail back through the crimp tube _and through several other beads already strung on the piece._ Using your round- or chain-nose pliers, gently pull the tail taut, taking out any extra slack in the strand, as shown in Figure A-10.

Here, you're hiding the tail and closing up any gaps at the same time.

Figure A-10:
Pull the slack out of the strand before crimping it.

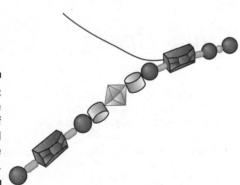

3. Using your crimping pliers, close the crimp using the two-phase crimp method (described in Chapter 2) to secure the clasp.

4. Use wire cutters to trim away any excess wire. Tuck the tail down into the closest bead.

Index

• *R* •

BUSINESS, CAREERS & PERSONAL FINANCE

0-7645-9847-3

0-7645-2431-3

Also available:
- Business Plans Kit For Dummies
  0-7645-9794-9
- Economics For Dummies
  0-7645-5726-2
- Grant Writing For Dummies
  0-7645-8416-2
- Home Buying For Dummies
  0-7645-5331-3
- Managing For Dummies
  0-7645-1771-6
- Marketing For Dummies
  0-7645-5600-2

- Personal Finance For Dummies
  0-7645-2590-5*
- Resumes For Dummies
  0-7645-5471-9
- Selling For Dummies
  0-7645-5363-1
- Six Sigma For Dummies
  0-7645-6798-5
- Small Business Kit For Dummies
  0-7645-5984-2
- Starting an eBay Business For Dummies
  0-7645-6924-4
- Your Dream Career For Dummies
  0-7645-9795-7

HOME & BUSINESS COMPUTER BASICS

0-470-05432-8

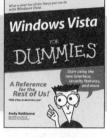

0-471-75421-8

Also available:
- Cleaning Windows Vista For Dummies
  0-471-78293-9
- Excel 2007 For Dummies
  0-470-03737-7
- Mac OS X Tiger For Dummies
  0-7645-7675-5
- MacBook For Dummies
  0-470-04859-X
- Macs For Dummies
  0-470-04849-2
- Office 2007 For Dummies
  0-470-00923-3

- Outlook 2007 For Dummies
  0-470-03830-6
- PCs For Dummies
  0-7645-8958-X
- Salesforce.com For Dummies
  0-470-04893-X
- Upgrading & Fixing Laptops For Dummies
  0-7645-8959-8
- Word 2007 For Dummies
  0-470-03658-3
- Quicken 2007 For Dummies
  0-470-04600-7

FOOD, HOME, GARDEN, HOBBIES, MUSIC & PETS

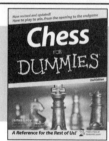

0-7645-8404-9

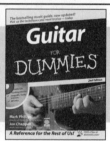

0-7645-9904-6

Also available:
- Candy Making For Dummies
  0-7645-9734-5
- Card Games For Dummies
  0-7645-9910-0
- Crocheting For Dummies
  0-7645-4151-X
- Dog Training For Dummies
  0-7645-8418-9
- Healthy Carb Cookbook For Dummies
  0-7645-8476-6
- Home Maintenance For Dummies
  0-7645-5215-5

- Horses For Dummies
  0-7645-9797-3
- Jewelry Making & Beading For Dummies
  0-7645-2571-9
- Orchids For Dummies
  0-7645-6759-4
- Puppies For Dummies
  0-7645-5255-4
- Rock Guitar For Dummies
  0-7645-5356-9
- Sewing For Dummies
  0-7645-6847-7
- Singing For Dummies
  0-7645-2475-5

INTERNET & DIGITAL MEDIA

0-470-04529-9

0-470-04894-8

Also available:
- Blogging For Dummies
  0-471-77084-1
- Digital Photography For Dummies
  0-7645-9802-3
- Digital Photography All-in-One Desk Reference For Dummies
  0-470-03743-1
- Digital SLR Cameras and Photography For Dummies
  0-7645-9803-1
- eBay Business All-in-One Desk Reference For Dummies
  0-7645-8438-3
- HDTV For Dummies
  0-470-09673-X

- Home Entertainment PCs For Dummies
  0-470-05523-5
- MySpace For Dummies
  0-470-09529-6
- Search Engine Optimization For Dummies
  0-471-97998-8
- Skype For Dummies
  0-470-04891-3
- The Internet For Dummies
  0-7645-8996-2
- Wiring Your Digital Home For Dummies
  0-471-91830-X

SPORTS, FITNESS, PARENTING, RELIGION & SPIRITUALITY

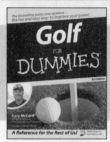

0-471-76871-5

0-7645-7841-3

Also available:
- Catholicism For Dummies
  0-7645-5391-7
- Exercise Balls For Dummies
  0-7645-5623-1
- Fitness For Dummies
  0-7645-7851-0
- Football For Dummies
  0-7645-3936-1
- Judaism For Dummies
  0-7645-5299-6
- Potty Training For Dummies
  0-7645-5417-4
- Buddhism For Dummies
  0-7645-5359-3

- Pregnancy For Dummies
  0-7645-4483-7 †
- Ten Minute Tone-Ups For Dummies
  0-7645-7207-5
- NASCAR For Dummies
  0-7645-7681-X
- Religion For Dummies
  0-7645-5264-3
- Soccer For Dummies
  0-7645-5229-5
- Women in the Bible For Dummies
  0-7645-8475-8

TRAVEL

0-7645-7749-2

0-7645-6945-7

Also available:
- Alaska For Dummies
  0-7645-7746-8
- Cruise Vacations For Dummies
  0-7645-6941-4
- England For Dummies
  0-7645-4276-1
- Europe For Dummies
  0-7645-7529-5
- Germany For Dummies
  0-7645-7823-5
- Hawaii For Dummies
  0-7645-7402-7

- Italy For Dummies
  0-7645-7386-1
- Las Vegas For Dummies
  0-7645-7382-9
- London For Dummies
  0-7645-4277-X
- Paris For Dummies
  0-7645-7630-5
- RV Vacations For Dummies
  0-7645-4442-X
- Walt Disney World & Orlando
  For Dummies
  0-7645-9660-8

GRAPHICS, DESIGN & WEB DEVELOPMENT

0-7645-8815-X

0-7645-9571-7

Also available:
- 3D Game Animation For Dummies
  0-7645-8789-7
- AutoCAD 2006 For Dummies
  0-7645-8925-3
- Building a Web Site For Dummies
  0-7645-7144-3
- Creating Web Pages For Dummies
  0-470-08030-2
- Creating Web Pages All-in-One Desk
  Reference For Dummies
  0-7645-4345-8
- Dreamweaver 8 For Dummies
  0-7645-9649-7

- InDesign CS2 For Dummies
  0-7645-9572-5
- Macromedia Flash 8 For Dummies
  0-7645-9691-8
- Photoshop CS2 and Digital
  Photography For Dummies
  0-7645-9580-6
- Photoshop Elements 4 For Dummies
  0-471-77483-9
- Syndicating Web Sites with RSS Feeds
  For Dummies
  0-7645-8848-6
- Yahoo! SiteBuilder For Dummies
  0-7645-9800-7

NETWORKING, SECURITY, PROGRAMMING & DATABASES

0-7645-7728-X

0-471-74940-0

Also available:
- Access 2007 For Dummies
  0-470-04612-0
- ASP.NET 2 For Dummies
  0-7645-7907-X
- C# 2005 For Dummies
  0-7645-9704-3
- Hacking For Dummies
  0-470-05235-X
- Hacking Wireless Networks
  For Dummies
  0-7645-9730-2
- Java For Dummies
  0-470-08716-1

- Microsoft SQL Server 2005 For Dummies
  0-7645-7755-7
- Networking All-in-One Desk Reference
  For Dummies
  0-7645-9939-9
- Preventing Identity Theft For Dummies
  0-7645-7336-5
- Telecom For Dummies
  0-471-77085-X
- Visual Studio 2005 All-in-One Desk
  Reference For Dummies
  0-7645-9775-2
- XML For Dummies
  0-7645-8845-1